Mason Stang and Udi Gal

The SAIL RACING BIBLE

ADLARD COLES
Bloomsbury Publishing Plc
50 Bedford Square, London, WC1B 3DP, UK
29 Earlsfort Terrace, Dublin 2, Ireland

BLOOMSBURY, ADLARD COLES and the Adlard Coles logo are trademarks of
Bloomsbury Publishing Plc

First published in Great Britain 2024

A catalogue record for this book is available from the British Library

Library of Congress Cataloguing-in-Publication data has been applied for

ISBN: PB: 978-1-3994-0515-7;
ePub: 978-1-3994-0514-0; ePDF: 978-1-3994-0513-3

2 4 6 8 10 9 7 5 3 1

Designed by Louise Turpin
Typeset in Effra by louiseturpindesign.co.uk
Printed in UAE by Oriental Press

FSC
www.fsc.org

MIX
Paper | Supporting
responsible forestry
FSC® C004800

To find out more about our authors and books visit www.bloomsbury.com
and sign up for our newsletters

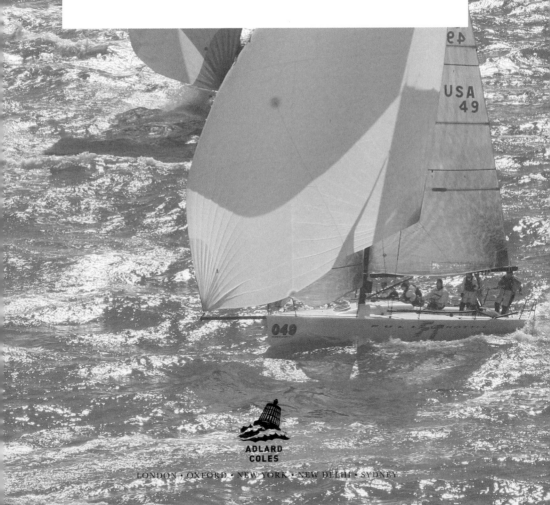

The
SAIL RACING BIBLE

Mason Stang and Udi Gal

The Complete Guide for Dinghy and Yacht Racers

ADLARD
COLES

LONDON · OXFORD · NEW YORK · NEW DELHI · SYDNEY

CONTENTS

INTRODUCTION

I first met Udi Gal at a practice with my school's sailing team. I was racing upwind in an FJ dinghy in the big breeze and waves of the port of Redwood City, when a dark grey RIB thundered up to me. I saw Udi standing tall at the centre console – or rather I heard him first. 'Trim in the jib! Press the boat! Hike lower!' His instructions boomed out across the water. Instantly I complied, and the boat took off. I was young at the time and I was just learning about racing. Udi was coaching my high school team. Despite my inexperience, all it took was one day of Udi's intense instruction on the racecourse for me to get hooked on racing. Little did I know the life-changing journey that lay ahead of me over the next five years.

When Udi began coaching here in the San Francisco Bay Area, he brought an unprecedented level of coaching to the youth sailing scene. From this area that has fantastic heavy weather sailing conditions, Udi has produced some of the best sailors in the U.S. These results I credit in part to the strong winds of San Francisco for providing my teammates and me with the skills to sail in any condition, but really to Udi's unparalleled expertise as a sailor and as a coach. Coming to us with his experience as a World Champion and four-time Olympian from Israel in the 470 class, twice as a sailor and twice as a coach, Udi has raised the level of his sailors here in the Bay to such heights through not just his expertise in the 420 (the double-handed youth class we sail), but through his intense coaching style.

You see, if you make a fundamental mistake in a race, Udi lets you know loud and clear. Udi's the coach that every sailor and coach on the water hears from across the racecourse energetically critiquing his sailors in his distinctive Israeli accent after each race.

But at the same time, Udi is more dedicated to his sailors than any other coach I've seen. I believe his constant dedication is what really separates him from the rest. Udi makes himself heard when we make mistakes on the racecourse, but he's also the coach that will stay at the boat park late into the night to help his sailors finish any repairs or boat work before the next day of racing.

Needless to say, Udi's coaching style has led to strong results. The sailing organization he started, HPC (High Performance Center), quickly rose to the national stage. I'd like to take this moment to thank my longtime teammate Timmy Gee for sailing with me for all these years. He's the quintessential 'student of the game', and I couldn't have asked for a better sailing partner with whom to spend years of dedicated training and competition. I'll never forget the first Club 420 Midwinter Championship Timmy and I won, and how it propelled us to finish runner-up in both the National Championship and in the Triple Crown Series. To cap off our high school sailing career, we represented Team USA in Italy at the 420 World Championship.

At some point I approached Udi with the idea of writing a sailing book. I've been incredibly fortunate to have learned from a world class coach such as Udi, but I know that most sailors are not so privileged to have access to a source of sailing knowledge like him. With this book I have an opportunity to share the knowledge that I have gained with other sailors. The lessons I've learned from Udi's coaching is information that I've never heard from any other coach or seen thoroughly presented in any book. I knew that the coaching I'd gained from Udi was unlike anything else that was out there, and that I had to get this stuff down on paper.

So I wrote this book as I neared the end of my high school sailing career – I wrote using the knowledge that I'd gained over the years, as well as from a series of interviews with Udi to hear his sailing advice as well as his personal stories. I wanted this book to include not just technical sailing content, but also Udi's experiences from his own sailing career, interspersed among the lessons on racing tactics and strategy. Throughout my process of organizing the book, writing the chapters, and creating the diagrams, my goal was to create the most comprehensive book possible for raising your level of sailing, covering the months or years of training and preparation before an event up to the very last race.

So, who is this book for? Serious sailors at any level who are motivated to look closely into the details of their sailing will benefit from reading this book. Novice sailors will take a deep dive into the steps to approaching pre-regatta preparation and each area of the race course, and advanced sailors will gain a new perspective on racing tactics and strategy. What we've created here is a chronologically ordered, practical guide to raising the level of your racing, from the beginner to the advanced racer, at every point around the racecourse.

Although I wrote this book, you'll notice that it reads from Udi's perspective as a coach. I believe this is the best way to replicate on paper Udi's voice. Just as he's coached me all these years, he'll coach you as well. I hope that Udi's lessons will reach you through these pages.

Mason Stang

PART 1

PRE-REGATTA PREPARATION
A regatta is won or lost before the first race even begins

Imagine that you're leading a regatta on the final day of racing. The pressure's on. You only need to sail well for a few more races and you've won the series. You comfortably accelerate off the start line, and you fall into the familiar pattern of your upwind strategy. You're around the top mark and onto the downwind, boat lengths ahead of your competition, and you plan to keep it that way – suddenly, disaster strikes! A moment's concentration is lost, and you've steered a few degrees too low down a wave. You push the tiller in vain, but already you've wiped out to windward. The boom crashes over, and you find yourself swimming while the fleet surfs by...

Or maybe it's the beginning of the last race, and you've decided to go for it and win the pin end of the start line. You get set into position, but you misjudge your layline. At 30 seconds to the start you see that you won't clear the pin end boat, but you continue to fight for your position, drifting sideways, refusing to bail out and duck the fleet. The gun sounds

and you find yourself parked on the anchor line, wishing you could rewind the clock while you watch the rest of the fleet sail off...

Many sailors have experienced similar, if not identical, near-disaster scenarios. We've all been there. On the first day of the 2007 470 World Championship, the first of two qualifying regattas for the 2008 Olympic Games, my teammate and I suffered one of the worst performances of our lives – at least, on the first day of racing. The regatta was to be held at Cascais, Portugal, and we were confidently expecting strong wind conditions. As a team with great technique and boat speed in strong wind, we had become accustomed in the previous years to using a stiffer mast and sails with a relatively closed leech, which improved our performance in the light wind. This way, with our equipment geared towards lighter conditions, we were fast in the light wind, and we relied on our technique to be fast in strong wind as well. However, only a few weeks before the 2007 World Championship, knowing that the wind would be consistently strong, we decided to switch back to a stronger wind setup to give us even more of an edge in boat speed: a softer mast and more open sails. This turned out to be the mistake that gave us so much difficulty throughout the rest of the Championship.

We were so well tuned to our old equipment that we could adjust our rig settings to any condition in under a half minute. In every situation we knew exactly how to adjust the shrouds, the spreaders, the tension, and the sail controls. However, we were not as well tuned with the new, strong wind oriented mast and sails. During the World Championship, every change in rig settings took us a few extra precious minutes, and we spent much more time on the racecourse with our heads in the boat, making sure that the boat was set up to be fast. As a result, we forgot to assess the conditions, our opponents, and look outside the boat at the big picture. We made so many mistakes on the race course that by the end of the first day it was unlikely that we would even qualify for the finals – even though the only time we hadn't qualified for the upper fleet had been our very first 470 regatta ten years earlier. Furthermore,

this year's championship was the most important event for Olympic qualification, and our main competition was in the top ten. The pressure was on.

After our disastrous first day, we simplified our game and took the championship race by race, leg by leg, and improved our performance. Fortunately, by changing our game and with a bit of luck, we were able to climb back in the standings and win the bronze medal. Needless to say, if I'd been smarter about my preparation before the regatta, I wouldn't have had such a poor performance on the first day of racing, and it might have saved me the championship.

The truth is that every successful championship is a process that begins weeks and even months before the few days of racing. Regattas are won or lost before the first day of racing even begins. To win races, you must do every bit of preparation you can before the first start to give yourself the greatest advantage when you're on the water.

It takes a considerable amount of preparation to set yourself up for success at a sailing regatta. The following chapters list the steps I have taken before every regatta that have led me to be successful.

Chapter 1

ON LAND

So you're preparing for your most important event of the year. These are the steps you should take before going out sailing to ensure your success, ranging from weeks before the regatta to the morning of each day of racing.

THE WEEKS BEFORE

☀ Read the Notice of Race (NOR). Review the dates, location, and eligibility information. In addition to reading the NOR months before the regatta to help you make travel plans, be sure to read it again before the first day of racing so that you don't miss out on any important scheduling details or rule changes.

☀ Register for the regatta as soon as registration opens online. Be aware if there is a cap on the number of boats that can enter. A few of the youth regattas in the United States, for example, are often limited to the first 100 entries, and fill up in just minutes after registration opens. If you want to be there, plan ahead, put it on your calendar, and make sure you're at your computer when it's time to register.

☀ Organize your travel plans. Book your flights and hotel, if applicable.

☀ Make sure you will have a boat to sail! Organize the shipping of your boat and sails, or book a charter if you need one. Check your boat thoroughly to ensure that everything is in proper working order.

☀ Carefully pack everything you will need when you travel. This might include a toolbox with the tools and spare parts that are appropriate to your boat, sailing gear for a range of conditions, sails, etc. Be sure that you have all your gear. If you will be sailing a boat that you do not use on a regular basis – for example, in the United States, West Coast sailors might keep a boat on the East Coast – I suggest that you snap a few photos of your boat after each regatta so that before the next one, you can look back and see exactly what you have in the boat and what else you need to bring.

☀ In the weeks or even months before the event, try to practice in the anticipated conditions of the regatta, even if you are not at the regatta location. Start tracking the weather trends of the venue. Monitor the weather over the time before the regatta. Often the wind conditions are determined by the seasons.

☀ Arrange some time to train in the area where you will compete. I prefer that youth sailors train a few days at the venue before national-level championships. In the 470, I began training at the site over a week before each World and European Championship. By getting used to the venue, you are gaining a valuable 'home field advantage'. Learn any trends in the wind, current, sea state, or other strategic knowledge that is specific to that location.

☀ Reread your past regatta notes. This is where your notebook will come in handy![1] Review any notes you made previously about the current and wind conditions in the area of the regatta to help inform your racecourse strategy.

☀ Learn anything else you can from resources online. Look at multiple online weather forecast models, either to just get a feel for the speed, direction and trends of the wind at the venue, or to get a long term estimate for the conditions during the regatta. Also look at nautical charts that show the depths in your racing area. The depths around the course can affect the current, sea state, and even whether a turtled capsize could land your mast in the mud.

☀ Talk to the locals! At the end of the day, local knowledge can give you the greatest advantage going into race days. Generally, most local sailors will be happy to share with you the tips and tricks of their location. For example, the breeze clocks towards the shore when the sun goes down, there is current relief on the left side, etc.

☀ Read the Sailing Instructions (SIs) and the Notice of Race word by word. This is a rule that I cannot stress enough. Take the time to make sure you know the courses, the schedule, and any rule changes. Depending on the complexity, either memorize the important points the night before or print out a copy to keep onboard the boat. I can't tell you how many championships have been lost by sailors who, for example, didn't realize they were only required to do a single turn to exonerate themselves, sailed the wrong course, or were otherwise unprepared.

☀ Depending on the regatta, you should look at how many boats are registered, who your main competition is, the racecourses the race committee plans to run and any other factors that might fit into your strategy going into the first day.

☀ Once you have your boat at the venue, be sure that it is race ready. Make any necessary upgrades or modifications, polish the boat, and make sure everything is in working order.

☀ Complete a checklist for your boat before the first day of racing and each day of racing after you come off the water. Inspect your boat from top to bottom and make any repairs that night, not the next morning. The checklist – a routine inspection list of

---

[1] See *Build Your Season* for details about keeping a notebook.

everything on the boat to check after each day of racing – will be different for every type of boat, but it is essential to your success the next day on the water.

❋ Get a good night's sleep. I like to organize and pack all my sailing gear the night before so I don't have to think about it the next morning.

EXPERT TIP

In all of my sailing career, in all the World Championships I have sailed, I have never had a breakdown that could have been prevented. Not many sailors can say the same. This is because every single day after racing I flipped my 470 on its side to check the gasket, all blocks, all lines, all fittings, all tape markings, and any weak parts of the boat to spot potential problems before they happen. It may take some extra time, and you may be one of the last to leave the boatyard each day after racing, but you will be reminded how it improves your results on the water when a competitor suffers a breakdown and retires from a race while you sail off to victory..

THE MORNING OF

❋ Arrive early enough that you will not be stressed for time to rig your boat, have a team meeting, and get to the racecourse with time to spare.

❋ Check the Notice Board for any schedule changes, changes to the SIs, and any other notices.

❋ Check the weather forecast. Look at multiple sources online as well as what you notice for yourself in terms of wind, clouds, and temperature. Check the tides as well – take note of how big the tides are, and note the time of the low tide and high tide that day. Discuss the anticipated conditions with your coach and/or other sailors.

❋ Rig and prepare your boat. Each type of boat is different, but stick with what works for you. Select your initial rig settings.

❋ Stretch and warm up.

❋ Put on your sailing gear and have a team meeting. When in doubt, overdress. It is much better to be overheated than freezing out there on the racecourse. Being cold and shivering drains your strength, energy, and mental acuity, so don't hesitate to bring aboard that extra jacket or warm hat. Note what the locals are wearing as well.

✳ Sail out to the racecourse. Depending on the type of boat, your skill level, and the regatta, aim to arrive at the racecourse at least 45 minutes before the first warning to give you some time to prepare.

One final note: the start of a regatta is not the time to try anything new, or you might have a similar experience to mine at the 2007 World Championship! Do not use new equipment, try a new rig setup, or change your technique of how you sail the boat, or you could encounter unexpected issues with your speed or equipment. Stick to what you know and keep it simple. Wait for your training sessions to test new equipment, boat settings, or sailing styles.

WHAT DOES IT TAKE TO GET YOUR BOAT IN RACING SHAPE?

While a race day is never the right time to try new equipment or test out different rig or sail settings, definitely take the time to try out new things during practices. Here are some of my suggestions for getting your boat in racing shape:

✳ Mark everything! The jib sheets, the vang, the spreaders, the centreboard, the spinnaker halyard, the tackline – whatever systems your boat has, make sure they are well marked. Marks allow you to instantly replicate settings that you know are fast. Have you ever had one of those moments when you were a rocket on the race course, and you seemed to have an unexplainable speed advantage over all the boats around you? Well, the next time that happens, check your markings and remember your sail trim and rig setup so that you can replicate it in the future. Marks also allow you to instantly change between your modes of sail trim when conditions change, without taking a costly extra look at your sails. The more automatic your sail trim and boat speed can be, then the more you can focus your attention on everything else.

✳ Read your Class Rules and see what upgrades are allowed. Many One Design Class Rules are 'closed', meaning you are not permitted to make changes to the boat unless they are specifically mentioned in the Class Rules document. This makes it easy to read through the document and find the legal modifications you can make to upgrade your boat.

✳ Check out what the fast guys are doing and look at their boats. I've heard coaches tell sailors 'Plagiarize in sailing, not in school'.

✳ Many sailors like to have every line in their boat a different colour. Even in boats with complex sail controls such as the 470, you'll rarely see the same line twice. This is so that even in those extreme wind and wave conditions when you're just hanging on, the fleet is chaos around you, and you can barely see through the waves and white water spraying into your eyes, you can quickly and confidently grab the right line in your boat without any accidental mix-ups.

✳ Keep your hull, blades, and gasket (if applicable) in tip top shape. Check especially the leading and trailing edges of your rudder and centreboard/ daggerboard/keel for any chips or scratches. A single chip in the gelcoat won't affect your racing, but the accumulated drag caused by many scratches, chips, and bits of damage to your hull and blades will slow you down.

✳ Keep a toolbox that is specific to your boat. As a coach, I've noticed a consistent trend that youth sailors' toolboxes grow bigger and bigger each year as they gain experience and a better understanding of their boat. At a minimum, make sure you are well prepared to carry out the normal maintenance for your boat, and carry out repairs for simple breakdowns. Each class of boat will have its own specific needs, but some common items included in most sailors' toolboxes are: a knife, Sharpie, rig tension gauge, pliers, electrical tape, sail tape, tape measure, splicing tools, screwdrivers, spare line, spare

shackles and blocks, and spare sheets.

Many boats also have rig settings, which are generally set before racing and may or may not be changed on the water. Depending on the boat, these settings include the tension on the stays, the angle, height, and length of the spreaders, the mast rake, the mast step location, backstay tension, etc. Rig setup varies greatly between boats (a 470 and a J-105 are wildly different) so I won't go into too much detail about the specifics behind each control, but in general, the rig setup affects two key things: the sail shape and the balance of the boat.

Think of it this way. Have you ever raced in five or six knots of wind, barely moving, scanning the water over the rail for any puff of wind that could power up your sails? Or have you ever sailed in extreme strong wind conditions, spray flying everywhere, massive gusts filling the sails and pushing the boat over, sails flapping, unmanageably overpowered, wishing if only that mainsail were a little bit smaller?

That's where rig settings come in. Each different rig setting optimizes the sails for a corresponding wind or sea state condition by either powering up or depowering the sails. Your settings for light wind should straighten the mast and increase the mast rake, giving the mainsail a deeper, more powerful shape that can take advantage of every gust of wind. By contrast, your settings for overpowered conditions should increase mast bend and decrease the mast rake, flattening out the sail and depowering the boat. Sail with depowered sails in five knots, or sail with powered up sails in twenty-five knots, and you will be slow, so it is crucial that while sailing you identify if you are either looking for power or if you want to depower, and that you are able to change your settings when conditions change.

Secondly, rig settings affect the balance of the boat – whether the boat wants to turn up into the wind while sailing upwind (weather helm) or if it wants to turn away from the wind (lee helm). To set up our settings to sail fast, we first need to understand the two main points of force that act on the boat: the Centre of Effort – you can think of this as the geometric centrepoint of your sails; and the Centre of Lateral Resistance – this is the centrepoint of your boat's sideways drag created by the keel, rudder, and hull, around which the boat pivots. If the Centre of Effort is farther forward than the Centre of Lateral Resistance, the bow will naturally be pushed away from the wind; if it is farther back, the boat will turn into the wind. While a small amount of weather helm upwind is sometimes beneficial, our goal is to balance these forces so that the boat will sail in a straight line upwind without requiring constant

input from rudder (this creates drag and is slow). So if you notice, for example, that you need to use significant rudder to prevent the bow steering off the wind, and small adjustments to your technique (sailing with a bit more heel, trimming in more main) are not enough to fix the problem, bring the Centre of Effort forward with adjustments to your mast rake, mast step, headstay tension, and any other adjustments applicable to your boat.

In boats with daggerboards or centreboards, sailors can also change the centre of lateral resistance for certain conditions, adding another layer of complexity. In the 470, for example, when sailing upwind in overpowered conditions, the centreboard should be raised as needed in order to reduce weather helm – this moves the centre of lateral resistance farther back in the boat, reducing the bow's tendency to turn up into the wind.

You will not be fast on most boats without a solid understanding of the rig settings. Wherever you are in the process of learning how to set up your boat to be fast, I recommend that you absorb all the information you can. Reach out to your coaches, your training partners, and other boats that are fast, and learn the ways of your boat. Most sailmakers also publish 'Tuning Guides' for each of their sails, with instructions for how to set up their boat in each wind condition. These are helpful starting points, but don't just blindly follow the tuning guide. I view these guides more as rough guidelines – ultimately, you need to experiment until you find the perfect setup for your crew weight and style of sailing. Don't be afraid to go out to practice with a little more tension, or a straighter mast, and see what happens. With experimentation and meticulous attention to how you set up the rig each day, analysing what works for you and what doesn't, you will find your own settings.

Finally, to be truly 'race ready', complete your boat's Checklist regularly and especially after each day of racing to make sure that there are no malfunctioning cleats, worn out ropes, loose bolts, corroded parts, or anything that looks like it could quickly turn into a race-ending problem on the water. There are no excuses for foreseeable equipment issues! If you see a rusting wire or a shackle or pin that looks like it might be past its prime, don't hesitate to replace it. It's better to be safe than sorry. You'll appreciate your efforts when one of your top competitors at a World Championship drops a sail or loses their rig due to a preventable equipment breakdown, allowing you to climb to the top spot (trust me, it happens).

A balanced boat has its Centre of Effort in line with its Centre of Lateral Resistance.

Chapter 2

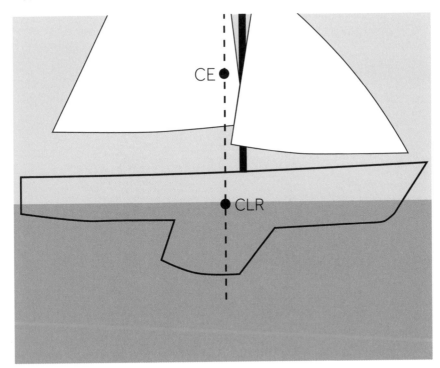

ON THE WATER: THE RACECOURSE ROUTINE

Finally, we're on the water! But there's more work to do before the first gun. Once you're out there get a feel for the conditions. If you have to sail a significant distance to get to the race course, don't just float over there. This is a great time to maximize your boat speed as if you were racing and get used to the conditions on any point of sail.

When you reach the racecourse the game of preparation changes completely. Now you must switch gears from land-based boat preparation to preparing yourself and your team for racing. During this time while executing your Racecourse Routine, you will narrow your focus to two main things: fine tuning your boat speed and boat-handling, and assessing the conditions.

You should give yourself a minimum of about 45 minutes before the first start to prepare in the racing area. Use the time before the start to tune your boat to make sure that you are fast. Find a couple of other boats and do a 'line-up' upwind. Each boat should set up 2–3 boat lengths apart on an upwind course and even to the wind, as if you were going off an even start line. The boats should get into position and accelerate at the same time. Do at least 2 or 3 line-ups on each tack, and reset yourselves and start again if a boat loses its lane.

The goal of doing line-ups is not to win the drill! It is to start evenly with each other and see how your speed and pointing compares to the other boats, so that you can make any necessary modifications to your sails, boat settings, or sailing techniques. For example, if you had great forward speed during a line-up but realized you were pointing much lower than the other boats and you quickly lost your lane, you might decide to make some minor adjustments with your boat setup or technique (for example, trim in your sails, close the leech,

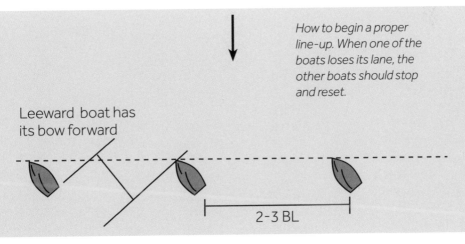

How to begin a proper line-up. When one of the boats loses its lane, the other boats should stop and reset.

Leeward boat has its bow forward

2-3 BL

shift your weight forward, and use a bit more heel to point higher). If you are overpowered or underpowered compared to the other boats, you may need to adjust your rig setup. This is the time when a coach can motor behind you to see your setup in comparison with other boats and help you tune your boat to sail faster. Continue with this exercise for 10–15 minutes upwind until you are confident that your sails, rig settings, and sailing technique are race ready.

Line-ups both upwind and downwind are critical to making sure that you have the proper speed, point, and boat set up before the start. Tune yourself now so that you are at full speed before the first race. Also be sure to throw in a few tacks and gybes to make sure that your boat handling is on point. If your courses include reach legs, be sure to sail on a reach on both tacks to get a feel for the angles you can sail.

While tuning your boat speed during your line-ups, don't forget to look outside the boat and analyse the conditions around you on the racecourse. If you are sailing with a compass, keep one eye on the numbers, looking out for any shifts or movements in the wind. See if you can find any trends in the wind shifts. If the wind is oscillating, try to determine the magnitude and duration of the shifts back and forth. I recommend writing down

the farthest-left and farthest-right compass numbers that you see while sailing upwind for both tacks, so that off the start line and during the race upwind you can easily determine what phase of the wind you are in (whether you are headed or lifted). On most dinghies I find it's convenient to write down your numbers on the boom with a grease pen, your starboard numbers on the starboard side and your port numbers on the port side, so you can see them and adjust them while sailing upwind.

Additionally, look for any trends with the wind direction and wind speed. Sometimes gusts or lulls will come with a shift in a recurring direction. Consider, how does the observed wind direction and wind speed compare to the forecasted weather? Look for any differences in the wave state across the course that might indicate differences in wind strength or current. Be aware of any clouds, wind changes or temperature changes that might predict a change in the conditions on the racecourse.

Here are some questions you might ask yourself during your Racecourse Routine before the start to help you analyse the conditions:

❋ Does one part of the course have significantly more or less wind?

❋ Is there a pattern to the shifts? Write down your lifted and headed compass numbers on each tack upwind, and keep an eye on them to see how the shift range changes during your Racecourse Routine.

✳ Is there a pattern to the gusts and lulls in the wind? Is the wind speed patchy or is it consistent? Is the direction shifty or consistent? Is the sea state flat, choppy, or is there ocean swell? Be aware of how these factors affect your technique and sail setup.

✳ Is there any current? Is it different from one side of the racecourse to the other?

✳ Is there anything else you notice (perhaps specific to that venue) indicating that one side of the racecourse is biased or favoured?

✳ If the top mark and start line have already been set, notice if the first beat is unusually long or short. Is the top mark biased to the left or right side of the racecourse looking upwind?

✳ How are the conditions across the course changing (wind speed, wind direction, current, etc)?

✳ Is the wind at the top of the beat different from the wind at the bottom?

One particularly simple, yet effective exercise that you can use to see if one side of the course might have an advantage is a 'split tack'. Once you are tuned up, grab another boat that has similar speed. Depending on the size of

the race course and how much time you have before the start, you might both choose to do a five-minute split tack, or longer. To begin the split tack, one boat ducks directly behind the other, at which point both boats start a five-minute timer and sail at full speed upwind. After approximately five minutes both boats tack and converge back together, seeing who comes out in front. Note that you don't want to sail blindly to your side and only be looking at your timer. It's a common mistake for sailors doing a split tack to tack exactly at five minutes, while the right thing to do is to take the best opportunity that you get from your side of the course. If you get a header at 4:45, for example, tack on that and take the advantage. If you see a gust farther out to the side, it's okay to sail a bit farther to get into the better pressure and tack at 5:15. This way, each boat takes the best of their side, which makes this an accurate representation of how you would come out from your side in the race. If one boat is significantly farther ahead when the boats cross, this might indicate that the side of the course that boat sailed is favoured.

It's easy to get caught up with tuning your boat speed and practising manoeuvres before the first race, but the last thing you want to do is miss the start because you got too far away and lost track of time. Always make sure that you know the starting time for the first race and that you periodically check the time on your watch, so that you can turn around with enough time to return to the starting area.

As a final note, races quite often don't start on time. The wind may die, or shift significantly, or the race committee may make an error and postpone the race. While you are waiting under postponement, it's okay to 'switch off'. As a sailor you can feel a lot of pressure to perform well, especially during important regattas, and the time before the start can be especially stressful. Take some time to eat some snacks, talk with friends, and relax, but be prepared to 'switch on' again into racing mode once the AP flag comes down or when you start to see the weather situation stabilize. Once your class flag is raised, remember to trust your skills. Enjoy the experience. You have already done all you can to prepare, and now is the time to race.

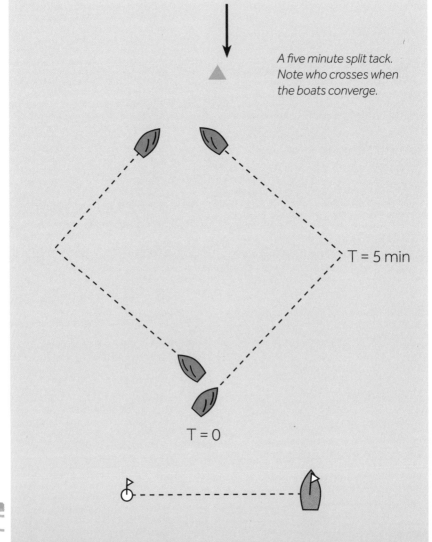

A five minute split tack. Note who crosses when the boats converge.

T = 5 min

T = 0

A BREAKDOWN OF A RECOMMENDED RACECOURSE ROUTINE

TIME TO START	CONTENT
60 minutes or earlier	Double check your boat before launching, launch, check in if specified (onshore or on the water), assess the conditions on the way out.
50 minutes	10–15 minutes of upwind, line-ups, checking and exploring the upwind area of the race course. Assess your speed and if necessary make small fine-tuning adjustments to sails, settings or technique. Recommended to get to the mark 1 area if possible. Record upwind compass numbers, make observations about the conditions as you go.
40 minutes	Downwind line-ups, check your speed, technique, manoeuvres, gybes and boat-handling.
30 Minutes	Quick break and assessment of your speed, boat-handling, and the conditions on the racecourse. Double check set-up & settings, make any rig changes to best suit the conditions you anticipate in the race. At this point you should be confident with your boat speed and boat-handling. Find a partner and do one or two split tacks.
15 minutes	Drink, snacks, continue to observe the conditions, race course, and other boats. Change clothing if necessary. Mind-set (relax or hyped-up). Rough assessment of the factors on the race course.
10 minutes	Begin your Pre-Start Routine.[2]
5 Minutes	Final assessment and plan – Racing time.

[2] See *Do Your Homework: Pre-Start Routine.*

PART 2

START
You can't win the race from the start,
but you can definitely lose it.

This start has a boat-end bias and is very
crowded. The boat with the black mast, sailed by
Udi Gal and his teammate, wins the boat end.

Chapter 3

DO YOUR HOMEWORK: THE PRE-START ROUTINE

Try to think back to the best start you've ever had. One that's memorable, where you looked back at the boats behind you and thought to yourself 'wow, how did I do that?' Before the gun you most likely had control of the windward boat with space to leeward, you were covered from the watchful eyes onboard the race committee boat, and you were able to accelerate early, build up to full speed, and punch out from the boats around you as the gun sounded. Everyone has experienced getting a great start in one race or another – the challenge is doing it every time. Consistently achieving these elements in every start isn't easy. In fact, every good start is a product of executing the right steps long before you're racing off the line. In this chapter I outline the elements of the starting process that have led to my success, and I hope that they help you as well.

The clock is counting down to the start, but there are just a few more steps we must take to ensure a winning start and a successful upwind strategy before lining up with the fleet. All the top racers in the world have a Pre-Start Routine – a routine that they do before every single start in order to determine their strategy for that start and for the upwind leg. Having already done your Racecourse Routine (see the previous chapter), you should by now be warmed up, have done some manoeuvres, line-ups, split tacks, and you should be confident about your boat speed and boat-handling. At about 10–15 minutes before the first start (5–10 minutes before the warning signal), it's time to shift from your Racecourse Routine to your Pre-Start Routine. The Pre-Start Routine encompasses everything you should do from that point forward, until it's time to get into position on the start line approximately 1–2 minutes before the start. With experience the steps of your Pre-Start Routine will become automatic, but I've laid them out clearly here.

STEP 1: GATHER INFORMATION

The first step is gathering information. You already have a feel for the conditions and explored the upwind beat during your Racecourse Routine. Hopefully you've also made some observations about the racecourse while you were sailing that will give you a competitive advantage. Ask yourself: Did I notice more wind on one side of the course? Was there a pattern to the shifts? Was there any current? Did my split tack(s) show that one side of the upwind leg has an advantage, and does this make sense with my other observations?

ASSESSING THE UPWIND LEG
We will use all this information to develop a strategy, or game plan,

27

for the upwind leg, but we need more information in order to set ourselves up for a successful start. In particular, here is the information you should collect before the start sequence:

✻ First of all, go above the starting line, stand up in your boat as high as you can and take a big, wide look at everything around you. The higher up you are, the better you will see the wind on the water. Look at the start line, the upwind leg, and the rest of the racing area to get the most expansive view possible of the racecourse, and notice anything that jumps out at you. Do you see any differences in the waves across the course, or darker patches of water, indicating differences in pressure?

✻ Are there any major weather events – a line of clouds, thunderstorms, rising temperature or sunny skies, etc – that might affect the wind on the racecourse? Are there any visible current lines that might indicate differences in current?

✻ How important a factor will the shifts be in this race? Are the shifts large or small? How long does each shift last; what's their rhythm? How many shifts will we potentially see in this upcoming leg?

✻ Is there any current on the racecourse? Is it consistent across the course, or does one side have more favourable current? How will the tides and current change throughout the day?

✻ Based on the forecasts, local knowledge, and your own observations, how do you predict the wind and weather will change over the course of the day? Try to identify major trends (eg the wind is very light right now, but veering right and increasing velocity as the sea breeze builds.) You might consider how the conditions have changed since you first left shore.

✻ Is the upwind mark biased to the left or the right side of the upwind leg?

Assessing the above factors, make a prediction on whether you think the left or right side of the first upwind leg is favoured – in other words, that you would gain an advantage by sailing to that side. This might be due to more favourable current, wind, an anticipated weather event, or any combination of the above factors. It might also be the case that the conditions are so shifty or the pressure is so inconsistent that you must wait to see which side has more pressure in the final couple of minutes before the start, or that it is impossible to predict which side will give an advantage. Whatever the case, remember your prediction, because we will use it in a moment to formulate a strategy for the start.

ASSESSING THE START LINE

❋ Look at the length of the line. Then check the number of boats in the fleet. Does the length of the line strike you as being especially long or short for the size of the fleet? As a result, do you foresee the start being especially crowded or uncrowded? This will become easier to judge as you gain experience from doing hundreds of starts.

❋ Is there any bias on the line? If so, which end is biased, by how much?

Line bias refers to one end of the start line being farther upwind than the other. If you are sailing with a compass, the bias is easy to calculate. One method is to sail directly along the line and record your heading. Then, find the compass number of the direction the wind is coming from, by either using your boat's instruments or doing a 'wind shot' (recording your heading while turning your boat directly into the wind). With some quick mental maths, you should be able to calculate the difference between these two values. If the

Before the start I like to imagine a 'midline' that goes straight upwind from the start line, dividing the racecourse into two halves. The location of the windward mark in comparison to this midline affects our upwind strategy. For example, if the mark is significantly farther to the right, especially with a relatively short upwind leg, then there is generally a strategic advantage to getting over to the right side of the upwind leg as early as possible, by either starting on the right side of the start line or taking the first opportunity to get onto port tack.

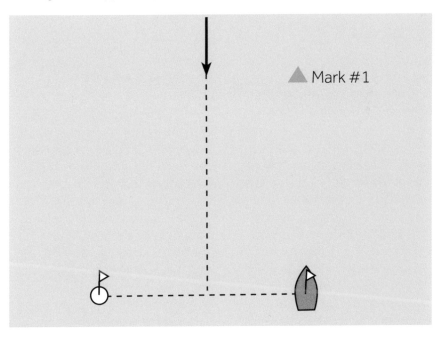

Mark #1

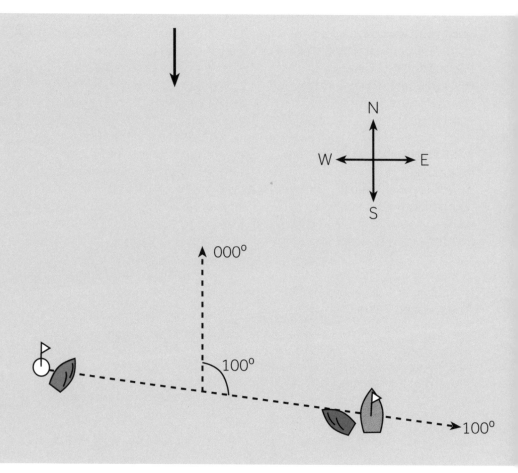

In this example, the pin end of the line is favoured by 10 degrees. Sailors can find this by calculating the difference between the bearing of the start line and the bearing to the wind. The line bias is also obvious from the boat sailing upwind on port near the pin end of the line, clearly lifted and crossing the boat on the boat end.

line is perfectly square, you will get a difference of 90°. The amount that your calculated value differs from 90° is the magnitude of the bias. You can figure out which end is favourably biased from your calculated value and the direction that you sailed along the line (see diagram above).

If you are sailing without a compass, you will need to visually judge the line bias. An easy way to detect a significant line bias is to sail close-hauled upwind from the pin or the boat end, and judge visually if you are headed or lifted compared to the line. Or, find another boat sailing close-hauled and judge their angle relative to the line.

Perhaps the very simplest way to quickly determine the line bias is to position yourself on the line and point your bow straight into the wind. Then, look at your traveller bar, and see how it is angled to the line. Although not very precise, this method is useful if you are short on time.

ASSESSING THE FLEET

Ask yourself:

❋ Who is your greatest competition in this fleet? Is there any possibility of falling into a match racing situation with another boat?

❋ What is the level of the fleet? Where do they fall on the scale from newbies to Olympians?

❋ Are you getting any idea about the general mindset or mood of the fleet? (eg Ultra-competitive, aggressive, chilled-out). Are the other competitors joking with each other on the water, or are they crowded around the RC boat furiously practising their tacks and accelerations?

Here is an example of a mental image you might create from your observations of the weather, the racecourse, and the fleet. You will use these observations to develop your strategy for the start and the upwind.

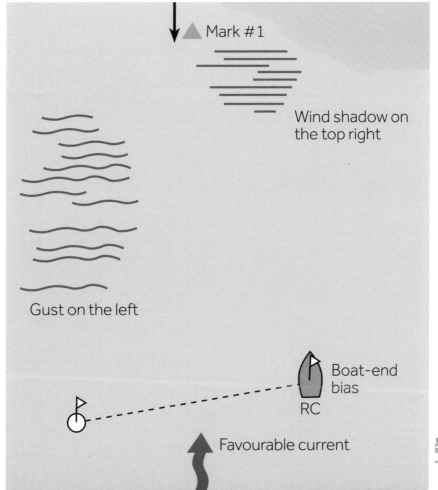

Mark #1

Wind shadow on the top right

Gust on the left

Boat-end bias

RC

Favourable current

✳ Even if the start sequence hasn't yet begun, does it seem like the fleet is crowded together at one end of the line? Additionally, a big line bias is usually an indication that the favoured side of the line will be very crowded.

At this point you should have a good idea about these three things:

1 The strategy of the upwind leg.
2 The bias of the start line.
3 Any relevant information about the fleet.

Using all this information, I like to construct a mental image of the starting line and the first upwind leg, just to make it all clearer to myself. This information will help determine the starting strategy.

I like to divide the start line into four quadrants.

STEP 2: MAKE YOUR GAME PLAN

Next, using the information we collected in Step 1, we need to come up with a game plan for the start and for the upwind. The following are the details of our game plan that we should either decide or at least have a solid idea about before we go into the starting sequence:

WHERE ON THE LINE SHOULD I START?

This is one of the most commonly asked questions going into a start, and rightly so. Starting in the right place on the line won't automatically hand you a winning start, but it can set you up for a successful start and is the first step to carrying out your upwind strategy.

The three main factors determining your initial assessment of where you should start are:

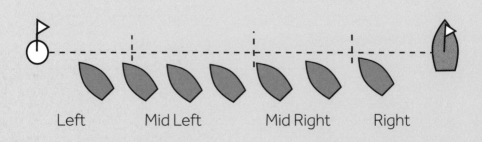

Left   Mid Left   Mid Right   Right

WHERE ON THE LINE SHOULD I START?

PIN END			BOAT END
FAR LEFT	MID LEFT	MID RIGHT	FAR RIGHT
LEFT BIAS		RIGHT BIAS	
LEFT STRATEGY LIGHT WIND	RIGHT STRATEGY STRONG WIND	LEFT STRATEGY LIGHT WIND	RIGHT STRATEGY STRONG WIND

This chart makes the likely assumption that the fleet is starting on starboard tack.

1 The bias of the line
2 Your upwind strategy (where on the racecourse you generally want to go)
3 The strength of the wind

Sound familiar? This is why we collected all that information about the racecourse and the starting line. It all comes together when we formulate a plan for the start.

You can use the chart above as a rough guideline for deciding where on the starting line to start, according to the three factors.

To apply this chart to your starting process, think of a significant line bias as restricting your start to only the favoured half of the line. The longer the line, the more important it is to stay connected to the favoured end. Then, choose where you want to start on that half according to the other factors. In light wind and a left upwind strategy, start farther to the left. In strong wind and a right strategy, start farther right. I find that dividing the starting line into four sections as I have done in this chart makes it easy to formulate my strategy and to communicate the plan to the crew. Telling your teammates 'Let's plan to start in the middle left' gives everyone on the boat a much clearer understanding of the game plan than saying 'Let's start somewhere in the middle', and it makes sure that you've chosen to do so for the right reasons.

Instead of just memorizing this chart by rote, it is important for sailors to understand the reasoning behind it. It is generally obvious to people why it is beneficial to start on the favoured end of the starting line: you are literally starting your race with a head start, farther upwind and closer to the windward mark than the other sailors. See the example page 34:

33

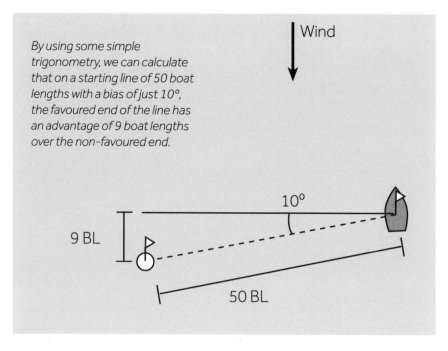

By using some simple trigonometry, we can calculate that on a starting line of 50 boat lengths with a bias of just 10°, the favoured end of the line has an advantage of 9 boat lengths over the non-favoured end.

It is also quite clear why if one side of the racecourse is favoured, it is advantageous to start on that side of the starting line: by starting closer to the strategically favoured side of the upwind leg, you will be one of the first boats to reach those more favourable conditions. But less obvious to most sailors is the understanding that there is generally an advantage to starting to leeward of a pack of boats in light wind, and to starting to windward of a pack of boats in strong wind. The reason has to do with how sailing boats sailing upwind 'lose their lane' to another boat (see diagram opposite).

There's no need to memorize the Starting Line Strategy chart – it's just to help you understand how choosing where on the line to start is a matter of balancing these three factors (line bias, upwind strategy, and wind strength). Keep in mind, these factors don't usually hold equal weight. If one or two factors are of much greater importance than the others, they should play a greater role in determining where you should start. For example, if the left side of the course were incredibly favoured because it had much stronger wind than the right side, then a few degrees of bias to the right side of the start line suddenly becomes much less of a significant factor – of course you should start a bit closer to the pin end, and be one of the first boats to reach those more favourable conditions. Any early advantage to starting by the boat end would quickly be more than cancelled out by the faster speed of the boats on the left.

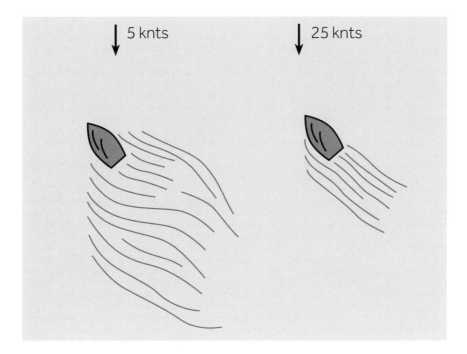

When sailing boats sail upwind, they create an area of turbulent 'dirty air' around them, as shown in the above diagram. When a second boat sails in the first boat's dirty air, it loses performance because the wind powering its sails is blocked or is very turbulent, which disrupts the flow over its sails. As a result, the second boat can't point as high into the wind, slows down, and falls farther and farther into the first boat's wind shadow of dirty air. This is how a boat loses its lane.

In light wind, a significant amount of air is deflected by a boat's mainsail into the area directly to windward of it (to the right side of a boat sailing upwind on starboard tack). This turbulent dirty air is what gives the leeward boat an advantage in light wind over a windward boat – the windward boat is at a greater danger of losing its lane from the leeward boat's larger area of dirty air.

In stronger wind and overpowered conditions, however, the force of the wind is strong enough to take the air deflected from the sails along with it, thereby making the area of dirty air around each boat smaller. The effect of the air deflected to windward by the mainsail is especially reduced, but each boat still creates a significant wind shadow directly to leeward of its sails. As a result, with less dirty air deflected into the windward boat, the leeward boat is now at a disadvantage. The windward boat is now in a position to drop its bow a few degrees (speeding up significantly with the lower angle and stronger wind) and roll over the top of the leeward boat.

Therefore, I recommend that you use the chart on page 33 as a rough guideline, or as a starting point to developing your game plan. It is up to you to weigh the importance of each factor and decide which should most determine your position on the line.

HOW CLOSE DO I WANT TO BE TO THE LINE?

When and where (how early/late, how close/far) do I want to go into position? This is the second question you should ask yourself before the start. You've already decided your starting position along the line, but it's important that you go into the start with an idea of how close or far you want to be from the line compared to the other boats while lining up with the fleet.

Note that I'm not referring to how close you should be to the line at start time. Your goal is to be at full speed crossing the line exactly as the gun sounds. I'm referring to your approach to the line before zero – do you want to get in position early and be one of the boats in front defending your position as the fleet drifts closer to the line in the last minute, or do you want to hang back a little and wait for the right time to find a hole and accelerate? It depends on three main factors.[3]

1 Line Bias
2 Strength of Wind
3 Crowded vs Uncrowded

Remembering this rule will instantly upgrade the level of your starts. The reasoning behind this rule is all about access *to the line*. In the last 30-60 seconds before the start, you always want to have

> ### THE KEY RULE
>
> *As the line becomes more pin favoured, the wind gets lighter, and the start is more crowded (a short line for the size of the fleet), you want to get into position earlier and stay closer to the line. As the line becomes more boat favoured, the wind gets stronger, and the start is less crowded, you should get into position later and stay farther from the line.*

control over access to the line. In other words, you have control over when you choose to pull the trigger and accelerate, and when you do, there are no boats in front of you or locking you from leeward, and you have open water in front of you to punch the line. A pin bias, lighter wind, and a crowded fleet all reduce your access to the line, which is why in this environment you definitely want to prioritize being in the front row as the boats line up, and not get trapped in the second or third row.

Why does a pin bias reduce your access to the line? Because it increases the sailing distance you need to sail in order to cross the start line. Lining up before a line with a pin bias (assuming you

---

[3] Current is another factor. Its effect will be discussed in more detail in *Starting In Current.*

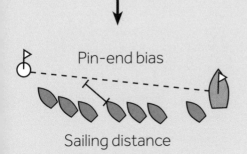

Pin-end bias

Sailing distance

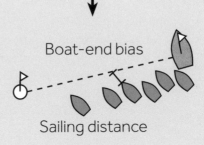

Boat-end bias

Sailing distance

are lining up on starboard), your upwind course to sail to the start line is much less direct than if the line were boat end favoured (see diagram above). As a result, you have to travel farther than you would otherwise to reach the line, and it will take more time. The boats to leeward of you will also tend to have their bow out farther while lining up, meaning there is a greater possibility of a leeward boat luffing into the wind and preventing you from moving forward. And finally, even with the same number of boats, a starting line with a pin bias will seem more crowded than one with a boat end bias, because all the boats are lined up angled sideways to the line rather than straight at it (each boat taking up more space). All of this means that you need to make sure you are in the front row early on, you need to begin your acceleration to the line earlier, and you need to line up closer to the line than you would otherwise.

Light wind also reduces your access to the line, for two reasons: first, in light wind you move slower than in medium or strong conditions. This means that from

A pin bias increases your sailing distance to the line. A boat bias decreases your sailing distance to the line.

X position before the start it will take you longer to reach the start line. Secondly, the dirty air and wind shadows created by the boats is much more pronounced in lighter wind. In fact, the air actually rises up and over the fleet in light wind, spelling disaster for any boat caught in the second or third row and unable to move forward. For both these reasons, in light wind it pays to stay closer to the line and be careful not to get caught behind the fleet.

It should also be obvious that a crowded line reduces your access to the line. Unless you're in the front row, chances are there will be boats in front of you, and you will have to get past them to get a first row start. With everyone hoping to reserve a spot, crowded fleets also tend to line up into position earlier in the start sequence, in some fleets at around 1.30 minutes on the countdown timer, or even earlier. If you end up being one of the last boats to get into position on a crowded line, you may find yourself in the unfortunate situation of reaching behind a line of transoms, unable to find a gap to stick your bow, panicking as your watch counts down to the gun. So stay close to the line, get your bow out in front, and reserve a spot for yourself.

By contrast, when we have a start line with a boat end bias, stronger wind, and a less crowded fleet, we have the opposite situation. You can sail a more direct upwind course to the line, you can move faster through the water with less hindrance from dirty air, and there's less likely to be boats in front of you blocking your access to the line. According to our Key Rule, in this environment we should get into position later and stay farther from the line, before doing a controlled acceleration that punches the line at full speed. In an environment where it is easy to access the line, there is no reason to unnecessarily push forward from the pack and risk getting too close to the line, being forced to slow down, and losing flow while the rest of the fleet surges forward.

Now we have a solid plan for where we want to position ourselves before the start. But remember, your plan can adapt and change! As other factors play themselves out during the sequence, such as a shift in the wind or a traffic jam at one end of the line, you can adapt your strategy. The purpose of this

process of developing a strategy before the start sequence is just to get you in the right general location, to make sure you are mindful of your strategy, and that you have a reason for everything you do.

In very light wind with a very long start line – the kind of conditions where everyone is barely moving and it would take you many minutes to float from one end to the other – it becomes even more important that you do this process early. At three minutes before the start, you wouldn't want to develop a strategy to start at one end of the line only to realize it will take you five minutes to get there!

HOW MUCH RISK SHOULD I TAKE?

Here is a final question to consider before going into a start, specifically when the starting line has an obvious bias to one side. How much risk do you want to take?

During the starting sequence you'll find that when there is an obvious and significant bias to one side of the upwind or one end of the start line, that end of the line becomes extremely crowded, with boats lined up two or three rows deep fighting to start there. As any observer can see, with so many boats fighting for such a short area of the line, very few of them will actually get good starts. One or two guys will blast out of there looking like winners, but most will

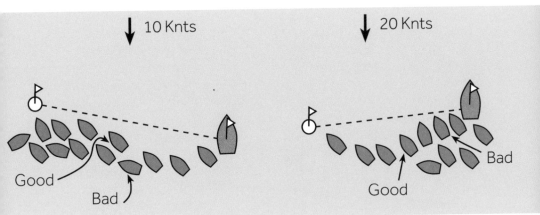

*Look at the above situations **45 seconds before the start**. In the left situation we have light wind, a pin bias, and a crowded line, so you definitely don't want to be hanging back, but instead fighting at the front and going into position earlier. In the right situation we have strong wind, a boat end bias, and a less crowded line. Since we have easy access to the line, there's no reason to put yourself in a vulnerable, risky position in front of the other boats during the approach.*

either end up in bad lanes or will be over the line early and disqualified. But the few that get off cleanly will be starting the race in the prime position. In these situations, competing in the crowded area on the start line, which is usually one of the ends, is a game of high risk and high reward.

Going for a more risky start means starting on the biased end of the starting line in the crowd of boats, or in the pack. Starting in the middle of this pack means there's a lower chance of getting off the line clean, but there's a greater reward if you do. A more conservative start, on the other hand, would mean starting outside the crowd, most likely giving up on some of the strategic advantage from starting in the more crowded area but having a higher chance

of a good lane off the line. In other words, lower risk, lower reward. (Remember, if one end of the line is very crowded, then the rest of the line will be much less crowded than an average line.) Experienced sailors know that sailing consistently well is a matter of risk management. This is the aspect of starting that you must take into account to your starting strategy if you want to have a consistent performance over multiple starts.

If there's a boat-end line bias and a right strategy, for example, then yes, the optimum place to start would be at the boat end – but if everyone in the fleet knows this, then the boat end will be an absolute traffic jam. Maybe just one in ten boats starting at this end of the line will get a good start. In this sort of situation I find that

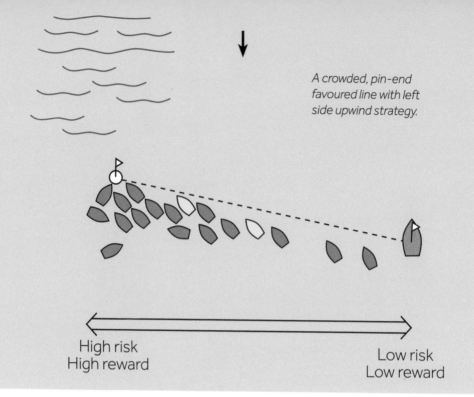

A crowded, pin-end favoured line with left side upwind strategy.

High risk
High reward

Low risk
Low reward

it generally pays to start a few boat lengths to leeward in a less crowded area, where you'll have a greater chance of a good start. But ultimately, deciding how much risk you want to take comes down to a couple of factors, summarized below:

HOW CONFIDENT ARE YOU OF GETTING A SUCCESSFUL START IN THE PACK?

The greater confidence you have in getting a good start from within the pack at the favoured end of the line, the more you can and should start closer to that end.

This is where assessing the fleet becomes relevant, and it helps if you have competed against the other sailors before. Are you one of the best sailors in the fleet, or do you always seem to

get rolled over by other boats once the gun sounds? Are all the sailors in a friendly, laid-back mood, or are they getting ready to tear each other apart on the starting line?

In most cases, especially in a tight fleet, the best sailors on the racecourse will be there fighting for the favoured end, while the farther away from that end you go, the lower the level of the sailors starting there. That's another reason that makes fighting for the favoured end so risky. If you aren't confident that you can defend your position in the front row of the pack and hold your lane off the line, especially in a fleet of aggressive boats who are going to pounce on any mistake you make, it's probably not the best idea to start there. Go down the line until the fleet thins out a bit, trade a little more reward for a little less risk, and

EXPERT TIP

Just to clarify, when I refer to a 'good start', I mean a start where you have a solid lane and are holding a similar VMG (Velocity Made Good) with the boats to leeward and to windward, and you could continue for at least a minute or more comfortably on starboard without losing your lane and being forced to tack. This is a good outcome – you don't have to win the start, and the sailors who do try to win every start will be quickly out of the running after one or two failed starts. Any racer's goal should be to consistently start in a clear lane that gives them options to execute their upwind strategy. A bad start is a start where you almost immediately lose your lane and fall into the dirty air of other boats, or it is obvious that you will in the next 20-30 seconds, and you are forced to tack away behind the fleet.

get a good, solid start that might not give you a head start over the fleet, but that you can hold a lane in and that gives you options to carry out your upwind strategy.

But if you know that you can hold your own with the other boats, and you're looking to win races, don't be afraid to fight for that top spot on the line. After all, in a competitive fleet, chances are that top finishers of each race will be those who have taken their chances starting near the favoured end.

(The only case that this might not be true is if you are so much faster or smarter than the other boats that you can consistently win races even when starting away from the crowded end of the line. In this case, start in a more conservative, safe area of the line,

prioritize consistency, and you have a sure win!).

WHAT IS YOUR SCORELINE?

To determine before the start how much risk you want to take, you also need to look at the big picture of the entire regatta. Your scoreline is something to take into account.

Most regattas these days have at least one 'throw-out race'. This is when after a specified number of races are completed, your worst result is dropped from the scoreline. This is one of the ways that race organizers incentivize sailors to take risks. It's part of the game. So you must take some risk in order to get your best result at an event, but there are situations during the regatta you should be aware of where you want to take more or less risk.

Imagine yourself in a variety of scenarios. It's the first start of a four day regatta, over which the race committee plans to complete 12 races. You get one throw-out. This is a situation in which you probably don't want to put yourself in the highest risk position on the racecourse. No one wants to start the regatta with a disqualification for being over the line early, and spend the rest of the races worrying about getting another bad result now that you already have your throw-out race. On the other hand, if you are preparing for the start of the last race and you haven't had a single 'throw-out score' (a bad race), by all means go for that higher risk start, because there's nothing to lose if it goes wrong. In general, if you haven't yet had a very bad result in the regatta, then you can take a little more risk in each of your starts, especially later as there are fewer and fewer races to go. But if you've already used your throw-out race, meaning you already have a disqualification or bad result, be careful not to risk a letter score or a bad start on the pin – but then don't let being too conservative hurt your score line either! It's a tricky skill to start and sail well with the mental pressure of knowing you need to perform well.

FINAL CONSIDERATIONS ON BALANCING RISK

A final consideration: it is much more risky to start in the pack on the pin end of the starting line than on the boat end. This is because since the fleet usually starts on starboard, if you do have a bad start on the pin end, it is much more difficult to bail out and find a good lane on port. On the boat end, even if you get a bad start, you often have the option to tack to port early and be one of the first boats going right, usually in a good lane. Your only option then will be the right side of the course, but you will have started with a head start on the favoured end of the line and/or you will be sailing towards the favoured end of the upwind leg. That's much better than getting a bad start on the pin end, being forced to tack out, and ducking the entire fleet. In general, in an important championship with a crowded fleet, you should only fight for the pin if you are 100% sure that you can win it.

Overall, starting is always about striking the right balance between risk and reward, and you have to look at the big picture to get it right. The challenge is taking enough risk during the start to set you up for the best race results that you are capable of, without losing the race before it has even begun. In general, I find that it pays to stay out of the super crowded areas as much as you can. At the Olympic level, all the boats know the value of starting in the least crowded area possible. That is why if you look at Olympic starts, all the boats are spread out evenly across the line. By contrast, if you look at the starts of a much lower level fleet, you will most likely see a crowd of twenty boats jammed together at the favoured end, all fighting for a two or three boat length advantage while the other three quarters of the line are virtually empty. Let me tell you, your chances of getting a good start in a pack like that, without being OCS (on course side), are close to zero. It is generally a better strategy in the long run, especially in regattas lasting multiple days where it pays to prioritize consistency, to lose a few boat lengths of bias on the start line but greatly improve your statistical chances of a successful start.

OTHER THINGS TO DO DURING THE PRE-START ROUTINE

Now that we have our strategy in place, there are other things we should do to make sure we are best prepared to start cleanly off the line.

☀ Practice the manoeuvres you will use on the start line. These include accelerations, holding position at minimum speed, double tacks, and any other manoeuvres you might use. Aim to do 2–3 reps of each, just to make sure you're warmed up and performing at your best. (These manoeuvres are covered in greater detail in *Defending and Upgrading your Position*.)

☀ Check in with the coach to get their opinion/advice on the conditions and on your upwind and starting strategy.

☀ Stand up in your boat and look for all the marks on the race course. At a minimum, make sure you can see the Mark #1 at the top of the course. Preferably, identify where the other marks of the course are as well. Identify what they look like, and their general positions. Check for anything strange or out of place, like the bias of the gates or skewed legs of the course.

☀ Do a final check of your boat to make sure you're ready for the start. This is your last chance to bail out any water, check that your rig settings are suited for the conditions, and put any heavy bags or gear with your coach. This is also the time to do any 'housekeeping', which means organizing all the lines in the boat, making sure the mainsheet isn't wrapped around your foot, etc.

☀ Get a line sight, if possible (see below).

A line sight, sometimes called a transit, is an incredibly helpful tool that will instantly improve your starts. How? It gets us a little bit closer to that ideal situation of having an imaginary starting line drawn over the water. You use a line sight to gauge how close you are to the line during your approach and to tell when you are on the line, which provides innumerable advantages.

For one, knowing where the line is allows you to confidently hit the line at go. This is most useful in long lines when starting in the middle of the line, because you can use it to prevent being a victim of 'line sag' – a phenomenon that often occurs along long lines as a result of boats in the middle having a weaker sense of where the start line is compared to the boats on the end, and therefore hanging back at the start.

Starts with less experienced sailors will generally have more line sag than with higher level sailors. In a start with lots of line sag, you can use a line sight to confidently start 1–2 boat lengths ahead of the line of boats around you, without being over the line. Even in starts with less line sag, a solid line sight that gives you the confidence to start just a half boat length ahead of the boats around you will completely transform your starts. Once you start making line sights a part of your routine in every start, you'll quickly be surprised how few other boats in the fleet actually take the time to get a line sight. Trust your line sight and start ahead when you can – the boats around you might all think you're crazy, until the Race Committee doesn't sound a recall!

A line sight can also tell you when to hold back, so that you don't risk an OCS.

As you can see, a line sight only works if there is land, an anchored boat, or another stationary object to the left side of the pin end. If all you can see is the open ocean, getting a line sight on the pin end won't work. In that case, try getting a line sight looking through the boat end of the line. Just reverse the process above.

You'll find that you have to be in the front row as the boats line up in order to use your line sight, because you need to be able to look under your boom and see the pin end of the line without other boats blocking your vision. But if you took the time to get a line sight, chances are you're looking to get a winning start anyway.

In addition to having a line sight, I like to make a mental picture of everything to the right of my line sight on shore as well. In a tightly packed start in which you might lose sight of the pin end in the last 30 seconds or so, you will find that this becomes incredibly important. Don't just watch for when your line sight is behind the pin, indicating you are already on the line – watch the movie of the landmarks ashore moving past the pin as you approach the line in the last minute. By being familiar with the landmarks on the windward side of your line sight, you can gauge how quickly you are closing in on the line during your approach before you are actually on it, helping you to know when to push forward and when to hold back. For example, if you look behind the pin end flag 30 seconds before the start and see

This is big fleet line sag. If you have a line sight and others don't, this is a great opportunity to start in the middle, knowing that you'll get a good start and a clear lane just by accelerating earlier than the boats around you.

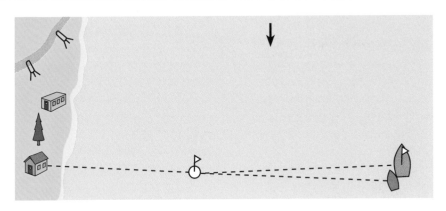

Here's how to get a line sight before the start. As shown above, come right up next to the Race Committee boat from behind and bring your bow right up to the line, next to the starting flag. Then, you and your crew look under the boom and remember the object or landmark that you can see while looking through the pin-end flag. This could be a tree, a brightly coloured roof, the edge of a building – anything that is noticeable on the shore. This is your line sight. During your real approach to the start, you will again look at the objects on the shore moving past the pin-end flag as you sail forward. When you see your line sight behind the pin, that means you are on the line.

If your boat has a bowman who will be calling the distance from the bow of your boat, you can skip the step of lining your bow up with the line because you don't have to account for the length of the bow. Instead, stop by the right side of the race committee and find the point on land that forms a line with both starting flags. The bowman will use this point or landmark as the line sight.

a landmark that you know is far from your line sight, that lets you know that you can push forward and bring your bow even with the boats ahead. This would give you the confidence to accelerate early, before the boats around you. Conversely, if you see that you are only a few landmarks away from seeing your line sight behind the pin, that lets you know to hold back, keep your number covered by the boats around you, and do a more conservative acceleration.

Finally, make sure to recheck your line sight before every single start. The Race Committee may have made adjustments to the line between races, making your previous line sight inaccurate. Be aware if the Race Committee moves the pin or if the guy on the front of the RC boat fiddles with the anchor line, which would also mess up your line sight.

SUMMARY

Congratulations! You've done your Pre-Start Routine and you now have a plan going into the start. You now know the general area on the line where you are going to start, how close and how early or late you plan to get into position, how much risk you are willing to take, and you have knowledge about the upwind leg that will become incredibly useful to your upwind racing strategy after the start. You also have a line sight and you've practised some of the manoeuvres that you will use during the start, both of which will help you cross the line at full speed at go.

You might be thinking to yourself, 'How will I ever fit all this in before the start!' But don't worry. With experience, this entire Pre-Start Routine will become almost second nature. Sailing is all about taking in information, processing it quickly, and forming an optimal plan from that information. You will see that this holds true on all areas of the race course. But it is

before the start that we have the most time to take in this flood of information and figure out what to do with it. Keep at it, follow these steps, watch what the best starters do, analyse your own performance for each start at the end of every race day, and you will see consistent improvement.

Generally, you will do your Racecourse Routine once, before the first race of the day, to get you warmed up and to do an initial analysis of the conditions.[4] About 10 minutes before each start you will repeat your Pre-Start routine. All the same information applies before each start, but by the second or third race you will have much better knowledge of the conditions, having already sailed a previous race and seeing what worked and what didn't. Apply what you observed from either your Racecourse Routine or the previous race to help determine your upwind strategy, follow the steps to developing your starting strategy, and you will be all set for the race.

We've done our homework, and we have our game plan. Now it's time to put it into action. In the following pages I will go into detail about the three stages of the start that take place in the final 1–2 minutes before the gun: getting into position, defending and upgrading your position, and executing the acceleration.

[4] See On The Water: The Racecourse Routine.

This start is a great example of line sag in a big fleet.

Chapter 4

GETTING INTO POSITION

There are now only 1–2 minutes before the start. Having completed your pre-start routine, at this point you should already know the approximate location along the line where you plan to start and have an idea about how early you want to get into position. With this in mind, I suggest that you hang around the area where you want to start. Get comfortable with this area, get a feel for the port and starboard upwind laylines to the start line, keep your eyes open and be aware of your surroundings. Let other people know that this is where you're going to start. Show your dominance in this part of the line, especially if you have a reputation as an aggressive starter. This makes it clear to other boats that they'll have to fight you if they want to start there, which can clear up the space around you and give you a slight advantage. Especially in light wind, stay close

to your target area of the line – you wouldn't want to get caught on the wrong end of the line in a drop in the wind while the clock is ticking and not be able to make your way back.

THE EAGLE WATCH

We're all accustomed to reaching back and forth and circling with the other boats along the line in these last few minutes before the start, with everyone finishing up their Pre-Start Routines, making final preparations, or just killing time. Then suddenly, there's that moment when everyone starts lining up before the start line, getting into position. In bigger, crowded fleets this moment tends to come earlier, sometimes as early as 1.30 minutes in the sequence. As you see the boats around you trickle one by one into their positions on the line, this is the time to make your final call of where you want to set yourself up. You are no longer looking at a macro picture of the line – you've already established which end of the line you're starting on. This is the time to zoom in your focus, look at a micro picture of the boats around you, and make a final assessment as to where exactly you want to position yourself relative to your opponents – is that area too crowded? Do I want to be to windward or to leeward of that pack of boats? I see a good gap over there and a few possible spots to leeward of that pack. Should I start next to this guy?

I call this final assessment the 'Eagle Watch'. At about 2.00 minutes in the sequence, position yourself a little bit below where you want to start and observe how the fleet is positioned. Chances are that some boats are already lined up in position, some are still reaching back and forth, and you will have to find a spot among the boats that are already in position. Choosing the spot in your micro area of the line that will give you the highest chance of a successful start is dependent on a few key principles: stay out of crowded packs of boats, and position yourself in areas where you can take advantage of line sag. Additionally, as I mentioned earlier, in strong wind it pays to be to windward of a pack, while in light wind it pays to be to leeward of a pack.

Setting yourself up in a good position on the line according to these principles depends on your ability to predict what will happen in the next couple minutes. This requires an understanding of the patterns that tend to happen as the fleet lines up. For example, if you see a relatively uncrowded area of the line but you also see a large pack of boats two or three rows deep directly up the line (directly to the right looking upwind, in other words) from that uncrowded area, you can expect that many of those boats will sail down to the less crowded area to leeward as they desperately look for an open spot. In this situation, knowing that this area will soon become crowded, you can choose to either set yourself up there early, before the crowd comes, and use your skills to defend your position, especially if you are confident in your abilities to successfully start in a crowded area; or you can look for another area on the line to start where you are more confident the fleet will be less crowded, where it will be easier to get a good start. Anticipating what the fleet will do before it actually happens is what allows you to make decisions that consistently put you in areas where you have the highest chance of success.

In another example, let's say you see that a pack of boats is lined up a few boat lengths farther from the line than the rest of the fleet. This means that you can likely expect some line sag in that area at the gun. Later in the sequence, if you are able to identify this line sag better than the boats around you, you will be able to take advantage of it and accelerate earlier than the pack around you without being over, essentially handing you an easy start (this is where using a line sight can be a game-changer!). The good news is that the less crowded areas of the start line tend to have more line sag, while the boats fighting each other in crowded packs tend to drift forward and push each other over the line – a double win for staying out of the crowd.

The Eagle Watch is also your final time to look at the wind conditions up the racecourse. I suggest spending a few seconds sailing full speed upwind on starboard tack just before your Eagle Watch so that you can do a final check of your compass numbers and see if you are in a right phase or a left phase, as well as do a final check on the setup of your boat. I like to be upwind of the fleet to do this, between 2 and 3 minutes before the start. If you see a new gust of wind or a cloud on one side of the course or if you've noticed a big wind shift that completely changes your starting strategy, you might still have time to make your way to the other end of the line.

A final consideration for choosing where to position yourself is knowing who will be directly to windward and leeward of you. If you pass by the sailor who's leading the regatta, it makes sense to (smartly) avoid starting next to them so as to increase your chance of a successful start. Quite obviously, you wouldn't want to start next to one of the top sailors in the fleet and have a difficult time holding your lane with a very fast sailor after the gun, even if you are one of the top sailors yourself. In fact, it is a well known tactic among top sailors to start next to 'marshmallow sailors' – less experienced sailors who will be easier to compete with during your start. In smaller fleets you will most likely know who the beginners are and who the more experienced sailors are, but even in large fleets you can often spot the less experienced sailors by how they sit in the boat, how aware they seem to be of their surroundings, and even by the sailing gear they're wearing. Ever wonder why the top boats in the fleet always seemed to start next to you last season? Maybe you were the marshmallow! (This is why it pays to build a reputation as an aggressive starter. You'll notice that the pack of boats around you during each of your starts seems to clear up as other sailors actively try to avoid you.)

Identifying the good spots to start on the line requires keeping your eyes open to the information around you and making constant assessments about the fleet. After all, that's why we call it the Eagle Watch. You can imagine yourself as an eagle looking down

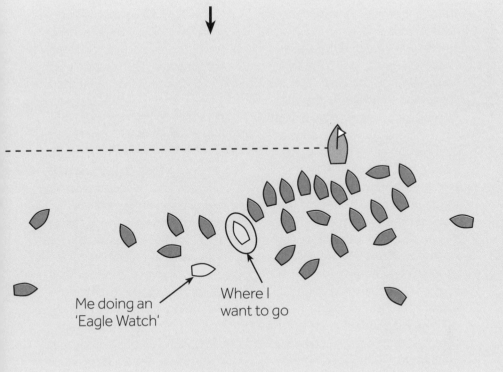

Me doing an
'Eagle Watch'

Where I
want to go

In this example, I decided that I would start near the committee boat end of the starting line due to a slight boat end bias. However, during my Eagle Watch as I'm making my final call for where I want to position myself, I'm thinking: 'There is a very crowded pack next to the committee boat. I definitely want to stay out of that pack because if I were to start in that crowd I would have a very low chance of getting a good start. In addition, they seem to be set up very close to the line, even though there is over a minute until the start. This tells me that many of these boats will end up very close to the line in the final seconds before the start – many of them will lose flow and have difficulty accelerating, while the few boats that do end up getting a good start from out of there will likely be OCS. However, I do like the area directly to leeward of this pack because in that position I would still be relatively connected to the boat end bias, but it is also much less crowded, and in this light wind the leeward position will put me in a favourable position over the pack to windward. However, since it is light wind, and since I can expect that many of the boats in the pack by the committee boat who don't find a position will end up sailing down to leeward anyway in search of more space, I'd better get into a spot there to leeward of the pack earlier rather than later and be extra careful to defend my leeward hole.' This is the type of analytical thought process that you should apply to all of your starts as you make the final call for where you set yourself up. As you gain experience this decision-making process becomes instinctual, but for beginner and intermediate level starters, this is the kind of thinking that will help you improve.

at the fleet around you as you make judgements and look for opportunities. This process can be overwhelming for beginners, especially for those who are not comfortable with the boat or with starting in a big fleet, but as with any aspect of sailing, it becomes easier as you gain experience. It may feel like an exhausting and repetitive process, especially over a long day of racing with many starts, but this is essentially the starting process that all top sailors do before every single start.

As you can see, finding your position on the line is the point at which the starting process switches from being strategic to being tactical. Most sailors generally define strategy as playing the racecourse and the natural environment around you in order to get around the racecourse as fast as possible. This includes staying in pressure, starting at the favoured end of the starting line, staying in phase with the wind shifts, etc. We generally refer to tactics as any sort of boat-on-boat interaction, such as making the decision of whether to duck or lee bow a starboard boat, positioning yourself to have an inside overlap at the leeward mark, defending your hole on the start line, etc. This is when the game of sailing gets especially fun. However, at the same time, it's not easy to manage everything going on around you when all the boats come together for the start, and especially for novices not used to

sailing in big fleets it can be quite overwhelming. We will next explore the methods that you can use to take advantage of the messiness of the pre-start and get into your initial position.

ATTACKING FROM BEHIND

When you're the boat who's looking to get into position on the line, you're the attacker. Think of this as being the boat on offence, while the other boats who are already lined up on the line on starboard, luffing their sails and manoeuvring at slow speeds, are on defence. As I like to tell my sailors, you are the 'shark' looking to swoop into someone's leeward hole, and chances are that they're going to fight you for it. However,

EXPERT TIP

This term shark is an especially important term to remember! A shark is any boat approaching from one side or another threatening to steal your leeward hole while you're set up on the line. Currently it's one of the newer vocabulary terms in the world of sailing, but it's becoming more and more popular and I will be using it frequently throughout this book.

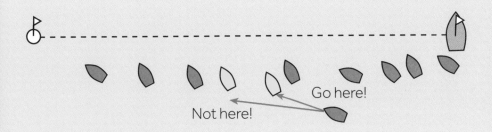

Building your leeward hole and controlling the windward boat begins with your initial position on the line.

an experienced starter will know the strategies at their disposal for getting into a great position.

Before I can get to the specific strategies, we first need to establish this basic principle: your goal when lining up for the start is to be close to the windward boat and far from the leeward boat. In other words, your goal is to maintain a 'hole' of empty water on your leeward side until your acceleration in the final few seconds before the start. This hole gives you a great advantage over the boats around you once it becomes time to accelerate: with space to leeward, you can put your bow down and accelerate on a lower angle, giving you greater speed as you cross the line. You will also be left with a larger gap between you and the leeward boat once you start racing upwind, making it much easier for you to hold your lane off the line. Finally, this position gives you complete control over the windward boat. As you are the boat with leeward rights, they cannot put their bow

down and go forward – instead of worrying about the windward boat accelerating first and rolling over you, you decide when to pull the trigger. Building up and defending your hole is a process that happens throughout the start, but it starts with getting into your initial position as far to windward as possible and squeezing up to the windward boat.

When you find a nice hole on the line using the Eagle Watch process, sail up to it from behind on starboard tack and position yourself directly to leeward of the boat on the windward side of the hole. If they offer no defence, great! You've just landed yourself a prime position on the starting line. However, a smart sailor will almost certainly take defensive manoeuvres to prevent you from stealing their leeward hole. Most likely, they'll be positioned almost head to wind on the line moving at very low speeds and luffing their sails, but as soon as they see you coming from behind, they will recognize the threat and

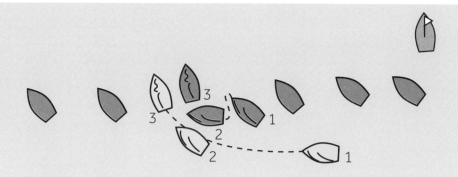

In this example, the yellow boat spots an open hole on the line. The light coloured boat who had built that hole tries to defend against the boat from behind by bearing away, but it had seen the threat too late and the boat from behind is able to gain an overlap to leeward and force the windward boat to head up, now in control of the gap to leeward.

immediately drop their bow to a reaching angle and build some forward speed, tempting you to head up behind their stern and take the position they were just in. This is a trap! As soon as you head up, your opponent will head up as well and use their momentum to coast back upwind to leeward of you, effectively trapping you on their windward side while maintaining a (somewhat smaller) hole to their leeward. Instead of falling for this common trap, you have two options for getting a good position when you attack from behind.

Your first option is this: when the boat on defence bears away to tempt you to go to windward of them, simply keep sailing to their leeward side. By coming in on a reaching angle from behind the fleet, you should have better speed than your opponent, who only a moment before was parked

head to wind. Remember that all you need to do to take their leeward position is to overlap your bow with their stern. At that point you gain the right of way as the leeward boat under Rule 11. Once you've gained an overlap, force your opponent to head up until they are head to wind (be vocal!) and lock them from leeward.

'Locking' the windward boat is a term that describes when you take the position to leeward of another boat and have complete control over that boat. It is especially important that you don't just create a marginal overlap, but that your bow is far forward enough that the windward boat has no option to drop their bow and head down over the top of you. At a minimum, your bow should be overlapped with the windward boat's shrouds or mast. If your bow is just barely overlapped with

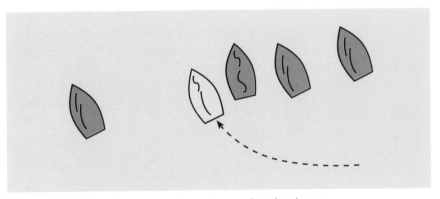

Successfully locking the windward boat means that they have no space to bear away and sail forward.

their stern, you may technically have leeward rights under Rule 11, but you'll be surprised by how many sailors who, whether they're clueless beginners or just willingly breaking the rules, will put their bow down over the top of you anyway, despite your cries claiming 'leeward boat!' and potentially destroy your start and your race. Then, when you return to shore after a long regatta day, what are you going to do? Find the sailor that headed down over you out of a hundred other sailors in the boat park and protest them? You'll still have had a bad start and most likely bad race. This is why I tell my sailors 'Don't be right. Be smart'. Go forward and lock the windward boat so that they physically cannot head down without clearly hitting you. Put yourself in a position where you shouldn't have to be vocal – your boat's position should speak for itself.

Locking the boat to windward while maintaining a gap to leeward is the ideal position before the start. The windward boat has no room to drop their bow, so now you decide when to go forward, you decide when to pull the trigger to accelerate, and you will almost certainly have a better start than them. Just be careful not to go so far forward that the windward boat has space to duck their bow below your stern. In that case, your opponent would be able to easily drop their bow and come to leeward of you with speed and flow. You would have essentially switched positions and now you'd be the boat in trouble!

Let's now look at your second option: if you are unable to establish an overlap to leeward of the defending boat and they don't seem to be giving up on their defence anytime soon, your second option is to accept their trap and head up to windward of them. Knowing that your opponent will turn back into the wind in order to regain their height as soon as they see you head up, your goal is to maximize the gap between you and your opponent when that happens, as this gap will essentially become your leeward hole. To do this, show the boat in front of you that you have every intention of hooking them to leeward. The more that you can get them to bear away in their defence, the better. Head below their stern and build as much speed as you can. You might even fake them out by quickly diving your bow 10 or 20 degrees lower, provoking them to bear away even more. Then, without warning, turn your boat head to wind with a sudden manoeuvre that prevents your opponent from heading up in sync with you. If they delay only 1 or 2 seconds before heading up and you use your speed properly to rebuild your height on the line, then you've already achieved a very sizeable hole to leeward.

When you actually do head up, don't just push the rudder and expect the boat to turn! Use proper technique to maximize the windward height that you gain. First, create a leeward heel and over-trim your main to help the boat make a quick turn to point straight into the wind. Use your speed and momentum to coast into the wind, jib off, even steering slightly past head to wind if you have the space above you and enough momentum to do so without losing flow over your rudder. Make sure that the leech of your main is engaged. If you prevent your opponent from

heading up in sync with you and if you use proper technique to convert your speed into height to windward, you should be left with a sizeable leeward hole which you can continue to upgrade in the time remaining in the sequence.

ATTACKING FROM PORT TACK

The goal is exactly the same when you tack into position from port tack as opposed to coming into position from behind on starboard tack. The priority is still to be positioned close to the windward boat and have a gap to leeward. Some advantages of a port tack approach include the fact that you usually have a greater visibility of the gaps between the boats lined up on starboard, making it easier to identify a good spot, and your attack into one of these spots can be more sudden and unexpected. However, the process of attacking from port tack is slightly different.

At the simplest level, all you have to do is tack to leeward of a boat on the windward side of a nice hole on the line. Again, if they don't defend, easy! Do a nice, slow tack and position yourself close to leeward of them, bow even. However, an experienced sailor will defend their hole by bearing off and heading straight towards you, forcing you to make a manoeuvre to keep clear as the give way boat under Rule 10. The defending boat's intention by doing this is to force you to either pass behind

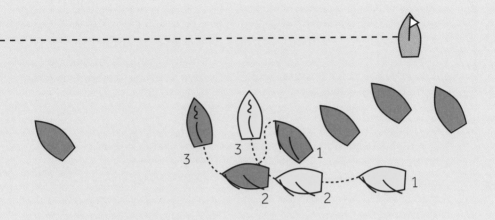

As the boat on defence bears away to defend their hole, the boat from behind continues to threaten to take the leeward position before making a sudden turn into the wind which the defending boat cannot match, producing a gap to leeward for the attacking boat.

them or to do a fast tack onto starboard, after which they will use their speed and technique to immediately head back up into the wind and rebuild their height to windward.

As the attacking boat on port, you have two options in this situation. The first is to simply pass behind the defending boat and look for a less aggressive sailor to attack. If you see that there are more open spots on the line, this is usually the better move, as you will have a much more comfortable start by not being next to a crazy aggressive sailor.

However, if there are few spots left on the line and if most of the fleet knows how to defend their

gaps to leeward, your second option is to tack to leeward of the defending boat and take the position. Understand that your opponent's intention is to barrel at you on a reaching angle, likely yelling 'Starboard!', and as soon as they see you begin your tack they will make a big turn and coast head to wind to build a gap between you and them. A strategy that sometimes works here is to begin a slow tack onto starboard, and if you see your opponent immediately luff up into the wind before you've actually crossed head to wind, you can bear off slightly onto port and take another 1 or 2 seconds to drift closer to your opponent before finally completing your tack directly to their leeward. This is a small but crucial way that you can take advantage of a defending boat's mistake and gain complete control over the windward boat. That said, be aware that this trick won't work all the time, as an experienced sailor will keep their bow down and wait for you to complete your tack onto starboard before they head up again.

One particularly neat trick that you can use in order not to elicit a defensive manoeuvre from a boat lined up on starboard tack is not to make eye contact with your opponent. In fact, don't even turn your head towards your target

BELOW In this example, the blue boat bears off to defend their leeward hole from the yellow boat on port. The yellow boat has two options: pass behind the defending boat in search of easier prey, or tack onto starboard as close as possible to the windward boat.

boat; keep facing forwards as if you were just passing behind them to continue on your way, but keep them in the corner of your eye. A starboard boat luffing their sails on the line won't bear away to defend if they don't believe they need to, because in doing so they burn up their leeward hole. So your goal is that they don't see you as a threat and therefore don't defend their hole – until you suddenly swoop into position by making a quick tack to leeward of them before they have time to react. By the time they realize your intention, you'll have already hooked them to leeward and taken the position.

The starboard tack approach and the port tack approach are

RIGHT Some of the boats are in competitive lanes while others are in bad lanes. It is very important to have the correct timing to hit the line at go.

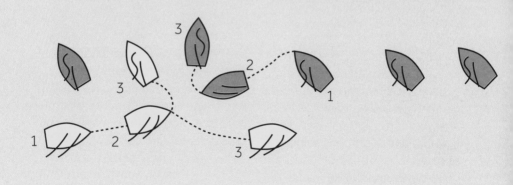

different methods of achieving the same goal. Many sailors prefer one or the other and use the same method every time. I suggest that you try out both and see which one works for you.

STARTING AT THE ENDS

There are many advantages to starting on the ends of the line, either close to the committee boat or to the pin. If one end of the line is biased, or if one side of the upwind leg is favoured, you will be in the best position to take advantage of that line bias or get to the favoured side of the upwind leg before anyone else. Additionally, it is much easier to judge your distance to the line when you're close to the committee boat or to the pin, making it easier to cross the line at the gun.

However, starting at the ends also comes with some challenges that should be taken into consideration. The ends of the line tend to be more crowded than areas closer to the middle, especially when there is a clear bias to one end of the line. There is also usually less line sag near the ends – as I think of it, less line sag that you can take advantage of if you have a better judgement of the line than the boats around you (use a line sight!). This happens because near the boat or pin ends it is easier for everyone to judge their distance to the line. This means that to punch out from

the boats around you, you likely won't be able to take advantage of line sag using your line sight and start ahead, which means that maintaining a leeward hole and executing a perfect acceleration becomes even more crucial. This also means that to have a better start than the boats around you, your chance of being OCS is much higher. The following are some principles for starting near the ends that will help keep you out of trouble.

First, know your laylines. It can be all too easy to set yourself up too far to the right of the committee boat, too high on the line, and have no space to cross the line at the start. Remember that since Rule 18 does not apply at starting marks, leeward boats have no obligation to give you room at the committee boat. On the other end of the starting line, one of the most disastrous situations that can happen during the start is when you set yourself up too low on the layline to the pin end and you don't make the pin, at which point your only option is to tack onto port and duck the entire fleet.

A rule that I constantly remind my sailors is to stay in the 'Starting Box'. This is the area enclosed by the start line, a parallel line a few boat lengths downwind of the start line, and the upwind laylines to the boat and pin ends of the start line. Positioning yourself in this box when lining up for the start will ensure that you will have access to the line and that you aren't late to the start.

Note that the laylines of the Box aren't necessarily your normal upwind sailing angle on starboard. Rather, these are your laylines while you are sailing at low speeds, which is how you usually approach the line in the last minute or so. In light wind, flat water, and with proper technique, your approach to the line might be a higher angle than your normal upwind sailing angle, while in strong wind and waves your low speed approach to the line might be a lower angle. You can build this awareness of the starboard laylines to the boat and pin ends of the starting line by making a few practice approaches to the line during your Pre-Start Routine.

Your understanding of the Box becomes especially important when fighting for one of the ends of the line, especially when you're starting on the pin and you're deciding whether or not to continue fighting for a leeward position. When you're lined up to start on the pin and you need to head down to defend against an attacker or hook another boat to leeward, you must make an instant assessment of whether or not you will be able to lay the pin. This comes from your ability to visualize where the layline is to the pin, and to judge whether you will be able to stay above that layline until the start. Making this judgement involves taking into account many factors, such as your distance to the line, the time left in the sequence, how much

Using the Starting Box will your increase your chances of successful and consistent starts.

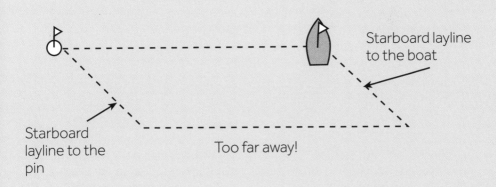

Starboard layline to the boat

Starboard layline to the pin

Too far away!

flow you will have, and your skills at holding your position without drifting sideways. As much as the area is more crowded and your boat has less flow or control in the water, give yourself a bigger safety gap to the pin layline. As I mentioned before, the pin is usually an area of high risk and high reward. Get it right and you'll win the start, but get it wrong and you'll find yourself in serious trouble.

Finally, be aware of how wind shifts as well change the laylines of the Box. A right shift will make it easier to make the pin while also making it easier to get shut out at the boat, while a left shift has the opposite effect.

A second principle that's important to consider when starting on the ends is to anticipate the movement of the fleet. In virtually every class, the boats lined up on the starting line holding their position and luffing their sails will almost certainly be drifting sideways, or to the left looking upwind on starboard tack. (This is why it is very important to practice the skill of minimizing your sideways drift, called leeway, while holding your position at slow speeds.) This happens to all the boats, so you might not notice it while you are lined up, but this phenomenon can sometimes open up a gap on the boat end of the line which you can take advantage of.

However, chances are that you won't be the only sailor on

the water anticipating the fleet drifting sideways in the last 1 minute, which is why on a boat-end favoured line you will almost always see boats positioned above the boat-end layline, waiting for the fleet to drift down. Even if you aren't there to take a spot next to the committee boat that magically opens up in the last 20 seconds, it's important to understand how the fleet drifts so that you can stay inside the box and have a proper start.

While it's important to start at the favoured end of the line, I generally recommend against being the boat on the pin or the boat on the boat end. It's just too risky. Sure, the sailor who wins the pin will blast out of there looking like a winner, but with each successful pin end start comes a high rate of disastrous starts as well – and in a big fleet of competitive sailors, consistency is everything. A competitor may win the pin once, but the next time they try it they'll end up starting the race last, and their scoreline over multiple races will be poor. If you want to really go for it, I suggest starting a few boats down from the boat end or a few boats up from the pin end. This reduces much of the risk associated with these high risk starts, such as not making the layline or being forced over the line, while still putting you in a great position to be one of the top few boats off the line if you can beat the crowd.

Chapter 5

DEFENDING AND UPGRADING YOUR POSITION

At this point you're in your spot on the line. In small fleets and low density start lines there might be only 45 seconds left in the sequence, while in large fleets and crowded lines you might have over 1.30 minutes to kill before the start. In any case, your starting process is far from over. In a way, it's only just begun. Every manoeuvre you do from this point forward is made for one of two reasons: defending against sharks and upgrading your position.

DEFENDING AGAINST SHARKS

Sailing can at times seem like such a complex and unfamiliar sport that sometimes it helps beginners to think about it in terms of ideas more commonly associated with other sports – namely, 'offence' and 'defence'. I am a fan of basketball myself, and any basketball fan knows that it is always very clear which team is on offence and which team is on defence. The offensive team is making moves in order to score on the defensive team, who must take action to prevent that from happening. Like basketball and other sports when the other team gets the ball, your mindset when you get into position on the line should switch from an offensive mode to a defensive mode. Now that you're in position, your first priority is defending against sharks – other boats not yet in position who may try to steal your

leeward hole.

Defending from sharks flips your role from the attacking process covered in the previous chapter. Now, instead of focusing your attention on looking for a spot on the line, at least one person on your boat must keep a constant eye out for anyone who might present a threat to your leeward hole. As I once heard another coach mention about leeward holes on the start line (as well as in reference to a certain movie), 'If you build it, they will come.' The bigger a leeward gap you build, the more boats there are around you, and the earlier it is in the sequence, the more likely it is that another sailor will try to take it.

When a shark engages with you to steal your hole, the earlier you see them the easier it is to defend. Let's first look at the example of a shark approaching from behind. As soon as you see a boat sailing behind you on starboard who might present a threat, make sure that you're not parked head to wind, but that you are at approximately a close-hauled angle and you have just enough flow over your foils so that you can steer down if necessary. If it looks like the boat coming in from behind intends to set up within about 1–2 boat lengths to leeward of you (this is the gap you'd like to preserve as your leeward hole), start heading down, flatten the boat, trim your sails properly so that you gain as much speed forward as you can, and bear away as much as it takes for the boat behind you to head up and go to windward of you – they might try to play with you a little bit or stubbornly continue to try to hook you to leeward, but if you properly drop your bow, it usually doesn't take more than a few seconds for your opponent to fall to your trap. As soon as you see them heading up (or moving to the next boat down the line), make a big turn and regain your height using the proper technique that I discussed before: use proper heel to turn the boat back into the wind, trim in your main, keep the leeches of your sails engaged, and use your new speed and momentum to coast into the wind, ideally locking your opponent. Your leeward hole may now be a little bit smaller than it was before, but the most important thing is that you now control the windward boat and there is no one to leeward controlling you

Alternatively, the attacking boat may be sailing on a reach on port tack towards your hole, hoping you'll let them do a slow tack to leeward of you. As soon as you see them closing in within a few boat lengths, aggressively drop your bow, point straight at them, gain as much speed as you can, and call 'Starboard!' if you think the situation calls for it. Your goal here is to remind them that you're the right of way boat under Rule 10, thereby forcing them to either pass under you and find someone less aggressive to mess with, or to do an earlier, more rushed tack onto starboard. In either case, as soon as you see the other boat pass behind you or complete their tack, immediately turn back up again and use your new speed to either coast back into the wind, do a double tack,

Bear away until you see the attacking boat go to windward of you, at which point use your new speed and momentum to luff and rebuild your leeward hole. It is important to 'lock' the windward boat so that they cannot make any manoeuvres to further mess with you.

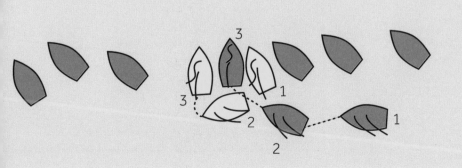

or use any of your available manoeuvres to regain your height to windward.

Knowing how to do a proper defensive manoeuvre like this is crucial if you want to get good starts, but you shouldn't use this technique in every situation. If you see that a boat is non aggressively setting themselves up a couple boat lengths to leeward of you or more, or that they are a lower level boat than you and unlikely to present a threat, leave them be. Remember that doing defence like this burns up your height on the line and usually takes you forward, so in some cases it's not worth it to engage with them. The purpose of doing defence is mainly to prevent a boat from coming close to leeward of you and locking you – at that point you would have no ability to bear away from head to wind, and therefore no ability to sail forward, no real options to attack the line, and your

As you see the port-tacker approaching you, bear away, gain speed, and use your speed to regain your height as soon as you see them complete their tack.

only hope would be to bail out of there and find a new spot on the line. The bottom line is that if you see an attacking boat threatening the space to leeward of you that's absolutely necessary for you to do a proper acceleration and execute a good start – usually within around 1–2 boat lengths – that's the time to do a defence. Find your spot, defend it like crazy, and you'll have the means to execute a great acceleration when the time comes and get a jump off the line.

Additionally, keep in mind that doing multiple defensive manoeuvres during a start is more conducive to dinghies than to larger keelboats. Dinghies are faster to bear away and get up to speed, while keelboats take more time and distance to turn and accelerate. This means that in a keelboat, you should do defence more sparingly as you will lose more height with each manoeuvre, and you must see sharks earlier so that you can execute a proper defence in time.

As a final note here, I'd like to acknowledge that it's not always possible to maintain as big a gap

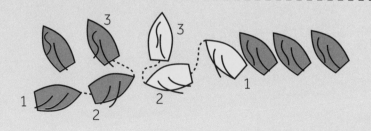

from the leeward boat as you'd like. In a tight line and a crowded fleet, no matter how many defensive manoeuvres you do, there will always be a boat close to leeward of you. There's a point when you have to realize that instead of losing all your height on the line by bearing away to defend against every shark threatening your hole, your best option is to let a marshmallow sailor go to leeward of you and not let any other boat get between you and them. The idea here is that since someone will inevitably be on your leeward side, why not make sure that they are a less experienced sailor who is less skilled at holding their height during the approach, less likely to make any moves on you, less likely to be fast, and who will be less likely to present a threat to you once the gun sounds? Then, build a good gap between you and them later in the sequence as soon as you see that there are no more sharks behind you, punch the line at the gun, and you should roll right over them.

UPGRADING YOUR POSITION

Your second priority when you're lined up with the fleet, whenever you're not occupied with defending against sharks, is upgrading your position to give yourself the best possible position for a great acceleration and for holding your lane off the line. This means having a sizeable hole

to leeward, controlling the boat to windward, and maintaining a proper distance to the line so that you are close enough that you have access to the line, but far enough so that you have comfortable room to accelerate. You should spend the majority of your time while in position on the line constantly upgrading your position, but don't forget about your first priority: protecting your leeward hole. At least one person on the boat should always be aware of the traffic behind you so that you can spot any approaching sharks in time to defend.

The way that you can upgrade your position when you're already lined up with the fleet is by closing the distance between you and the boat to windward, thereby building your hole to leeward and locking the windward boat. There are a few different manoeuvres, or actions, that you can do to achieve this goal of gaining height to windward. Keep in mind that some of these manoeuvres are much more effective or are easier to execute in dinghies and smaller sailing boats than in larger keelboats. The main ones include:

1 Holding position
2 Coasting into the wind
3 Double tack
4 Jump

HOLDING POSITION

This first technique is not really a manoeuvre, but a skill that everyone does (with varying levels of success) on the starting line. That skill is holding your position on the line by pointing into the wind and luffing your sails, while minimizing your sideways drift, or leeway, as much as possible. Luffing into the wind is something that all sailing boats do during the start in order to hold their height. You must practice it so that you can minimize your leeway at low speeds. Everyone drifts sideways on the start line, but imagine if you were able to drift just slightly less than the boats around you. After a minute or so of holding your position, you would have a great hole to leeward and great control of the windward boat, seemingly without doing anything. The best way to practice this skill is to position your bow just behind a mark in the water and concentrate on staying next to it, using your steering, sail trim, and boat heel. You will find that you will drift sideways gradually, and you'll see how keeping flow over your foils reduces that drift. As you learn how to hold your height, building a hole on the line will become easier and easier.

The first step to holding your position without drifting is keeping 'flow' over your foils. Although your average angle while holding position is somewhere between close-hauled and head to wind, you always want to be moving forward through the water just fast enough to have water flowing over your rudder and your keel/centreboard. Think of this as the minimum amount of forward speed you need to keep control over your boat (also called 'minimum control speed'). Doing this maintains your manoeuvrability, reduces your leeway, and makes it easier to quickly bear away to defend against an approaching shark.

The second step is properly trimming the sails. You never want your main and jib on the start line to both be completely off and flapping in the wind, as I see many beginner sailors do. Instead, head into the wind and pull in enough mainsheet that the leech of the main is engaged (not flapping) except for in extreme overpowered conditions. This reduces the force pushing you sideways and helps keep your bow into the wind. There should be minimal boom vang in the pre-start, as this would also create leeway and will make it difficult to accelerate. The jib can tolerate more flapping, especially when pointing higher into the wind, but ideally its leech should also be engaged as to mirror the main. Our goal is to see the leeches of the main and jib just tight enough to be engaged, while the luff of each sail is flapping. Most importantly, never have the jib trimmed in while the main is flapping. All this will do is push your bow down, and as you compensate with the rudder you will drift sideways.

Finally, have a proper heel angle. Windward heel is something to avoid at all costs while you're luffing on the start line, except for situations when you're trying to bear away quickly, because it will cause you to slide sideways. Think about keeping your boat vertical or with a slight leeward heel so that the maximum depth of the centreboard or keel plants you in the water. From the smallest dinghies to keelboats, holding position without going forward while minimizing leeway is a very important skill during the start, and a skill that I highly recommend practising.

COASTING INTO THE WIND

The second technique is coasting into the wind. This can be done throughout your process of holding position. The idea here is that whenever you have speed, then build a slight leeward heel, turn into the wind, and use the boat's momentum to coast into the wind. If you have the speed and the space to windward, even try coasting a little past head to wind, thereby gaining height to windward, at which point you'll start to see the jib flapping on the starboard side of the mast. On smaller boats you might even slightly backwind the main for an extra slide. Then, when you feel you are about to lose flow over the rudder, head back down to approximately a close-hauled angle on starboard to regain speed. This is a great manoeuvre for larger keelboats in which it's difficult to execute a quick

double tack without gaining lots of distance forward or needing a large gap to windward. As with any other manoeuvre, it requires communication between the helm and the crew because the jib must be off and the leech of the main engaged when heading into the wind.

DOUBLE TACK

This is another highly effective move during the pre-start, but it requires a fairly sizeable gap to windward for most boats. Whenever you want to build your hole and you see a gap of at least a few boat lengths between you and the windward boat: bear away slightly and trim your sails to gain some speed, make a quick, strong tack using leeward heel, lots of rudder, and a roll (for dinghies), and bear away as much as you can before executing a second tack to leeward of the windward boat. Essentially, you are doing two quick tacks in a row in order to gain height on the line. You want to make sure you use the proper sail trim and heel so that you can execute this quickly, and you generally want to bear away to at least a beam reach after the first tack so that you don't gain too much distance to the line in the process. Find a time to do your double tack when the windward boat loses flow, is stuck head to wind, or doesn't seem to be paying attention – that's when they won't be able to do a strong defence against your attack.

JUMP

This is a manoeuvre that's really only possible in relatively small and light dinghies. A 'jump' is essentially a very quick double tack that requires aggressively rolling the boat, in which you never really complete your tack onto port. To do a jump, have enough speed to turn your boat slowly into the wind, at which point the sailor(s) on the boat aggressively press on the windward rail of the boat, fanning the sail forward and effectively paddling with the centreboard, as the helm steers past head to wind but not quite onto a close-hauled angle on port, depending on how much space there is to windward. Then, the sailors aggressively press on the other rail of the boat (the left side), which paddles with the centreboard again and pivots the boat back onto starboard tack. The advantage of this manoeuvre is that you can gain around a boat length of height to windward without going much distance forward, you don't need much space to windward to do it, and you don't need much flow to begin the manoeuvre. In my experience competing in the 470, a jump was an extremely common move on the start line. Doing jumps in the 470 and similar dinghies is a must, because it allows you to squeeze up to the windward boat in situations where you don't have enough space to complete a double tack.

EXPERT TIP

Remember to consider the rules whenever you do a jump or another manoeuvre in which your bow passes head to wind. Until you pass head to wind you have the right of way over the boat to windward of you on the line, but as soon as you pass head to wind you are no longer a leeward boat – you are a tacking boat, meaning that now the windward boat has the right of way. Under RRS (Racing Rules of Sailing) Rule 13, you must return to a close-hauled angle on starboard tack in order to regain your leeward rights. For this reason, manoeuvres such as jumps play in a gray area of the rules: if your opponent to windward doesn't react as you build height up to them, then you haven't broken any rule, but if they bear away at you just as you pass head to win during a jump, then they may have a case against you in the protest room. Remember to consider the rules, as well as how large the gap is between you and the windward boat and how likely they are to defend it, whenever you go for a manoeuvre.

PUTTING IT ALL TOGETHER

It's important to practice these four manoeuvres so that you have them in your toolbox and can execute them in the appropriate situations. Master them, and they will completely change your game on the starting line. Understand that the goal of these manoeuvres is to gain height to windward without going forward towards the line. In your execution of them, it's an important and difficult skill to keep your flow and height by moving sideways back and forth rather than forward, so that you maintain your distance to the line.

Techniques for holding or upgrading your position.

This toolbox of manoeuvres for upgrading your position on the line is incredibly useful, and everyone on your boat must have them practised to perfection. Just as sailors on a large keelboat have multiple ways of dousing the kite, and whenever a code word such as 'windward douse' or 'leeward douse' is called out everyone knows exactly their role to execute the manoeuvre, your team's execution of these manoeuvres should be almost automatic. This ensures that whenever you see an opportunity to use one of the manoeuvres in your toolbox, all you need to do is call out double tack, jump or another code word and everyone on the boat knows exactly what to do. Once you have

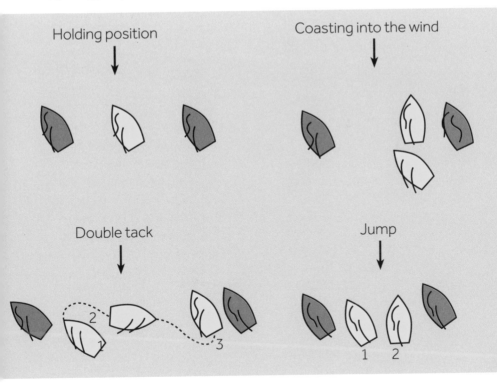

Holding position

Coasting into the wind

Double tack

2

3

Jump

1   2

them mastered, you will have an accurate sense of exactly how much space to windward you need to execute a double tack or a jump, how flat the water must be, how light or strong the wind must be, and how much speed you need to execute each manoeuvre. For example, coasting into the wind requires the least amount of space to windward, while a double tack requires at least a few boat lengths between you and the windward boat. Understand what it takes to execute your manoeuvres, and you will know which manoeuvre to select for a given situation in the pre-start.

These manoeuvres play a role in your defence from sharks as well. For example, if an attacking boat does get to leeward of you, either by tacking from port or coming in from behind, you must immediately look to windward and assess the size of the windward gap, and based on how much space you have, use your new speed from your defence to regain your height.

To sum up, your goal while lined up on the starting line is to be constantly upgrading your position (closing up on the boat to windward and building a gap to leeward) while defending your hole from other boats. You might be asking: When would I use these manoeuvres? Whenever you have to bear away to defend against a shark (thereby opening a gap above you), or whenever a boat squeezes in to leeward of

you, or any other time that you're uncomfortable with the boat to leeward and want to build your hole. That's the time to look at how much space you have to the starboard side of you, decide which manoeuvre is appropriate, wait for an opportunity when the windward boat loses flow and can't defend, and do it.

Sounds like a lot to do all at once? That's because it is. When you're in position on the line, everyone on the boat is constantly active, either with manoeuvres, holding position, or making assessments of the situation around you. As a coach from the outside, it is easy to see the boats who take this process seriously. Even when a boat is not moving, we can still see that those sailors are active – crew swivelling around on a constant lookout for sharks, non-stop communication about the gaps to windward and leeward, pointing up the course towards the next gust – in general, highly aware of their surroundings and highly aware of what they want to do in any situation that approaches them. To consistently start well in big fleets or at the high level, this is what it takes.

Now that we have our manoeuvres down, there's one principle that I'd like to share that helps sailors balance upgrading their position with defending from other boats: be off-sync with the leeward boat and in-sync with the windward boat.

On a crowded start line in which

you must fight for every inch of your gap to leeward, whenever you see the windward boat head up sharply or do a double tack, you want to be in sync with them. If the windward boat heads up and you have good speed, head up as well and coast into the wind so that you are always side by side with them. If the windward boat does a double tack, do an immediate tack to follow them and roll into an identical tack close to leeward of them as soon as they tack back onto starboard. Remember, 'Don't be right, be smart'. As you tack back onto starboard, lock the boat to windward so they can't illegally accelerate over the top of you. By matching the windward boat's manoeuvres in this way, you are both building your own leeward hole and preventing the windward boat from building a gap to leeward of their own, thereby maintaining your control over the windward boat.

On the other hand, when you see the boat to leeward doing a double tack, a jump, or otherwise turning their bow past head to wind, you want to bear away, build speed, and point yourself at them. In other words, be out of sync with them. Recognize that in this situation when the boat to leeward is on port or has headed past head to wind, you now have the right of way under Rule 10 or Rule 13 respectively. At this point, bear away as you would to defend against a shark coming in on port to steal your hole, be

intimidating and vocal about your right of way, force them to tack back onto starboard with a rough manoeuvre, and then use your speed to do the proper manoeuvre to regain your height according to the size of the gap to windward, whether that's with a double tack or simply turning and coasting to windward. If you were to allow them to attack your leeward hole like this without you presenting any defence, they would simply take the position to leeward of you and you would have no chance at surviving off the starting line.

As you can see, this process of bearing away to defend and then building your height to windward is all about the balance between defence and offence in the pre-start. The key is seeing the sharks or the leeward boat who tacks onto port soon enough to respond to their threat. At least one sailor on the boat must be aware of potential outside threats at all times. This is one of the ways that the crew on the boat must be active during the start.

Finally, as you focus on gaining height to windward, don't forget about your forward and backward position. Zoom in your view to the two boats on either side of you, and then zoom out your view of the fleet around you. In your zoomed-in view, make sure you're far enough forward that you're locking the boat to windward but not so far forward that they could duck to leeward of you. Also make

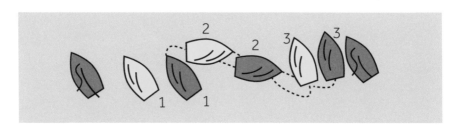

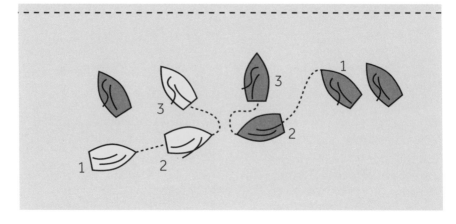

sure you're not too far bow back behind the boat to leeward. In general you want to be mostly overlapped. Then zoom out, look at the larger fleet spread across the line in each direction, and make sure the group of boats around you including yourself aren't either way too early to the line or buried behind the rest of the fleet.

Judge the distance of the fleet to the line, using your line sight if you have one. If you believe that the entire fleet is set up too far from the line, see this as an opportunity to take advantage of! Don't set up much closer to the line than the fleet (unless there are some other boats also setting up closer) as you will only draw the fleet up to the line. Instead,

By being in-sync with the boat to windward and off-sync with the boat to leeward, you maintain control of the windward boat and build your leeward gap.

hang back with the fleet, but have your bow slightly more forward than them, and wait for the right time to accelerate. Just keep your awareness of the boats around you and make sure you begin your final acceleration before they do!

If you see that the entire fleet around you is too close to the line, recognize early on that everyone's acceleration will be quite late. This makes it even more important to execute a perfect acceleration. So upgrade your position on offence, be aggressive with sharks on defence, and you'll have all you need to do a great acceleration.

Chapter 6

THE ACCELERATION

It's time to accelerate off the line. Depending on your sailing distance to the line, the wind strength, and how quickly your class of boat gets up to speed, you might begin your acceleration anytime between 15 seconds and 3 seconds before the gun.

Hopefully by now you've built yourself a good position relative to the boats around you: being close to the boat to windward, having a hole to leeward, and having enough distance to the line so that you'll have space forward to accelerate. Remember, a good acceleration means accelerating from low speed to maximum boat speed quicker than the boats around you, so that when all the boats cross the line at go, you punch out from the pack and have a positive lane off the starting line. This is when it all comes together. All the process of building your hole, upgrading your position, and defending from sharks has been to give you the best possible chance of success for this moment.

KNOWING WHEN TO ACCELERATE

You want to time the acceleration so that you cross the line at the gun. Here's the first factor that goes into this: you have to know your time and distance to the line at all times. Throughout the entire pre-start you should have your line sight in view and an idea of your distance to the line, as well as the time on your watch. The last 20 seconds or so before the start is the time to really make use of your line sight, as you're judging when to begin your acceleration. I like to track how my time and distance to the line changes as I approach the line, so I know if I'm on track to be early or late given my current approach speed. For example, if I hear my crew say '30 seconds, 5 boat lengths to the line' and then say '20 seconds, 4 boat lengths',

I'd know I can push forward more. Alternatively, if I hear my crew say '30 seconds, 5 boat lengths to the line' and then say '20 seconds, 2 boat lengths', I'd know to hold back.

A second factor that goes into timing your acceleration is being 'covered' by the boats around you. The easiest starts are when there is a lot of line sag, because with a line sight and good judgement of the line you can identify this, start ahead of the boats around you, and have an easy start without

risk of being over. The more difficult starts are when the fleet around you is close to the line or over the line. In crowded starts where everyone is pushing the line, being called OCS by the Race Committee is a real threat, so you want to make sure your sail number is covered by the sails of the boats around you from the view of the number callers on the starboard end (and possibly also the port end) of the line. If you believe you and the boats around you are over the line, keep

EXPERT TIP

Think from the perspective of the guy on the Race Committee boat calling numbers of boats over the line. You are much more likely to be called over if you set yourself up forward of the pack, sail numbers exposed in plain view on both sides, and sit on the line before the start. You're just inviting the RC to call you over, they'll remember your number, and they may call your number even if you become hidden in a pack that drifts over the line before the gun. Understand that the Race Committee specifically doesn't like boats that sit on the line because they draw the entire fleet up to them, causing more recalls. Instead, you're much safer if you keep yourself in line with the fleet, your number covered, and you come from behind and punch out from the pack at full speed at the start, even if you punch forward over the line 1 or 2 seconds early. The RC will always disqualify the sailor who sits on the line over the sailor who stays covered for the entire pre-start and punches over the line in the last second before the start. So don't be afraid to aggressively punch the line, but do so by staying covered before the acceleration. This is another example where crew communication is important during the start. The crew should communicate with the skipper whether you are exposed or covered on both ends before the start.

Good Bad

In a proper start we usually want to set up in line with the fleet and accelerate to hit the line at full speed. If we set up too close to the line, we will either be OCS, we will not have a good acceleration, or we will drift sideways to leeward, which are all bad outcomes.

your bow even with the boats around you so that with a good acceleration you will still hold your lane after the start, but only if you are absolutely sure that you are covered. Make sure the boats to windward block your sail number from the boat end, and if they are also calling numbers from the pin end, make sure you're covered to leeward as well.

Finally, it's important to have an awareness of when the boats around you accelerate. If you see the boat above or below you accelerating and you see you have enough distance to the line, go immediately! Otherwise they will be ahead of you at the gun and you'll have no hope of holding your lane off the start. As you gain experience you will be able to expand your awareness of the boats around you to not just the boat to windward and the boat to leeward, but to the larger pack on each side of you. Zoom into the boats next to you, and zoom out to see any possible threats a

few boats up or down the line. If you see a boat or pack of boats pushing forward, that's a sign for you to begin your acceleration as well.

Keeping all these factors in mind, it's up to you and anyone else on the boat to decide when to accelerate. I've found that the best accelerations don't happen when someone suddenly calls out 'accelerate!' and surprises everyone on the boat, but when it is a planned manoeuvre so that everyone is ready and in position. As you count down the final seconds to the start and judge your distance to the line and the boats around you, try saying 'let's go on six!' or 'let's go on eight!' This lets everyone know the plan before you actually begin the acceleration, and your manoeuvre to accelerate will be much more coordinated among the team members and the outcome will be much more effective.

Take an example scenario: you're lined up evenly with the

fleet and there's only 15 seconds before the start, and you can tell from your line sight that everyone is deep below the line. In this situation you know there's no need to be afraid of being one of the first boats to accelerate and take advantage of the sag. Stay relatively covered, but have your bow forward, say 'let's go on 10!' and make sure you begin your acceleration before the boats around you.

Alternatively, if you see that the fleet around you is quite close to the line, accelerating earlier than the other boats would put you at risk of being over. Instead, prioritize being bow even with the boats around you as well as covered from each end, and maintain your leeward hole. Build it up if you can, luff high into the wind, and work on locking the windward boat so that they can't head down to accelerate until you

do. Then, understand that you must do a better acceleration than the boats around you in order to punch out from the pack. Once you begin your acceleration, you're now committed to completing that acceleration and sailing forward. You never want to get nervous and slow down in the middle of the acceleration.

In this photo, boat 8088 is clearly the most punched out, which gives them a momentary advantage.

HOW TO ACCELERATE

Every class is different, but the manoeuvre to accelerate is essentially the same for each boat. And of course, the goal is always the same: cross the line, at the gun, at full speed. Before the acceleration, you will most likely be holding position luffing near head to wind. If you have a comfortable distance to the line and the fleet around you is moving steadily forward, you may be moving forward at about 20–30% of your upwind boat speed, an ideal situation as this makes it easy to accelerate to full speed. But it is most likely that before the acceleration you'll be holding position into the wind with the boats around you with minimum flow, at around 10% boat speed. If you got too close to the line too early or if the fleet is extremely close to the line, you may find yourself having to accelerate from 0% boat speed, which is the most difficult. Whichever situation you're in, try to build as much flow as you can before the acceleration without going forward on the boats around you. It's much more difficult to accelerate from 0% boat speed to 100% boat speed than from 50%, so any speed you have going into your acceleration will make punching the line that much easier.

The acceleration can make or break your start, so it's important to use the proper technique. It is a manoeuvre that must be practised and that takes the entire crew's coordination to pull off. First, the helm must bear away to a lower, faster angle, ideally somewhere between your close-hauled angle and a beam reach. If you have a boat close to leeward and you need to prioritize your height off the line to hold your lane, don't bear away as much for the acceleration, as doing so will burn up your leeward gap. If you do have a comfortable gap to leeward, however, then bear away a little farther to build more speed – but don't overdo it. Don't head down all the way to a reaching angle, as this will take you needlessly sideways. Hold this angle for only a second or two, building up speed. The sails should be properly trimmed – sheets generally eased and with the leeches not too tight, vang eased – to build forward speed. Once you've gained speed on this lower angle, create a leeward heel, trim in the mainsail, and use the sails, heel, and minimal rudder to head the boat up to close-hauled. As you reach close-hauled, press the boat. In a dinghy, aggressively flatten the boat as you would in a roll tack. In a keelboat, this means everyone needs to be on the windward rail, as long as there is positive pressure and the boat isn't underpowered. The flattening of the boat will accelerate you forward. As you trim in the sails for upwind, the main should come in just slightly before the jib. Be sure not to trim in the jib before the main, as this will close the slot and make it difficult to head up. Sail upwind full speed towards the line.

That leeward hole that you worked so hard to defend during the pre-start is what allows you to bear away to do a great acceleration, but knowing how to use it is the key. You will need to experiment in order to find how much of your leeward hole is optimal to 'use up' in your acceleration. On the one hand, if you were to reach across the entire length of your leeward hole for multiple seconds before turning up to a close-hauled angle for the start, you would cross the line at a very high speed, going possibly even faster than your maximum upwind boat speed, but you'll pay the price by having another boat close to leeward. On the other hand, if you accelerate by simply trimming your sails on a close-hauled course, by the time you cross the line you'll have maintained a great gap to leeward and you'll have a great lane in terms of your position, but you'll have a very slow speed, increasing the danger of the windward boat rolling over the top of you. With experience and by learning to do a proper acceleration, you'll find the balance between these two extremes.

As you punch out, judge what kind of mode you need to hold your lane. In very crowded starts all the boats are usually pinching off the line in order to hold their line, going high and slow. You can gain an early advantage in this battle to hold your lane by using your speed out of the acceleration to point a few degrees higher than close-hauled for a second or two, until you see the luff of the jib begin to bubble to windward. If there's no imminent threat of the windward boat rolling over you, using the slingshot effect you get out of the acceleration and converting that into height in this way can give you an early advantage by improving your lane, helping you pinch out the windward boat and giving you a more comfortable runway to leeward so you can put the bow down later on.

Finally, make sure all your control lines are properly set, such as the vang, sheets, and other sail controls. Your cunningham and outhaul should have been set before the start. Racing off the line is the time when every inch of performance counts, so make sure the boat is set up for maximum speed.

Like your other starting manoeuvres in your toolbox, the acceleration is one that must be practised to get it right. Even on regatta days, at the beginning of the day and before each start it's helpful to do a few practice accelerations. There's no way that your first acceleration of the day will be as good as your second or your third, so don't wait until the first start to fine-tune your technique.

Chapter 7

OTHER TIPS

TEAM COMMUNICATION DURING THE START

If you sail a double handed boat or larger, team communication is an integral part of the starting process. You may have raced on some boats where the helm runs their own show and you hear almost no communication within the boat before the start, which is an unfortunate tendency that is actually quite common when an experienced helm is sailing with a less experienced crew. This is not the right way to start a race. The start is usually the most complex and overwhelming area of the race, so the helm needs all the help they can get. There are so many different factors rapidly playing out to be aware of during the pre-start that as a helm, you will not be able to get consistently successful starts without constant communication and input from your crew. The communication on the boat should be of such use to you that you won't even be able to imagine how those Laser sailors can get the job done. The following are the pieces of information that crew members should be communicating to the rest of the team.

THE TIME

Someone on the boat must be calling out the time to the start. Simply having the time on your countdown timer on your wrist isn't good enough, because you need to know the time even when you're adjusting a sail, bearing away to defend against another boat, or otherwise have your hands occupied. Without the time there's no way to do a proper start, so make sure you have someone calling it out for everyone onboard to hear.

SHARKS

As we established earlier, once you're in position on the line, the sooner you see a shark, the easier it is to do a defensive manoeuvre to protect your leeward hole. Since the helm will be mostly looking forward and occupied with holding height, at least one other crew member should have a constant eye out for threats coming from behind or from leeward. A dependable crew member who alerts the helm early on of potential threats makes the helm's life a lot easier and ensures you will have time to bear away to defend.

CALLING MANOEUVRES AND STRATEGY

Even though most larger boats have dedicated tactician roles, it's always helpful when crew members communicate about any opportunities as they emerge. When someone on the boat sees a good spot on the line to attack, or an opportunity to do a double tack, call it out! The helm can't see everything – in fact, it's best if the helm focuses most of their attention on holding position and maintaining height on the line. It's up to the crew to look around for tactical opportunities and alert the rest of the boat to those brief chances.

TIME AND DISTANCE TO THE LINE

Someone on the boat must be calling out time and distance to the line. In some boats this may be done from the cockpit, while in larger boats a bowman may communicate distance using hand signals. It's important for you as the helm to receive both the time and the distance during the approach to the line, because with this information you can fine-tune your approach. Track your time and distance as you approach the line and see if you need to push forward or hold back. For example: if you have 30 seconds left in the sequence, you are 6 boat lengths from the line, and your distance to the line has been decreasing by about 1 boat length every 10 seconds, you would be 3 boat lengths late if you continued at your current approach speed. That's a sign to push forward.

Additionally, your crew can look to windward and to leeward and communicate whether you're covered or exposed from the ends of the line. This is the kind of important information that must be brought into the boat so that you know how far forward or back to position yourself.

TIMING THE ACCELERATION

Someone needs to call the acceleration, and it doesn't need to be the helm. On larger boats the tactician or bowman may call the acceleration, while on smaller teams of just a few crew, anyone who understands how quickly the boat accelerates can call out 'Let's go on five!' Whether it's the tactician making a calculated plan to time the acceleration or a crewmember who sees the boat to leeward trimming their sails and yells 'Go now!' input from the crew about the acceleration gives the helm one less thing to think about.

That said, the discussion on the boat should be a two way dialogue between the crew and the helm, not just one way. The helm should communicate their own observations, such as if they're losing flow or if they're uncomfortable with the boat to leeward. As a general rule, everyone onboard should communicate their own observations, whether that's alerting the team to other boats, suggesting a strategy, or calling time, and everyone onboard should know the plan going into the start. Experienced teams know that the boat sails best when the whole crew contributes to the tactical game, not just the sailors in the back of the boat.

STARTING IN SHIFTY CONDITIONS

Every sailor knows that the wind never blows consistently from one direction. At the least, even on those seemingly steady days there are small shifts that oscillate back and forth. These small oscillations of just a few degrees may factor into your upwind strategy as you sail the upwind beat, but they don't particularly affect your starting strategy. It's primarily on the 'shifty' days as sailors call them, when the oscillations are 10–20 degrees or more, that the final shift before the start plays a significant role.

Hopefully you identified what the wind is doing in your racecourse and pre-start routines. The key to making use of the information you collect is identifying patterns that you can use in the race. It is absolutely critical that you sail with an electronic compass that displays your boat's bearing, if your class allows it. Assuming you did your homework before the start, you will have written down or remembered the range of the shifts, the average duration of the shifts, and any other subtle patterns you may have noticed. I like to write down the minimum and maximum (max headed and max lifted) compass angles that I see on each tack on the respective side of the boom during my racecourse routine. Whenever I notice a new shift range while I'm sailing upwind, I write the new compass numbers a line below. With these numbers I can sail upwind on either tack, look at the compass and the numbers on the boom, and know instantly which phase of the shift I'm in. As the start nears I can also look back

at the lines of numbers I wrote down and track how the wind has changed since I've been out on the water. If the numbers seem to be trending in one direction, for example, that would be a clue that there has been a persistent shift which might continue into the first race. From these observations you can identify whether the wind is consistently oscillating back and forth, shifting inconsistently, or if there's a persistent shift in one direction.

Whichever type of shift you've identified, knowing the final phase before the start is an absolute necessity. About 2 minutes before the start while you're deciding where on the line to start, or during your Eagle Watch, sail upwind on starboard and check your compass numbers. If you're in a right or left phase, judge if that shift will hold until the start. Additionally, look upwind at the pressure and the clouds for clues to the next shift coming down the racecourse. This final phase before the start factors into your starting strategy in the following ways.

In the first type of shifty wind condition – *large, consistent oscillations* – your priority is to get onto the lifted tack as early as you can after the start. This means that if there's a right phase, make sure you get a good start that allows you to hold your lane off the line and continue on starboard. If you are in a left phase, your goal is to take the first good opportunity to tack to port off the line.

In your preparation during the pre-start, check the bias on the start line. Then, determine if one end of the line is favoured because that end was actually placed too far forward by the Race Committee, or if the phase of the wind is creating a temporary line bias. A right phase would make a correctly set line appear boat-end favoured, while a left phase would make it appear pin-favoured. This is important to distinguish, because if the bias of the line is only created by the phase of the shift, then starting on the favoured end is less important to fight for. What's more important to prioritize is getting onto the lifted tack. To illustrate:

When the final shift before the start is a left phase, start close to the boat to windward of you, pinch out the pack of boats above you after the start, and you may be able to achieve the ideal situation of tacking onto port and crossing the boats that were to windward of you. Easier said than done, right? In reality this is not usually possible to pull off. Instead, when the shift off the line is a left phase and the line is not so biased that the boats near the pin would be able to easily tack and cross, consider forgoing

the pin-end bias induced by the left phase – instead, start closer to the boat end of the line and do an early tack onto port. You may not look great on the fleet initially, but you'll be the first boat to fall onto port, the lifted tack. Even if the entire fleet follows you by tacking onto port, there's no reason to be concerned. You will make your money on the next shift once the wind clocks back to the right.

Similarly, when the final shift before the start is a right phase and the line is boat-end favoured because of this, understand that it is less important to start in the crowded area on the boat end. Instead, it's okay to go for a more conservative start farther down the line where it will be less crowded. This gives you the greatest chance of getting an easy start and having a clear lane on starboard tack so that you can continue sailing the lift. Don't worry if the boats to windward initially look forward on you – you will make your money on the next shift. Understand that by taking this option of starting farther down the line in a less crowded area you reduce your risk, but the trade-off is that you absolutely must get a good start for it to pay off.

See the examples on the right in which the start line is set for an average wind direction of north (0°). The wind is oscillating by 20 degrees. In each example the yellow boat doesn't look very good at the start, but it gets immediately onto the lifted tack either by continuing on starboard or by being the first boat to tack onto port, it waits patiently to make its gain on the next shift, and is in a very good position partway up the beat.

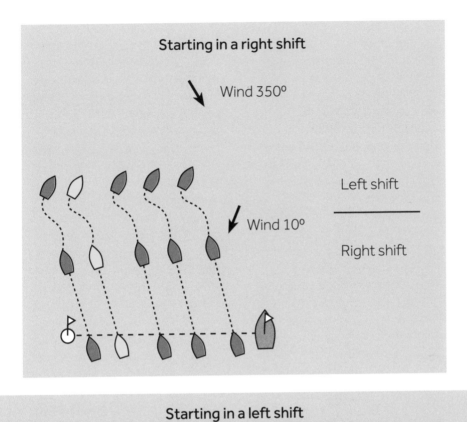

Starting in a right shift

Wind 350º

Wind 10º

Left shift

Right shift

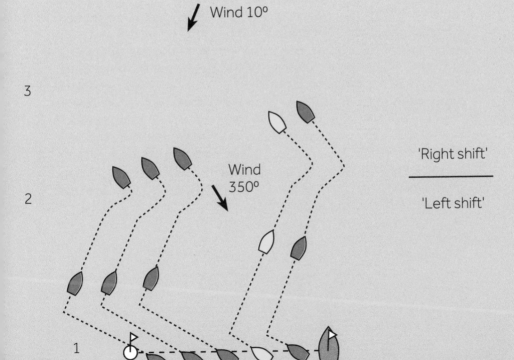

Starting in a left shift

Wind 10º

Wind 350º

'Right shift'

'Left shift'

3

2

1

In the second type of shifty wind condition – inconsistent shifts – more factors gain weight in your starting strategy. On days when the shifts swing back and forth seemingly at random or according to puffs of pressure that briefly appear in different areas across the course, it is especially important to keep your head outside the boat and look at the environment around you in order to make your best guess about the next shift. Prioritize getting onto the lifted tack as soon as possible after the start, but only if it plays into your prediction for where the next pressure or shift will come from. Again, the key is to look for patterns. Ask yourself as you speed-test before the start: Do the gusts come with a shift in one direction and the lulls with a shift in the other direction? Does more or less cloud cover affect the direction of the breeze across the racecourse? Then, looking up the course, do I see more or less breeze coming down before the start? Do I see more or less cloud cover approaching? Is there a cloud on one side of the course that might bring a shift in that direction? Is there darker water showing incoming pressure on one side of the course that I want to prioritize? Patterns and observations such as these can help you predict a shift before it reaches you. You want to start near the end of the line that gives you the best access to that next gust or shift you may spot during your Eagle Watch just before you get into position. To sum up, while it's important to know the final shift before the start, in crazy, shifty winds your upwind strategy (finding the next pressure, weather factors) holds greater weight in determining where you set up on the line.

Finally, in the third type of shifty wind condition – a persistent shift – your first priority is to start with a clear lane that you can hold and keep working towards the persistent shift. Your goal is to lead the fleet to that side of the racecourse, continually getting headed, so that you can eventually tack and cross most of the fleet towards the windward mark. The winning strategy in this type of race is the most obvious to the sailors, but it is also usually the most difficult, because it is what we call a 'closed course' situation. This means that one side of the racecourse has a clear advantage over the other. As a result, the boats that get a great start heading in that direction will have an easy life staying ahead of the fleet and arriving first at the windward mark, while the boats who fall behind will have very few opportunities to recover. Understand that you'll pay a high price for losing your lane going out to that side, so make sure to find a balance between risking it on favoured end and going for a more conservative start from which you can lead the fleet in a clear lane towards the persistent shift.

STARTING IN CURRENT

Starting in current is a complete game-changer for those who have never done it. Even for experienced starters, adapting your starts to strong current can take a while to get used to. As a coach in the San Francisco Bay, my sailors and I regularly train in the 2–3 knot ebb and flood that is such a defining part of this venue. But even in locations where you would measure the current before the start in boat lengths per minute rather than in knots, I can't overstate how important it is to do your homework and be aware of what the current is doing. Neglect it, and you may find yourself in deep trouble on the wrong side of a layline or the starting line.

The effect of the current on your race becomes greater as the speed of the current increases and the wind strength decreases. Each day, know what the tides are doing according to your tide book, and in your pre-start routine before each race take the time to stop next to a mark and see how the current affects your boat. Even better, toss a floating object

In this example, the current is coming down the racecourse. Notice how the bottom edge of the box is now much closer to the line, indicating that you must avoid drifting too far to leeward of the line. If you see that the bulk of the fleet hasn't noticed the current pushing them away from the line and as a result there is a deep sag, this is a great opportunity to accelerate early, punch out from the fleet, and have an easy start.

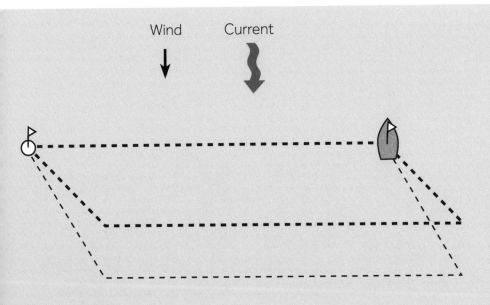

Wind   Current

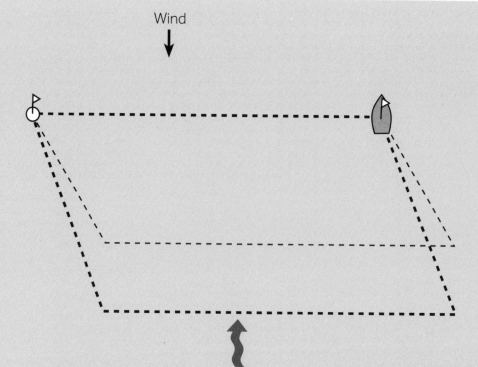

Wind

Current

In this example, the current is coming up the racecourse. Notice now how you shouldn't be afraid to set up farther than normal from the line. Pay special attention to timing your approach. Trust me, there are few worse situations in the start than realizing you're drifting over the line, and then you're desperately backing your main with 10 seconds to go as the fleet surges from behind.

into the water next to a mark and watch how it moves over the course of a minute (then retrieve it of course). Once you know what the current is doing, you can properly account for it in your approach to the start.

The best way we can understand how the current affects our starts is by looking

at the Starting Box.[5] This is the area enclosed by the start line, a parallel line downwind of the start line that indicates the farthest away distance from the line you should set up, and the upwind starboard laylines to the boat and pin ends. The following starting boxes have been altered to account for current.

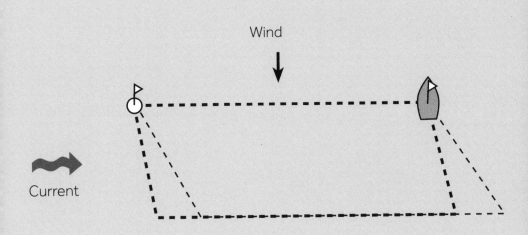

Wind

Current

The current is now from left to right. Notice how this makes the laylines to the boat and pin more vertical. As the boats drift from left to right on the line, it is easier to start on the pin with little risk of not making the line, while starting at the boat becomes more difficult as the likelihood of being shut out increases.

In general, starting on the up-current end of the line gives you an advantage on the first upwind, because the current will centralize you in the middle of the course as it pushes the down-current boats towards the layline. Additionally, especially in light wind and lower-level fleets, the up-current end of the line will be less crowded as the majority of boats are swept down to the down-current end. These reasons make starting on the up-current end of the line an appealing option.

As you can see, it's important to understand how current affects your distance and your laylines to the start so that you don't find yourself drifting away from where you want to be. After checking the current, stand up in your boat, take a wide view of the entirety of the start line, and imagine in your mind the correct starting box

5 See *Starting At The Ends* to understand the Starting Box.

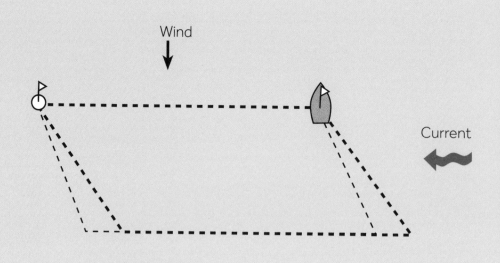

The current is now from right to left. Notice how this makes the laylines shallower. This means that it will be easy to squeeze in on the boat as the fleet drifts right to left, while it will be difficult to make the layline to the pin.

drawn over the water, adjusted for current. Then, imagine your boat approaching the line within the box, with wind and current considered. Just as a basketball player imagines the arc of their shot before taking a free throw or a baseball player stepping up to the plate envisions striking the ball deep into left field, making this mental image helps you envisage what you're going to do before you do it.

An additional tip: when there is strong current flowing downwind, do tacks in the pre-start instead of gybes. In strong current going against the wind, do gybes instead of tacks. This simple, easy rule

helps prevent you from getting swept away.

If you are on top of the current going into the first start of the first day of racing, I promise that it will upgrade your starts. It's unfortunately all too common for racers to be completely surprised by the current in the first start and have a terrible outcome, either missing laylines, starting way under the line, or scoring unnecessary letters. Realize that everyone will figure it out after a few races – by being aware of the current by Race 1 and recognizing it before everyone else, you'll have an early jump on the fleet.

STARTING UNDER PENALTY FLAGS

We've all seen the various penalty flags the Race Committee raises at 4 minutes: the I flag, the U flag, the black flag, etc. Most Race Committees won't start using them until a couple of general recalls under the P flag. Their purpose is to reign in the early starters by increasing the penalty for being over the line early. If you aren't sure what each flag means, be sure to read about them in the Racing Rules of Sailing. Memorizing their meanings is a must! If you can't remember them, have a sticker on your boat to remind you (available online and quite common on the decks of racing boats).

Race Committees don't want me to tell you this, but from my experience, I have found that you should start just as aggressively, when sailing under a penalty flag. Many racers will start really aggressively and fight for their spot in the front row in the first few starts under the P flag, but after a few general recalls when they see the U flag or the black flag, they become overcautious. They don't push the line as much, they don't bring their bow inline with the boats in the front row, and end up being much less likely to get a good start. This is wrong. You want to be just as aggressive starting under the black flag as you would under the P flag. I'm not saying to recklessly push the line and have a needless disqualification, but don't let the penalty flag change the way you start. In many cases, you'll actually see that the starts become easier under the black flag because the fleet around you will hang back more on the line. Most of the fleet will be less aggressive with pulling the trigger and accelerating forward. Just as when you identify a deep line sag in the seconds before the start and you use it as an opportunity to accelerate before the boats around you and punch out from the pack, see the black flag as an opportunity to take advantage of the fleet's tendency to be overcautious.

The reason for this principle is that in practice, there is virtually no difference in the penalty of being OCS under the P flag and being disqualified under a penalty flag like the U flag or black flag. There are some situations, such as if your Race Committee is using a radio or loudhailer to call the numbers of the boats that are OCS thereby enabling you to easily clear yourself, or if your fleet is very small and it is easy to identify yourself as the boat who's over, that it might make sense to take more risk under the P flag. But in most situations, especially in larger fleets, if you are OCS under any flag you won't know about it until the end of the race. You might feel some stress in the race and worry 'was I over the line?' (and you should feel this way after most starts because it means you were properly pushing the line) but you won't know for sure. And at the end of the day, an OCS, UFD (U Flag Disqualification), and BFD (Black Flag Disqualification) all carry the same amount of points. Yes, under a penalty flag you might have to make slight adjustments to your starting technique – don't be over the line in the last minute, and under the black flag don't be drawn over the line by the fleet around you when you see there's going to be a general recall, as you might under the P flag – but don't let a penalty flag make you a less aggressive sailor.

WHY WE GET BAD STARTS

To consistently get good, clean, and safe starts in clear air off the line, it's a good idea to study how bad starts happen. If you understand how your start may go wrong, then you'll spot the telltale signs of trouble and reposition yourself before it's too late. Here are the common causes of most bad starts:

* Getting into position too early
* Getting into position too late
* Losing your leeward gap
* Being outside the layline to the pin or the boat end (the Box)
* Being in a too crowded area
* Mistiming the acceleration

The first way a bad start might happen is if you get into position on the line too early. In a crowded fleet it's important to get into position relatively early, sometimes even earlier than 1 minute to the start in order to reserve your spot. However, when you go into position too early and too close to the line, you can run into serious trouble. Sitting on the line early in the sequence while the fleet comes from behind is one of the worst positions you can be in. Because you have no room to sail forward, your only option is to luff into the wind and stop, losing all your flow, your manoeuvrability, and you'll be sliding sideways on the line. This makes you a sitting duck for the pack of boats approaching from behind or from port. With zero speed and zero distance forward to burn, you will have no ability to defend your hole against a boat coming in to leeward. The probable outcome from here is that as the fleet fills in the space around you, the other boats will accelerate from speed and flow while you, with no speed and no hole to leeward to put your bow down, will accelerate from zero speed in the final second or two before the gun; the result is that you will be left sitting on the line as the fleet sails off. The other probable outcome is that you will not accept the idea of boats behind taking your hole or crossing the line with more speed, so you will defend and accelerate forward despite being already on the line, and the race committee will call you over.

The second way it can all go wrong is if you get into position late. This, of course, can happen in a variety of ways. Maybe your strategy was to hold back before committing to a position, but the line is crowded, everyone has their head swivelled backwards and are ready to defend against you, you can't find a spot on the line, and you end up starting in the second row or worse. Maybe you failed to look up the course and see that the wind was dying, and you find yourself too far below the line in the shadow of the fleet above you, with no chance of reaching the line in time. Maybe you even had a great spot on the line, a large leeward hole with no sharks and control over the boat to windward, and you had done everything right so far, but you forgot to get a line sight, you're late pulling the trigger to accelerate, and you're quickly pinched off or rolled over by the pack around you. Whatever the reason, being late to the line is the surest way to finding yourself in the back of the pack.

Thirdly, a sure way to struggle off the start is to lose your hole to leeward. Remember, there's a reason why we defend it: your leeward hole allows you to put your bow down to accelerate, and once you've crossed the line, your remaining gap to leeward becomes your runway, which is crucial to holding a comfortable lane. Sometimes a shark will

EXPERT TIP

When you punch the line maybe a second or two early but by coming from the back with speed, you're relatively safe; it's when you sit on the line early before the start, clearly exposed, and wait for the fleet to come to you, when the race committee sees your number clearly, has that extra motivation to penalize you for drawing the entire fleet forward, and is much more likely to call your number.

swoop into your hole and passively leave some room between you and them, especially if they are a less experienced sailor. If this happens, then as long as you do a perfect acceleration, cross the line on time, have control over the windward boat and hold a high mode off the line, you should have no trouble staying in the front row in clear air. But more often than not, if you don't defend your leeward hole, a shark will come from behind, coast right up alongside you, and lock you to windward. As their shrouds come even with your bow, you'll have no option but to steer higher into the wind, and as the pack around you bears away to build speed and punch the line, you'll be unable to accelerate.

Fourthly, you can't execute a proper start if you don't know your laylines. On crowded starting lines there is almost always a group of boats waiting above the layline to the committee boat, hoping for a gap to open up in the final seconds. This can sometimes work if you're the only boat fighting for the boat end and your plan is to tack early and go to the right, but generally I strongly recommend against doing this. Too many sailors now know the trick of starting late at the boat end, waiting for a gap to open up and making an immediate tack onto port, so if you're at all over the layline, you'll find yourself following a train of boats ducking committee, all of whom have the exact same plan as yourself. The result is that you'll never find the front row position you would have had with a proper start. On the other end of the line, misjudging your layline to the pin is even more painful. We've all seen or experienced the nightmare of going for that perfect pin end start, seeing that you're not going to make it, and circling around to duck the fleet as the gun sounds.

These are all things we try to avoid, but the reality is that they do happen. The fact is that the quicker you can anticipate trouble before it happens, the greater your chance of escaping from a disadvantaged situation and saving your start.

Chapter 8

CONCLUSION

As you can probably tell by the length of this section, starting is one of the most complex parts of a race. There is no other time around the racecourse that you have to take in as much information and make as many strategic and tactical decisions for the first beat and fight for your position on the line. Starting really is a game in itself. Master it, and you put yourself in a great position to win races. But make a mistake in a big fleet and you'll find yourself shot out the back. The start can make or break your race.

This part explains what you can do to prepare before the start and how you can perform a successful start, but putting all the pieces together in a regatta is another challenge. At the end of the day, practising starts will improve them more than anything else. In these pages I have laid out the steps to a very systematic approach to the start to help you make sense of the starting thought process, but it takes the experience from practising hundreds of starts to be able to connect all the dots successfully. Each time you do a start, whether it has a positive or negative outcome, hopefully you ask yourself why it did or didn't go well. With proper analysis after each start, your level should gradually improve as you try to replicate what led to your good starts and change what caused your bad starts. Sailors who have performed and then reflected on hundreds of starts have an instinct, almost a sixth sense, for knowing how much they can push the line, what gap they should go for on the line, whether or not they'll make a layline, and knowing what works and what doesn't. The information in this book can give you a head start on gaining this experience, but there truly is no substitute to on-the-water practice. So find some buddies to train with, get out there, set a line, and run some starts.

TIMELINE OF THE PRE-START ROUTINE AND THE STARTING SEQUENCE

TIME UNTIL THE START	CONTENT
60-10 minutes	Racecourse Routine: Warm-up and explore the conditions.[6]
10-3 minutes	Pre-Start Routine: Collect information. Make your game plan. Practice techniques and accelerations.
3 minutes	Sail upwind and check the compass numbers. Final assessment of the pressure and any weather events up the course. Find the area on the line where you want to start.
1.30–0.45 minutes	Usually at some point within this range it will be time to get into position. Do your Eagle Watch and find a good spot on the line.
1.00–0.10 minutes	Defend and upgrade your position. Time and distance to the line.
0.15–0.03 minutes	Begin the acceleration at the proper time
0.00+	Focus on maximizing boat speed and holding your lane. Shift your mindset to upwind strategy.

[6] See *The Water: The Racecourse Routine.*

The fleet in this start is clustered at the boat end because there is a boat-end bias. When this is the case, it's up to you to judge how much risk you want to take. A good strategy is to start just to leeward of the pack at the boat end – there is still a big reward but it is considerably less risky.

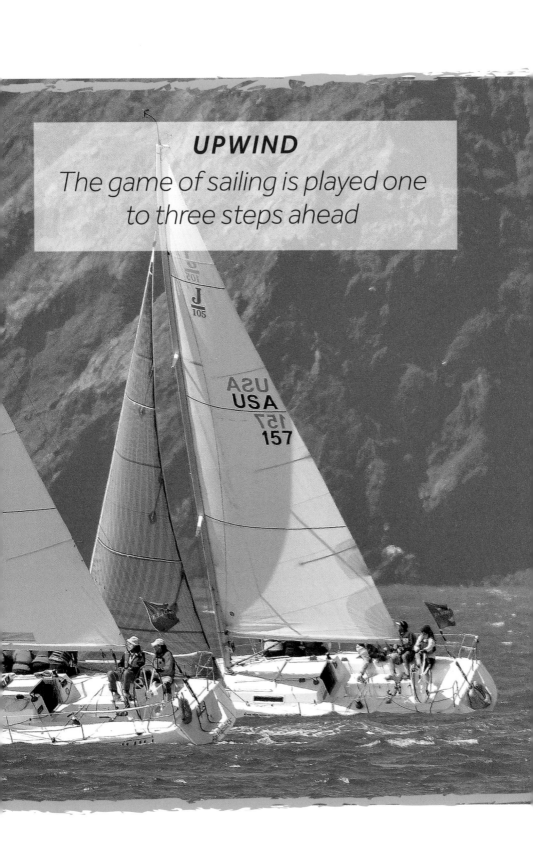

PART 3

UPWIND

The game of sailing is played one to three steps ahead

In a way, the upwind leg is one of the simplest parts of the race. After all, you have only two options: tack or continue. On the face of it, racing upwind couldn't be more straightforward. However, there are a great many factors that go into this seemingly simple decision of whether to tack or continue. There's the strategic component – getting up the racecourse as fast as possible according to the environmental factors around you such as the pressure, wind shifts and current, and the tactical component of executing a successful upwind leg – making the best moves relative to the boats around you. In this chapter I will go into detail about the tactical and strategic principles that made me successful.

Having started the race, you've already completed your Pre-Start Routine and you should have a basic plan for your upwind strategy.[7] Hopefully you started in an area of the line that allows you to go where you want to go according to your plan. Before I get to more advanced tactical and strategic principles, let's get some of the basics of upwind tactics out of the way.

The Basics:
- ☀ Stay in clear air
- ☀ Stay in pressure
- ☀ Cover the boats behind you
- ☀ Consolidate with other boats when you make a gain
- ☀ Don't get to the laylines too early
- ☀ Sail to the favoured side (if there is one)
- ☀ Stay in phase with the shifts
- ☀ Understand the current

These are the essential basics of upwind tactics and strategy that every racer should know. In this chapter I will expand on each of these principles, as well as dive into other more complex ideas.

Like the start, the upwind is its own game. To simplify the challenge of racing upwind, I break down the upwind leg into three main stages:

OFF THE LINE

This first stage is the race off the line, which occurs at the very bottom of the upwind leg. This is that time just after the start where you're holding your lane off the line and working hard to stay in the front row. It begins as soon as you accelerate to cross the line and lasts around 1–2 minutes after the start, once the fleet spreads apart and your options start to open up, making up about 5–10% of the upwind leg.

EXECUTING YOUR UPWIND GAME PLAN

This second stage, the largest, is when you actually execute your upwind strategy. This usually

---

[7] See *The Pre-Start Routine* for more information about making an initial upwind game plan.

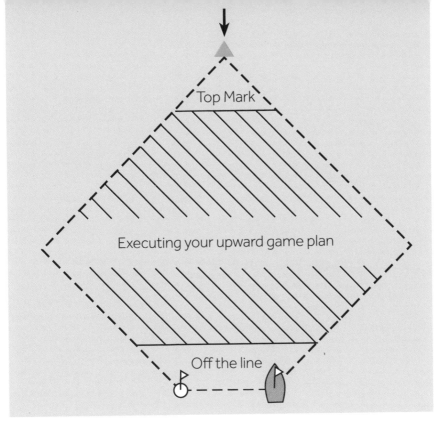

Top Mark

Executing your upward game plan

Off the line

The upwind leg broken down into three stages.

involves choosing a side according to your upwind strategy, staying in phase with the shifts, and consolidating with the fleet when you make gains. This stage makes up approximately the middle 60–80% of the leg, and it happens when the boats are most laterally spread out across the course.

THE TOP MARK

This third and final stage occurs at the top 10–20% of the upwind as the fleet converges at the top of the course. It's your last chance to consolidate or make another offensive move. Proper racing in this stage involves a mix of tactics and strategy: getting around the windward mark in the best possible position relative to the other boats, and determining your

initial game plan for the next leg (the hand-off).

I will cover each of these three stages in the following chapters. Note that this structure of breaking down the upwind leg is most relevant when you have a great or good start that allows you to execute your upwind strategy. If you have a bad start (ie you quickly lose your lane) and you end up in the back of the fleet early on, especially in a large and crowded fleet, then the game of the upwind is very different. Recovering from deep in the fleet is all about finding a clear lane and making the best of the options that are left to you. See *The Comeback* for how to escape from a bad start.

Chapter 9

OFF THE LINE

The starting gun fires. Everyone's racing off the line. You've just completed a high-action and potentially stressful start. Hopefully you've done well so far and you hit the line at the gun, at full speed, and on your upwind angle. If there's any time in the race for maximum effort and focus from the entire crew on the boat, it's now. When you're racing off the line in a big fleet, your ability to hold or even upgrade your lane with the boats around you can make or break your race. The first minute or so off the line is perhaps the most critical time of the entire race. The difference between holding your lane and losing it means the difference between comfortably controlling the fleet from the front row and being shot out the back. I can't stress enough that this is a game of inches. This is the time that everyone on the boat needs to hike (sit out) hard and be 110% focused on sail trim and producing boat speed. Just a few feet or inches of height or speed forward can determine your race.

ASSESS YOUR START

First, you want to assess your position compared to the boats around you. Do this right after you accelerate your boat, or even earlier if possible. Basically, you want to know as soon as possible if you have a good or bad start

This section of the upwind is the first one or two minutes of racing off the line.

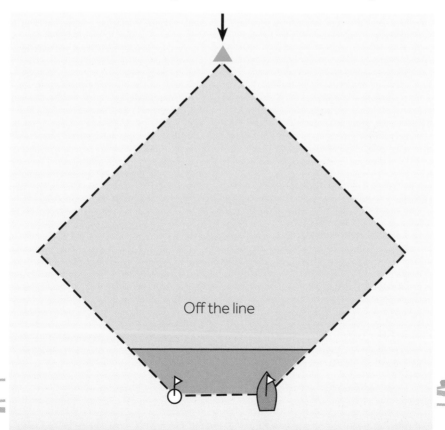

Off the line

The first 30–60 seconds after the start is perhaps the most critical moment of the race.

so that you can take the best of your options according to your situation. In my experience, the simplest and most effective way to do this is to assess your start quickly as plus, minus, or equal. The following are explanations of each type of start and your goals with each one:

☀ A *plus start* means that you got a great start compared to the boats around you. You punched out from the pack, you have a relatively comfortable lane with the boats to windward and to leeward of you, and you're sailing fast upwind relative to most of the other boats which are not in an optimal lane or at full speed. At this point you're likely to be in the top 10–20% of the fleet. This is essentially your best case scenario because you have options you can choose from to begin executing your upwind strategy. This means that you have the freedom to choose from different modes (angles) upwind, and you will soon have the freedom to tack without ducking boats as the front row thins out, if you don't have it already. Your goal here, in this free and open position, is to begin executing your upwind strategy/game plan while also making the right tactical decisions according to the fleet. Begin to play the shifts, look for the next pressure up the course, and get to the favoured side, but be sure to stay connected with your main competition, and stay

on top of the fleet behind you if possible. As any racer knows, life is easy at the front.

☀ An *equal start* means that you started even with the boats around you. You're confident you can hold your lane for at least a minute or two, but you will need to work hard to do so. This is the most complex scenario, because you must weigh your options of whether to continue holding your lane while probably compromising optimal boat speed/VMG or to tack and take another opportunity. My usual answer to this scenario is to bail out from this situation ONLY if you have another better and safer option. Stay in phase with the shifts and get to the favoured side, whether that means continuing on starboard tack to the left or tacking onto port, ducking some boats, and going to the right, but only if you can do so while staying in clear air. However, unless you're making an early tack to go right, your first priority is to have perfect boat speed and be mindful of your mode so that you can hold your lane for as long as possible. Understand that when the fleet crosses the starting line all the boats are more or less even, but as time goes on the fleet very quickly splits into two general groups: the leaders in the front row and in clear air, and the rest of the boats in the second row or worse, who are suffering in bad lanes and falling further and

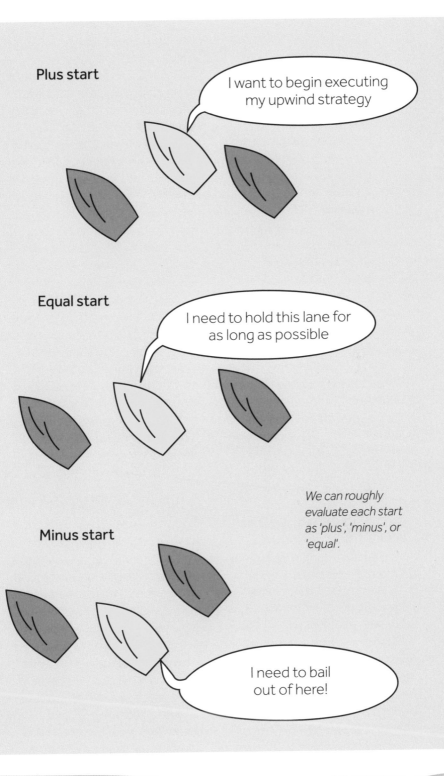

further behind. For every second that passes after the start, the distance between these two groups steadily increases. So, the greater amount of time you hold your lane without getting rolled over by the boat to windward or pinched out by the boat to leeward, the more likely you are to stay in that first group and the better position you will be in, relative to the rest of the fleet, when you are finally forced to tack out of there. If you never lose your lane but instead build up a nice gap around you, then congratulations: you've effectively turned your equal start into a plus start.

☀ A *minus start* is a bad start. You are either in bad air or you know you will lose your lane in the next few seconds. Or perhaps you thought you had an equal start but you made a mistake, or hit a bad wave, and got quickly squeezed out or rolled over. In almost all cases when you have a bad start you want to react right away. You should be looking for the first opportunity to tack, unless staying in this very bad lane will give you a much better opportunity later down the road. See *The Comeback* for how to escape from a bad start.

This assessment of your start is something that the crew can and should help out with. Remember, on the upwind leg especially, while the helm's job is to stay 100% focused on producing maximum speed, it's the crew's job to keep their head outside the boat and bring information in. What makes the best teams stand out in any class of sailing boat is their ability to divide up the roles among them and have constant and clear communication between themselves so that outside information is efficiently brought into the boat. Being in perfect sync with your team and having great teamwork is one of the hardest yet most critical things in sailing in my opinion. Trust me, it makes all the difference when the helm can focus on steering and they can trust the tactician or another crew member given the role of upwind strategy to call out from the rail 'plus start, let's sail a high mode to pinch out this windward boat so we can tack and get to that pressure on the right!' That said, if you're sailing single-handed, you'll have your work cut out!

MODES OFF THE LINE

It's also key to be deliberate with your mode, or angle, off the line. When people sail upwind, especially beginners, they all too often rely on the basic fundamentals they were taught when they first learned to sail – they steer the boat on a dead-straight angle to the wind. The result, of course, is that their boat speed upwind will suffer and they'll be baffled by how the more experienced sailors around them always seem to surge forward and get their boat into the better tactical position. The reality is that when sailing upwind, there are three modes you can have – high mode, low mode, and a proper VMG (Velocity Made Good) mode. On a basic level these are the three modes. As we get more advanced we can look at the fine-tuning of sailing between and combining these modes. Each of these modes should be used purposefully at different moments throughout the race.

First of all, any improving sailor needs to understand the concept of VMG. As we already know, sailing boats cannot sail straight into the wind; instead, to race upwind, they must zigzag back and forth. The speed that the boat moves towards the wind is called its VMG. Note that this is different from the speed the boat is moving through the water. Since we cannot sail directly towards the wind but rather at an angle to the wind, our VMG is just a fraction of our upwind boat speed through the water.

Most of the time we use what I call our 'VMG mode' when sailing upwind. This mode is the best combination of the speed of the boat and angle to the wind that will get you up the course as efficiently as possible. Not too high, not too low, but finding the perfect balance between heading low for speed forward and high for height. In most sailing boats this is about 40–45 degrees off the wind. However, there are times in a race that we want to sail a 'high mode', or point higher into the wind, and there are times that we want to sail a 'low mode'. Note that each of these modes is just a subtle difference from your VMG mode – the difference in angle between the high and low modes is usually no more than a few degrees. Sailors who've practised the technique to sail their modes properly can actually produce a similar VMG, or progress upwind, with each one. In a high mode the boat is sailing high and slow – this is often called 'pinching'. Sailors may also call this a 'point mode'. Sailors can use a high mode and still have a reasonably good VMG because while their boat speed may be slower, their higher angle means that they have less actual sailing distance to the mark. A low mode is just the opposite. We also call this a 'foot mode'. Instead of high and slow, a low mode means you're sailing low and fast. A boat may have more distance to zigzag back and forth to get to the windward mark, but it will be travelling faster through the water.

What factors should determine which mode you use? It all depends on your position relative to other boats and the conditions on the racecourse. To know which one to use off the line, you need to know what you're trying to achieve.

If you have an equal start, realize that your first priority is holding your lane. Think about it: the race off the line is essentially

Wind

Low mode   VMG mode   High mode

More sailing distance
but faster speed;
similar VMG

Normal sailing
distance and normal
speed; most optimal
VMG

Less sailing
distance but less
speed; similar
VMG

'Modes' for sailing upwind.

a temporary drag race that you just need to survive so that you can stay in the front row. Yes, you can perfect your boat speed and sail trim in order to be as fast as possible, but in a closely-matched fleet, the real tool you have at your disposal when you need to hold your lane with other boats is choosing the right mode and sailing it well.

To use this tool properly, in an equal start, you should choose your mode based on the modes of the boats above and below you, with the goal of separating from the leeward boat and staying connected to the windward boat. More often than not you will be starting in a tightly packed area, and nine times out of ten you'll find it's a pinching war as you sail off the line. This is how it happens:

one boat pinches hard in order to build up a gap to leeward, and so the boat above them will sail a high mode as well to hold their lane and pinch out the boat to windward of them, who will then start sailing high as well ... and the end result is that all the boats who got equal starts spend their first minute or two sailing off the line high and slow. In fact, in most fleets, especially as the fleet becomes more crowded and more competitive, sailing a high mode off the line is essentially an automatic thing that everyone does. And the sailors who either can't sail the high mode or just haven't had the memo will see after each start the leeward boat slowly but surely squeezing up to them within the first minute; their leeward gap will disappear, they'll slowly be squeezed out, and they'll lose their lane. So the most important thing to remember is that the high mode should be your go-to mode off the line. Even if it seems like the fastest way up the course is to put your bow down and sail fast, it's a good idea to spend those first few seconds off the line using your speed for height until you can see how the boat to leeward of you is sailing. If they're sailing high, then that's okay, you've already maintained your gap to leeward and you should have no problem holding your lane from now on. If they're sailing more of a VMG mode or even a low mode, then you've already built yourself a great gap to leeward – now is the time to bear away a few degrees and go for speed. After all, it's always easier to begin with height and later sail low when you need to, rather than burning up your leeward gap early on and then struggling to rebuild your gap in a tough lane.

There are times, however, when the boats around you will sail a VMG mode or even a low mode off the line. It might be because there's very light wind or chop and the sailors want to keep their boats moving, or it might be that everyone wants to get to favoured conditions on the left side of the racecourse as quickly as possible. Especially in very strong wind, sometimes sailing low off the start and getting

EXPERT TIP

As a simple rule, sail as high a mode as you need to in order to have a comfortable lane with the boat to leeward. If the leeward boat is sailing high, sail high as well to maintain your lane. Once they bear off, bear off slightly as well to sail a faster VMG mode. Additionally, keep an eye on the windward boats as well. See if they are bow forward, and what kind of mode they are sailing. If they are sailing low and fast forward, judge if there is any risk of them rolling over you. If so, you will have to be careful not to sail too high a mode. Sail a VMG mode or lower to protect your air to windward.

on a plane will give you an early advantage. In many keelboats, starting by gaining some speed on the low mode is necessary to get the keel working. Most commonly, this trend happens when the fleet is comfortably spread out across the line and everyone has a decent gap to leeward – since there's no reason to fight on a high mode to hold their lane, the sailors' best bet is to prioritize their VMG. Whatever the reason, identify this trend in the fleet as soon as possible as you assess your start so you know that you don't need to dig for height. In general, the low mode will have a slightly better VMG than an aggressive high mode, so go for the VMG mode or low mode when you have the space around you to do so. Again, this is a time when crew communication is a big help to the team. The crew bringing in information about external factors such as the modes of the boats around them and which modes seem to be working well frees up the helm to direct 100% focus to producing boat speed.

One of the benefits of having a plus start is that you have more freedom to choose your mode. If you have a plus start, you are no longer forced to sail a certain mode just to survive your lane off the start. Instead, you can choose the best mode according to your upwind strategy (the environment) and tactics (the fleet). This is explained in greater detail in *Executing Your Upwind Game Plan*, but essentially you want to sail a VMG mode when you have a plus start, unless you have a good reason to sail another mode. For example, you might sail high or low in order to position yourself to make gains from environmental factors, such as to stay connected to the edge of a puff that's to windward or to leeward of you, or to get to better pressure or

EXPERT TIP

The best communication is simple, clear, and efficient. As a helm, when you're sailing off the line and holding your lane the most important information you need is your relative speed and relative angle compared to the boats on each side of you. It follows that you can be either high and fast, high and slow, low and fast, or low and slow. When I sailed the 470, my teammate and I developed a very efficient method for communicating this information. As a crew, I would say just two words: 'high slow', or 'fast low', for example. I would choose to either say the relative angle or relative speed first – whichever one I said first was the one that was more extreme. For example, 'high slow' translates to 'we are sailing much higher and a little bit slower'. In that way I added another dimension to the information I was communicating, while only using two words. This efficient transfer of information is key to making quick decisions.

current on one side of the course as quickly as possible. You may want to pinch in order to 'kill' the boat to windward and force them to tack so that when a header comes, you have the freedom to tack. Overall, this freedom of modes that a great start gives you is so powerful that I can't stress it enough. Just by simply sailing fast on your VMG mode you will be extending away from the bulk of the fleet, because while the rest of the fleet sails high and slow in their pinching war with a less optimal VMG, you can put the bow down and rip, making huge gains.

Your modes upwind are useful at other times in the race as well, not just when sailing off the line. For the majority of the upwind leg you usually want to use your VMG mode as this, by definition, will get you up the course the fastest, but there are times when, because of strategic and tactical considerations, you might sail slightly higher or slightly lower than you would otherwise. For example, later in the race you might put the bow down if you want to consolidate with other boats (potentially sacrificing some height to reduce your lateral separation and risk in case of a header), and you might use a high mode if you're trying to survive a boat close to leeward or if you're trying to make a tight layline. While sailing on starboard tack, if you see better pressure on the left side of the upwind, anticipate a shift to the left, or see that the

pack to leeward of you is your greatest threat, you can go on a lower and faster mode (drop the bow a few degrees, adjust the sails, flatten out the boat) and get connected to those more favourable conditions or connect with that pack. Conversely, if you want to stay connected with the conditions or the pack on the right side of the upwind, or if you simply want to pinch out the boat to windward so that you can tack onto port tack, then sail on a higher and slower mode (head up slightly, adjust the sails, and keep slight leeward heel). So really, your modes become tools that you use constantly throughout the race.

As a final note on modes, it's important to understand how the conditions affect the modes available to you. In light wind and chop you generally need to sail a lower mode to power through that chop. In extremely light wind you also want a low mode just to keep the boat moving and to maintain flow. In these conditions the high mode doesn't work. You really just want to power through that chop and keep maximum flow over the foils and the sails. Conversely, in flat water and positive pressure the boat can tolerate a lot more time pinching without slowing down, making the high mode a much more available tool in these conditions.

The class of boat you sail also affects which modes work well and in which conditions. In overpowered conditions in most keelboats, it usually helps to sail a slightly higher mode and steer up slightly in the puffs. This reduces the power in the sails, reduces the heel of the boat and the weather helm, and makes sailing the boat a bit more manageable. In light, planing hull dinghies such as the 470, however, you make a big jump in boat speed by sailing slightly lower in strong, overpowering conditions. In general, as much as your boat is lighter and faster, you want to go earlier on a low mode in a big breeze because the boat will take off much faster. If your class of boat is relatively heavy and slow, the pinching mode is more effective because you have the momentum to use your speed for height without slowing down.

A NOTE ON BOAT SPEED: SAILING THE MODES UPWIND

So, how do you properly sail these different modes? First, let's look at the things you can control. The primary things you have control over on the sailing boat are your steering, sail trim, and the heel of the boat. When you want to sail an aggressive high mode, your goal is to use most of the speed you have and convert it into height. You want to ideally start with speed before you go for the aggressive pinching. Once you have speed, trim in the sails tightly. The leeches of the main and the jib should both be strongly engaged and the main should be

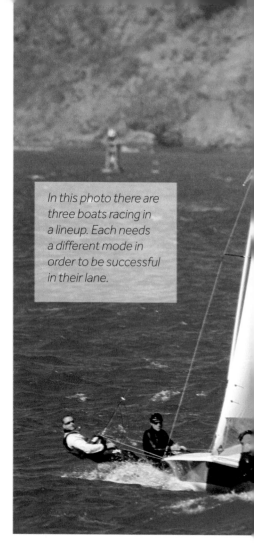

In this photo there are three boats racing in a lineup. Each needs a different mode in order to be successful in their lane.

slightly over trimmed, depending on how much flow you have over the sail and your attacking angle to the wind. Adjust the crew placement so that the boat has a slight leeward heel if it doesn't already. Doing both of these things will cause the boat to head up naturally a few degrees with minimal use of the rudder. Moving the crew weight forward will keep the v-shape of the bow down in the water, which acts as a second keel or centreboard and helps with height. Maintain the slight leeward

heel throughout the process so that you keep the boat as powered up as possible – avoid windward heel at all costs. As you feel the boat slowing down and losing the flow, head down a few degrees and ease the sails slightly to regain speed and flow, and then repeat the process.

When you want to sail a low mode, your goal is to maximize your forward boat speed by sailing a slightly lower angle at the expense of height. To do this properly, you want the boat to be relatively flat. Most dinghies definitely want to be sailed perfectly flat on the low mode, while keelboats should be sailed slightly flatter than the normal heel angle upwind and as flat as possible in strong conditions, otherwise the boat will have a tendency to round up and have more leeway (sliding sideways). In medium and strong wind conditions the boat will sail the fastest with maximum righting moment (ie maximum crew weight on the rail, sitting out fully, or crew fully down on the trapeze), while in light wind the heel angle can be gradually flattened out as you feel more power in the boat. Sails should be trimmed for maximum speed forward. In light wind this means keeping the leeches open to promote flow over the sail. In stronger wind, as you ease the sails slightly to maintain the heel angle, you want to keep the leeches engaged, usually through a combination of tightening the vang hard and lowering the traveller to leeward to increase the leech tension (adjust your sail controls such as cunningham, outhaul, and backstay accordingly as well). When depowering the main in this way, just make sure you are not disrupting the flow through the slot between the main and the jib. Although your goal with this mode is to sail low and fast, whenever you feel especially fast over the water don't be afraid to head up slightly and convert that speed into height. This will improve your overall VMG.

As you can see, it takes lots of practice and a solid understanding of heel angle and sail shape in order to sail these different modes effectively. It also requires you to actively sail the boat: constantly heading up and down between the modes and adjusting the sails to squeeze every bit of speed out of your boat. I recommend practising your modes whenever you sail upwind until they become second nature, an automatic

aspect of your upwind boat speed. Additionally, practice so that you can adjust effortlessly between your modes whenever a situation arises where you need to make a gear change. Having this second nature to drive the boat and make automatic gear changes frees up your cognitive ability so you can focus more on race management during the race.

Note that using these modes doesn't require drastic changes in your angle. Your high mode and low mode are usually just a few degrees higher or lower than your normal VMG mode. Because of this, working on your modes is all about fine-tuning your skills once you have the fundamentals taped. Focusing on sailing different modes

EXPERT TIP

Remember, when you change angle between the modes, use as little rudder as possible! Your steering should mainly come from the two other methods of handling the boat: sail trim and heel angle. When you want to head up, instead of using the rudder, tighten the main, create some leeward heel, and allow the boat to naturally round up a few degrees. When you want to head down, ease the sails slightly and flatten the boat.

is not something for the real beginner who's just learning how to sail upwind – it's a more subtle skill for intermediate racers to add to their toolbox of skills and for advanced racers to perfect.

(Note: In this book I've chosen not to go into much detail about boat speed. Every boat is sailed fast differently, and your local racers and other references dedicated specifically to developing boat speed will probably be your best sources for advice. However, these principles apply to virtually any sailing boat, from the smallest of dinghies to large keelboats. I hope you find them useful.)

BUILDING THE RUNWAY

The concept of the runway is closely related to your modes and it is important to think about whenever you have a boat close to leeward of you, especially off the line. When racing upwind, a boat that is close to leeward of you is a constant threat. As fleet racers know all too well, a boat sailing upwind creates an area of dirty air directly to leeward of its sails as well as to its windward side, especially in light wind, as the air is bounced off the mainsail and deflected back into the sails of any unfortunate boat on its windward hip. An important key to holding your lane and staying in clear air, then, is making sure you have a comfortable gap to leeward. I call

this gap while you're racing the 'runway'.

The reason I call it the runway is because having this solid gap between you and a leeward boat gives you the freedom to adjust your angle slightly up or down according to the feeling of the boat. In other words, the space allows you to sail the angle that is most comfortable to you. When you don't have the runway (ie you have a boat close to leeward threatening to squeeze you out), as a helm you feel uncomfortable, closed in, and restricted, because you can't push the boat in the way that you would like to. Instead of driving the boat for speed on your preferred mode, all you can focus

The runway allows you to sail your optimal VMG, without facing the leeward boat's turbulence or pinching unnecessarily.

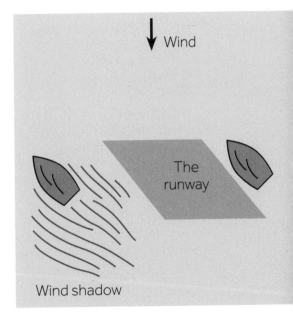

on is holding a high enough angle so that you don't risk falling into bad air.

You have a solid runway when you have a large enough gap between you and the boat to leeward that you feel more free, like you can breathe again, and you're a bit more relaxed. A few boat lengths to leeward is usually enough. When you have the runway, you no longer feel restricted with your angle but instead you can make slight steering adjustments up or down, on your own terms. Then, whenever you hit a wave or feel the boat slowing down, you aren't afraid to drop the bow a few degrees every so often to gain a bit of speed, and then take that speed up again. To sum up, what makes building and holding onto the runway so important is not just that it reduces your risk of losing your lane to the leeward boat, but that it also gives you room to play with your angle and do 'curving' upwind.

Even before you begin the acceleration for the start, take a look at your gap to leeward to see if you have a solid runway. If you do have a nice gap to leeward, great! You have some flexibility to put your bow down, so don't be afraid to accelerate on a nice low angle and punch the line at full speed. If you don't have a comfortable gap to leeward, make sure you don't lose too much height in your acceleration and hold a high mode off the line

to try to build up that runway as much as possible, hopefully at the same time pinching off any boats to windward. When we break the start down to its fundamentals, having a good start is all about building and maintaining the runway, so make sure you're always conscious whether or not you have a good runway to leeward, at any time throughout the race and especially off the line. Remember, it's always easier to prioritize height for the first few seconds off the line and then start sailing low when you have a solid runway to do so, rather than burning up your leeward gap early on and then struggling in bad air to rebuild your lane.

A NOTE ON BOAT SPEED: CURVING

I'm going to present you with one more nuance here about your modes upwind. Your VMG mode upwind – your fastest average angle to sail up the course – isn't actually a fixed angle. You might know, for example, that in your particular class of boat your average upwind VMG angle in a certain condition is about 40 degrees off the wind, but if you were to steer exactly 40 degrees to the wind for any significant stretch of time you would actually find that you would be slow. In reality, sailing your VMG mode upwind properly requires a small amount of constant adjustment to your angle. I call this 'curving'.

To sail your boat upwind as fast as possible, you need to curve. Curving means playing with your angle by a few degrees according to your speed, the puffs and the lulls, the waves, the balance of the helm, and the feel of the boat. Below is the key rule to using curving to produce great boat speed that you can remember all throughout the race.

As the helm, when sailing upwind the vast majority of your time should be spent watching only two things: the telltales on the jib and the puffs on the water directly upwind of you. But by simply having your hand on the tiller or the wheel and by sitting on the boat, you get a whole other dimension of feedback to help you produce boat speed. You can feel the response you get from the rudder, whether it feels neutral or if you have weather helm (the tiller pulling away from you and the boat trying to round up). You can feel the heel angle of the boat. And finally, you can feel if you're fast or if you're slow. Have you ever felt your boat move especially fast and light, like it's risen out of the water on a plane and aggressively powers through the waves? Or have you ever felt suddenly slow and sluggish, especially in light wind and chop, you feel a heavy response from the rudder, and the bow seems to slam to a standstill with every wave? All these things determine how you curve upwind, and to do it well, you need to have a good feeling for the boat.

Think of curving up and down when sailing upwind as if you were steering according to a sine curve. It's not just either going high or going low, it's the steady curving up and down according to the pressure and the feel of the boat. The timing of when you change your angle is extremely important here. As you begin to feel fast, first flatten out the boat as much as possible. Trim in the sails (especially the mainsail), make sure the leech is engaged and even slightly over trimmed, and allow the boat to head up naturally a few degrees with minimal use of the rudder. Head up as much as you can without losing your speed or the power you feel in the boat.

THE KEY RULE TO CURVING

On the upwind leg, when you feel fast, trim in the sails, head slightly higher, and flatten the boat. When you feel slow, head down slightly, ease the sails, and press the boat a bit less so that we have lighter flow on the rudder and easier flow on the sails. On the downwind leg, when you feel fast, flatten the boat, head down slightly, and ease the sails. When you feel slow, create some leeward heel, head up slightly, and trim in the sails.

This effectively converts your fast speed into height. Then, as you feel that you're just about to lose your speed/power, open the sails slightly, head down a few degrees to your average VMG angle or even slightly lower, and create a bit of leeward heel in order to rebuild the power and speed in the boat. As you feel fast again, trim in the sails, head up to a higher angle, and repeat the process. Generally as your timing gets better (heading down just as you begin to lose pressure, heading up just as you regain your speed),

the smaller your change of angle while curving needs to be. This perpetual cycle is the key to being fast upwind.

I want to stress that this curving requires very subtle changes in angle. I'm talking about steering only 3–5 degrees as you head up and down. It also requires only subtle changes to the sail trim, in a small dinghy maybe one or two inches in on the main as you head up, and one or two inches out as you head down. Larger boats may require a greater range of main trim. An

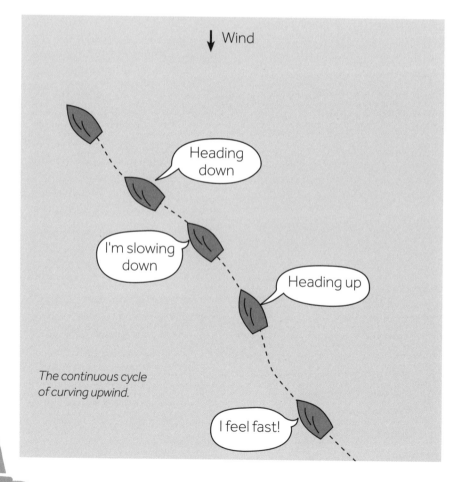

The continuous cycle of curving upwind.

entire cycle of curving – heading up with speed and then heading down to regain the speed – usually has a duration of somewhere between 5 and 15 seconds, but again, this all depends on the conditions and the type of boat. As you gain experience in your boat and develop a sense of how it feels when it's fast, how it feels when it's slow, how much is effective to head up and head down, and how long is effective to stay on each mode, curving will become an automatic part of your boat speed. Once you learn to do it effectively, you'll see just how much of a game changer it is on the racecourse.

As I mentioned earlier, while curving upwind is mainly a function of your speed and your feeling of the boat, there are other factors to consider such as the sea state and the pressure. As you're sailing, there are times when the water is flatter and there are times when it is choppier. Try to curve so that you're sailing a high mode in the flat water and sailing low in the chop. The most extreme example of this is when a motorboat crosses somewhere in front of you and creates a choppy wake. See this wake ahead so that you can put your bow down before it hits you and drive through it for a few seconds while powered up and maintaining speed on a slightly lower mode.

The puffs and lulls are also important factors in your curving. In almost every condition, puffs

and lulls in the wind come down the course, and you will experience these differences in pressure in the span of seconds as puffs and lulls hit your sails. The important rule to remember here is that you want to curve up and down according to your speed, not the pressure. Curve up because you have good speed, not just because you happen to be in a puff of wind. Perform this correctly and the trend you'll notice is this: when you're experiencing a lull you'll slow down, so when the next puff hits you'll probably enter the puff on a slight low mode. Then, once you've gained speed from the puff you can pinch higher again and trim in the sails. Coming out from a puff and into a lull, continue to point as your speed is maintained, but as soon as you feel the boat starting to sink in the water, head back down, ease the sails and build a bit of leeward heel to keep the pressure in the boat.

Let's now bring the concept of curving to your high mode and your low mode. In comparison to sailing a VMG mode, your high mode and low mode are both more of a fixed angle, but it is still effective to curve a small amount. An aggressive high mode can be extremely beneficial for building yourself a runway on a crowded starting line, but there is a point when pointing your bow too far into the wind slows you to a standstill and becomes a disadvantage. To keep your speed while sailing a high mode, don't hold a fixed angle. Instead, if you think of the curving that you do on your VMG angle as a 50:50 balance between heading up and heading down, then to sail a high mode, just allocate more time in that ratio to curving up for height – try sailing 80% of the time high and 20% low. Don't necessarily point higher, just spend more time on the high mode and be quicker to use your speed for height. Sailing the low mode is just the opposite. You're still curving just offset the balance of these two factors by spending more time going for speed on the low mode and less time using your speed for height.

Pretty much on all points of sail, curving should become a natural and automatic part of how you sail the boat. Experienced sailors do it almost instinctively. On the upwind, use the speed to head up, and when you feel slow, drop the bow to regain your speed. What it does take to do curving well is to have a good feeling for your boat, which you only gain through repetitions and consistent practice.

PLAY THE COURSE

Finally, as you fight for your lane off the line, don't forget about your upwind strategy. Always have someone on the boat looking up the course for the next pressure and making sure you're going to it. Check your options. Re-assess which side is better. Look at

your compass numbers and know what shift you are on. If you're on a lift, make sure you hold your lane because you want to continue on starboard (you definitely don't want to have to tack onto port). If you're on a header, look for the first opportunity to tack into a clear lane.

In addition, identify what is going on with the fleet. Are all the boats continuing on starboard? Has everyone tacked onto port? Or is the fleet split, with half the boats continuing to the left and half going right? And why? Did everyone tack because of a shift or another external factor? It's important to understand both what is going on with the conditions on the racecourse as well as what the fleet is doing while you consider whether to tack or continue. You want to put yourself in the best position according to what you think the weather is doing but still stay connected to the fleet.

This is what it takes to get off the line successfully, while keeping in mind your upwind strategy. The fleet will be tightly packed around you as you cross the line, but after a minute or two the space around you will clear up. The boats with good starts will shoot to the front, those with bad starts will most likely tack away. In the front, the space around you will clear up and you will find yourself in a safe, established lane. With a good start, you can now begin executing your upwind strategy. If you did fall into the second row or worse, now it's comeback time...

Chapter 10

THE COMEBACK

So that perfect start didn't work out quite as you planned it? Don't worry! It happens to everyone. Just because you lost the early advantage doesn't mean your race is over – you just have a lot of work ahead of you. The key to turning this race into a keeper score is keeping a level head and making the right moves after a bad start so that you can make the best possible initial recovery. From there, you have the entire rest of the race to fight back.

ESCAPE ROUTES

So, you're starting a race and you foresee trouble ahead (or maybe you're already in trouble) as the clock winds down from 30 seconds before the start?[8] Keep a level head and don't panic! Now that we've covered how the start can go wrong, let's look at our remaining options. We have a number of escape strategies at our disposal to make a quick recovery. Remember, a bad situation at the gun doesn't mean we will be in a bad position later in the upwind or in the race. There are always things we can do to make a good recovery.

The first and most important rule is to anticipate trouble before it happens, and then bail out as early as possible. More often than not, you'll be able to tell that it's going to be a bad one as early as 30 seconds before the start.

Fortunately, that's plenty of time to save your start. If you get to the line too early and you see that you're already over it or that you will be by the time the start happens, get out of there! Don't wait for the start to be over the line! If you have space to leeward of you, bear away sharply onto a

---

[8] See *Why We Get Bad Starts* to understand how the start can go wrong.

downwind course, create some distance from the line, and steer up sharply again to your new position farther from the line. I call this the 'dive'. Just remember to keep clear of any starboard boats below you. If there's a crowd around you and there's no feasible way to bear away to get farther from the line, another option is to sail forward over the line and circle around one of the ends (This only works under a P flag or I flag start. Under any other penalty flag this is not an option, as you will be penalized for sailing over the line within the last minute). If you're close to an end and you have the time on the clock to do so, this is a great way to reset your position and find a new spot on the line. A final option when you feel trapped in a crowd and you're drifting over the line is to back the mainsail and sail backwards. This works best in dinghies and small keelboats, but I generally don't recommend this method because the process of losing all your forward flow and then regaining it results in you drifting so far sideways that in a crowded pack you'll fall into any boats to leeward. Also, keep in mind that under Rule 21, as a boat backing a sail you are the give-way boat to everyone around you. If before the start you can tell that you're over the line and you need to get out of there at all costs, drifting backwards is a last-ditch option to save your start before the gun

sounds.

The same logic applies to when you find yourself outside the Box, when a shark takes your leeward hole, or when you fall into the leeward boat and are prevented from sailing forward. Bear away, tack out, circle around, back a sail, and do whatever it takes to get out of that position because when you know it will be a rough one, your best bet is always to bail out and look for other options. Don't keep fighting in a position that you know is never going to work out – don't wait for a miracle to happen.

Once you've escaped from your position on the line, you now have two options. The first is to find a new gap on the line if there is one and if there's still time on the clock, and get into it as fast as possible. The second is to get immediately onto port, sail full speed towards the boat end while ducking a big portion of the fleet, and punch off the line strong on port (we often call this a 'reverse rabbit start'). The earlier you do this, the better. You will almost certainly look bad initially, but you'll have a great chance of being the first bow going right once the gun sounds, and you are still well in the race.

If the starting gun has already fired and you find yourself in a bad lane, you can still recover nicely and have a competitive race. The following four escape routes can be used to find clear air after a bad start:

1 DUCK THE FLEET

Ducking the fleet is definitely the most common way of escaping from a bad start. Sounds simple, right? It is. But there's one thing that's incredibly important to making it work: doing it *early*. All too often sailors get a bad start or fall into a bad lane, but instead of tacking out immediately, either out of laziness or because they somehow feel that by tacking they're accepting a loss, they continue to hold that bad lane, insisting to themselves 'I can hold onto it for just a little bit longer'. The fact is that by staying in a bad lane, you are accepting a loss. The earlier you bail out of there, the greater your chance of finding clear air on the other side. Additionally, recognize that the longer you wait to bail out the worse air you fall into and the slower the boat becomes, so when you do go for a tack it will be heavy and slow. By bailing earlier you will fall onto port with a much stronger tack, so you will have a much better chance of then lee-bowing someone with good flow and speed or ducking aggressively and punching out on port with speed.

Boats that get a bad start need to be immediately looking for better options.

By tacking out and ducking the fleet, your goal is to be one of the first bows going to the right so that you will be in clear air. This is your advantage relative to most of the fleet. The longer you wait, the more likely it is that more boats higher up on the line will tack before you, and your chances of clear air on the right will be sealed off by port tackers. So as soon as you can tell that you'll have a *minus* start, bail and duck the fleet. If you do this early, even as early as 10 or 20 seconds before the gun, you'll have a great chance of being the first bow to the right.

Once you identify the final boat that you'll need to duck, make sure you do a proper duck! This means ducking early and then crossing behind their transom when you are already on an upwind course, (NOT heading up to close-hauled after you pass behind their transom), and using leeward heel and trimming in the mainsheet to head the boat up naturally, with minimal rudder. This is an important manoeuvre that needs to be practised. Note that as you duck their transom, you'll experience a small lift for a couple of seconds as a result of the air

When you bail from a bad start early, you have a much higher chance of finding a clear lane.

Bailing late

Bailing early

flowing sideways off their sails, so use that lift to build a bit of extra height. Doing a proper duck may seem like a small detail, but trust me, that extra half boat length or so you gain is incredibly valuable for holding your lane in the long run, especially if there are boats to leeward of you. From there, you'll be in clear air, sailing fast, and only a few boat lengths behind the leaders. You are still well within the race and you can get a great result from here! Start executing your upwind strategy, and you'll be back at the top in no time.

2 DOUBLE TACK

Another strategy for finding a clear lane after the start is simply doing a double tack – two quick tacks in a row – into a better spot above you on the line. (Note that this is a different manoeuvre from our double tack in the pre-start, in which the goal was to build height to windward but not gain distance forward.) The double

tack works well in light winds and in dinghies, where tacks are not very costly. As you feel that you're about to lose your lane, your first step is to look around for escape options. Make a plan B. Ideally a crew member should communicate possible options while the helm steers the boat. Knowing your possible escape options before you bail out of a bad lane really helps reduce the chaos of the situation. Usually the most viable option is to tack and duck the entire fleet. But if you see a gap or hole above you on the line that you could tack into and have a clear lane, and your strategy dictates that you stay on starboard, take it! If you haven't practised doing two quick tacks in a row before, I highly recommend it. Being able to rip a quick double tack is another one of those highly useful skills that can be a life-saver by enabling you to find a good lane after a bad start.

Double tacking into a better lane.

3 CROSS ON PORT

When the start is heavily pin-end favoured it's all too common to see a massive pileup of boats on the far left side of the line. A few of them will blast out of there looking like winners, but the majority of those boats will be toughing it out on starboard in bad lanes. Let's say that you are one of those boats (I can guarantee that you will find yourself in this situation more than a few times in your sailing career). One possible escape route is to tack and duck the entire fleet, but with such a pin favoured line this is incredibly unappealing. The rightmost boat is so far behind the pin starters that to duck everyone, you would have to sail almost downwind, and you would be worse off than you were before. Your best option, then, is to tack onto port and find a gap where you can break through the train of starboard tackers who are all sailing in a line and headed. Your goal is to make this critical cross on port before the majority of the fleet tacks onto port so

that you can get into clear air before all your options disappear. Remember, since the line was heavily pin favoured, once you cross one starboard tacker, you'll be ahead of everyone else to the right of them and you'll have complete access to the right side of the course.

Making this critical cross is difficult. It requires the crew (and likely the helm as well) looking under the boom for a gap you can make as you sail on port. It requires a strong awareness of the boats on starboard so that you can keep clear of starboard tackers, and good judgement of whether or not you can make the cross. Finally, it requires a very good level of ducking skill so that you can duck a starboard tacker in as strong a position as possible, because making the crucial cross on the next boat is a game of inches. Remember, a proper duck is a skill that must be practised to perfection on your training days! Misjudge a cross or lose too much height on the duck and you

Making the crucial cross after a pin favoured start.

might find yourself crash tacking to avoid a train of starboard tackers, or worse, repairing a hole in your starboard hull. Look for the first cross you can make, go for it, and you'll have the entire right side of the course to work with.

4 GO LOW

It's quite common that the leftmost boat off the start – the boat that 'won the pin' – actually doesn't look strong off the line. The boat that wins the pin usually just barely makes it. Maybe they had to pinch extremely high and slow to make it around the anchor line, or in their effort to get around the pin they got to the line early and began their acceleration at the gun, while the boats above that boat roll over them at full speed.

If you find yourself in this situation, getting to clear air

doesn't necessarily mean tacking. If you're the leftmost boat and the boats above are starting to roll over you, just sail a lower mode. Clear your air by heading down 5 or 10 degrees and picking up a couple of knots of speed forward, while the boats above you continue to sail high. Then, once you're no longer being rolled over by the boat(s) above you, head back up to your VMG mode. You'll lose some boat lengths in VMG initially, but you'll have clear air and space around you as you gain separation with the boats to windward. It's not my favourite strategy to start so close to the pin end and find yourself in this situation, but it's sometimes worth it in longer races and when there is a strong pin bias and left racecourse strategy. In a large and crowded fleet, this is usually a much preferable alternative to tacking and ducking the entire fleet.

STRATEGY FROM THE BACK

There are certain conditions where it is easy to make a strong comeback from a bad start, and there are other conditions where it is virtually impossible. On days with strong wind, a small fleet, a long upwind leg, big shifts, and an open course (there are equal opportunities across the racecourse), it is easy to find clean air and recover after tacking out. By contrast, in light wind, a big, competitive fleet, a short upwind and a closed course (one side of the racecourse is clearly favoured), a bad start is almost as bad as an OCS. In these conditions, even the best sailors won't be able to find clear air and make it back to the front of the fleet. Identify these conditions before the start even happens (as part of your Pre-Start Routine) so that you know whether to err on the side of caution or to aggressively push the line, start ahead of the boats around you at all costs, and have a higher risk start.

The trickiest starts are actually the ones where you can't tell whether you have a minus start or an equal start. In other words, you're not sure if you'll lose your lane in the next half minute, or if you'll end up surviving the pack around you and holding your lane

> **EXPERT TIP**
>
> *Remember, it's okay to get an OCS every so often. If you ever look at the scoring sheets of world champions or other top sailors, you will often see an OCS or BFD in a given championship, especially in light and steady conditions. If you're one of those sailors who never gets an OCS, it means you're not pushing the line enough!*

for as long as you'd like. Because you're unsure, you continue fighting for your lane to try your luck. These can turn into the worst starts, because if you don't survive as you hoped, losing your lane and tacking out after 30 seconds in a big fleet is the surest way to get buried in the back for the rest of the upwind. By that time, enough boats have tacked out to the right to seal off any viable escape paths, and unless you get bailed out by a lucky shift or puff, you are destined to be in the bottom group of this race. This goes to say that in a crowded fleet, if you have a significant doubt that you'll be able to hold your lane for much longer than a minute or so, making an early tack and bailing out early actually gives you a much better chance of saving your race.

That said, if you think you can hold your speed and position with the boats around you for at least one or two minutes, even if you don't have the greatest lane, then hold your lane, unless you see a safer option to tack into clear air. This is especially true if you want to continue on starboard for strategic reasons (such as staying on a lift, or going towards better pressure or current). Survive the lane for as long as possible while you wait for the bulk of the fleet to tack and the space around you to thin out. Then your options will open up without you having taken an initial loss. After all, racing in the front and in the back are completely different games. Leading in the front is easy – you have tons of clear space around you, you have a clear view of the entire fleet spread across the course and the weather coming down, and there's nothing stopping you from getting to each puff and nailing every shift. By contrast, in the chaos of the bottom half of the fleet, all your strategy goes out the window as you scramble back and forth for clear air. This is what causes the usual massive separation between the leaders and the rest of the fleet by the top mark – on the upwind, the rich get richer. Therefore, just by surviving a tight lane in the front row you are holding even with the leaders while the rest of the fleet is losing, making you well-positioned to stay in that top group.

In terms of your mindset after a bad start, you always want to be forward-thinking. Have confidence in your abilities and take back the initiative. As a great sailing coach once put it: 'It's not the first mistake that gets you, it's the second and the third.' Get back in phase, find clear air, and stay connected to the boats in front. If you do miss the first shift, make sure you don't miss the second. Most of all, be patient. Bail out of a bad lane, but don't 'bang a corner' or 'take a flier' and go to the opposite side of the course as the fleet when you know the better strategy is the other way. Don't try to win a race or a regatta right off the start. Keep calm, stay focused, and pick off boats one by one throughout the rest of the race. Look forward and make steady gains 'boat by boat, leg by leg, race by race'. Whenever you feel overwhelmed and everything feels like it's all falling apart, *do the next right thing*. I always tell my sailors to ask themselves after a bad start: 'What is the next right thing?' A bad start can be stressful and frustrating. Keep this question 'What is the next right thing?' in your mind to help you focus on looking forward to the next opportunity rather than getting caught up with what's already happened.

So, what do you do if your escape strategy didn't work? What do you do if you can't find clear air anywhere? Sometimes in a crowded fleet it is simply not possible to find clear air. Unsurprisingly, when you're completely buried behind the fleet, you have a tough race ahead of you. When this happens, go back to the basics. Keep it simple. Stay on the lifted tack, sailing towards pressure, and get to the best air that you can find.

Bad starts happen to everyone. If you get a bad start, don't lose hope. Keep a level head. You're still in it. I always tell my sailors: 'Having a bad start doesn't mean you're going to have a bad race.' I've seen plenty of sailors get a disastrous start on the pin end but then be the first to bail, duck the entire fifty boat fleet, and go on to win the race. What separates champions from the rest is their ability to use an entire race to fight their way back to the top. They may start a race in dead last, but by escaping early to clear air and sailing smart, they'll round the windward mark in 25th – already mid-fleet in a fleet of 50 boats. Then, they might catch a few boats on the gybe or find the inside at the leeward mark to pass five boats in the first downwind. They might take advantage of a wind shift to cross another five in the upwind. They might catch another five in the second downwind; making gains throughout the race not by taking a flier or banging a corner, but by sailing high percentage plays and picking off boats one by one: 'boat by boat, leg by leg, race by race'. Before you know it, by the end of a long race they'll be back in the top ten. That's a good keeper score. So never stop fighting. When you know the start is going to be bad, don't just stubbornly keep trying to make that pin layline or barge into a wall of boats. Be flexible and look outside the pack for other options. The point here is that getting frustrated after a bad start helps no one but your competitors. Keep a level head and have confidence in yourself, your skills and your strategy. Most importantly, take your first escape route, and from there, look to make steady gains up the fleet, not by gambling on a side against all prevailing strategy. There's a long race ahead, and the start is only the beginning.

EXPERT TIP

If you're bailing out and ducking the fleet on port tack, there's a starboard boat coming, and you're close but not quite making the cross, a common strategy nowadays is to ask them if you can cross by calling 'tack or cross?!' If they're smart, they will usually let you cross them rather than lee bow them, because it's a win-win situation for both boats – it would be to their disadvantage if you lee bow them. That said, if they don't give you a clear go-ahead to cross, it's almost always better to duck them rather than to lee bow, so that you can still get to clear air on the right.

Chapter 11

EXECUTING YOUR UPWIND GAME PLAN

This section is about the middle 60–80% of the upwind, the largest chunk, where you actually execute your upwind strategy. Once you've sailed off the line and your options have opened up, it's time to begin executing your initial upwind game plan that you made during your Pre-Start Routine.

There's no doubt that making a game plan before the start is important. Even if you're not right all the time, looking up the racecourse before the start and making a game plan means you're much more likely to be right than someone who hasn't. In addition to your upwind strategy, you must also sail with sound upwind tactics, which ranges from making the right moves in boat-on-boat situations to managing the entire fleet. Both your strategy and tactics must come together to sail a strong upwind beat. You don't, as some coaches put it, want to be an 'unguided missile' racing up the course. The goal in sailing is to be going fast *and* in the right direction.

In previous chapters I outlined a very systematic approach to preparing for a regatta and for the start. There are so many factors that go into the upwind, however, that I believe it's more

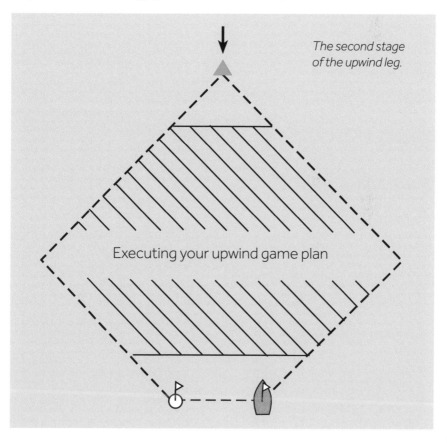

The second stage of the upwind leg.

Executing your upwind game plan

effective to speak generally about the guiding principles that work in combination with each other to determine your best move in any given situation. This chapter is structured around these general principles that lead to a successful upwind leg. Remember, there are the *strategic* principles – getting up the racecourse as fast as possible according to the environmental factors around you such as the pressure, shifts, current, and geography – and the *tactical* principles of executing a successful upwind leg – making the best moves relative to the fleet and other boats. I go into detail about both components of upwind performance in the following pages. You'll find that these principles will become virtually automatic to you as you gain experience racing, but most of them are certainly not intuitive or natural to beginners or even intermediate sailors. I hope that for the up-and-coming racers this section gives you a crash course in how to make decisions as you race upwind, and for the returning veterans of the sport a new perspective on upwind strategy.

STAY IN CLEAR AIR

First and foremost, find a clear lane. This is the most fundamental rule when sailing upwind and it almost goes without saying. To sail properly upwind you need to be in clear air. As I covered in the chapter on tactics for starting,

every boat creates an area of disturbed 'dirty air' around it as it sails upwind. Think of this area of disturbed air as a cloud that extends downwind and directly behind a boat's sails, and a short distance laterally to windward as well. This area is largest in light wind and shrinks as the wind becomes stronger. Sail in another boat's bad air and your sails will not work efficiently – you will feel that you have less power, and you will also notice an apparent header, both of which result in your boat speed taking a big hit. So whenever there are options available, getting to clear air is your first priority.

That said, there are certainly times around the racecourse when our best option is to sail in a bad lane. For example, when we are on the layline to the windward mark and there are boats directly in front of us, or when we have to sail in a bad lane until we can tack into a better one, or when one side of the course is so favoured that it is worth surviving in a bad lane to get there, or on a day with big and quick shifts where the first priority is to stay on the lifted tack. In situations such as these, the questions to ask yourself are probably: How much is it worth for me to stay in this bad lane? How much am I losing here? What are my options if I tack out? Are they better than staying in this bad lane? Can I do two quick tacks to clear my air? Understand how your boat is affected by bad air and weigh your options.

In the middle stage of the upwind there is the most lateral separation in the fleet. This is where you use racecourse strategy to make gains.

STAY IN PRESSURE

Unless the boat is seriously overpowered, more wind equals more boat speed. The tricky part is getting to and staying in that wind. There are some days when the pressure is consistent and evenly spread across the course, and so doing that is easy. There are other days, however, when the wind is incredibly patchy, and short-lived puffs materialize without warning and roll down the course from any side, seemingly at random (this is a common characteristic of offshore winds – when the wind approaches you by going over land rather than over water). Most commonly the wind will fall somewhere between these two types. Before you get racing, it's essential to identify what kind of day it is. Is the pressure consistent and reliable across the course, or is it patchy? Either can be the case in both strong wind and light wind. If the pressure is consistent, mentally realize that it is not something that you need to prioritize or think about much during the race. If it's patchy and inconsistent, pressure rises up the list of the most important factors in the race.

Once you identify that pressure is something to prioritize, you know to be on a constant look-out for it. The only way to consistently stay in pressure is to see it up the racecourse before it reaches you. For those who are new to 'calling the puffs', practice seeing the breeze on the water as it approaches you. This wind, or pressure, appears as darker patches of ripples on the surface of the water. Using polarized sunglasses and standing up in your boat to get a higher vantage point both make it much easier to see the pressure. During your Pre-Start Routine, stand up in the boat and look up the racecourse. If you see better pressure in certain areas of the course, that's important information to factor into your starting and upwind strategy. Throughout the race, especially on those puffy and patchy days, either a crew member or yourself must keep their head outside the boat at all times and continue to look up the course for where those darker patches of water are ahead of you. Realize that you'll be doing frequent tacks to stay in them. Your goal is to connect the patches of pressure together as you work your way up the course so that you can maximize your time in good wind.

OPEN COURSE VS CLOSED COURSE

Any race can be described as either an 'open course' or a 'closed course', and it is important to make the distinction between them.

A closed course is when one side of the racecourse is clearly favoured – a side day, in other words. This might be due to better pressure, favourable current, a persistent shift, or a land effect that shifts the wind in that direction farther up the course. Whatever the reason, every boat in the fleet will be fighting to get to that side, because they each want to get a piece of those favourable conditions. In a closed course it is easy to lead if you are in the front and it is difficult to fight your way up from the back, because your only option is to follow the train of boats in front of you. This is what makes it a closed course. Because the bias is so clearly to one side, there are few opportunities in other areas of the racecourse and therefore few opportunities to change your place in the race.

By contrast, an open course is when neither side is favoured and there are opportunities on both sides of the racecourse. This can describe days with shifty and patchy wind and variable weather, or days when the wind is consistent across the course. Because the fleet becomes so spread out to find clear air, it is much more difficult to take a definite lead over the fleet in an open course. It is also much easier to recover from deep in the fleet because there are more opportunities available: you can tack out from a losing position, disengage from the fleet, sail to one side, and find a favourable shift or pressure that will give you an advantage. Sailing an open course well requires you to really prioritize looking outside the boat

so that you can take advantage of those opportunities as they come your way.

During your Pre-Start Routine, communicate with everyone on the boat whether it's an open or closed course. Why is this important to identify? Because knowing whether you have an open or closed course directs your mindset of how you sail. Firstly, the start is much more important in a closed course, so you need to make sure you get a good start. In an open course, because there are more opportunities available, you can be a bit more conservative with your start, knowing that if you do need to tack out you have a greater chance of making a strong recovery.

Additionally, in a closed course you always have a goal you're working towards. Whenever you have the opportunity to sail to the favoured side in a clear lane, do it! If you lose your lane while working towards the favoured side, tack out but then come again at your next opportunity. Be persistent and keep working towards that direction when you can. In a closed course you want to sail very positionally. Try to be one of the first boats to get to the favoured side. If it's an open course, however, you have more flexibility to find opportunities on the other side of the course, so don't be afraid to disengage from the fleet when you're at a disadvantage. In an open course you want to sail more strategically,

Closed course

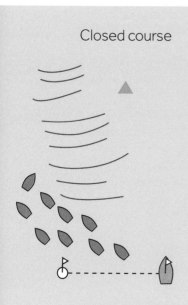

Open course

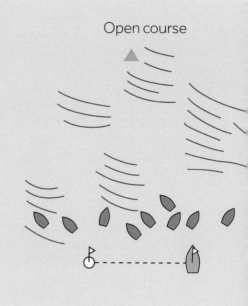

Open course vs closed course.

so prioritize keeping your eyes outside the boat for the shifts and the pressure and using these elements of the racecourse to your advantage.

THE 80/20 RULE

The 80/20 rule says that at any point on the upwind, you always want to have at least 20% of the remaining sailing distance to get to the windward mark to be on one tack, and no more than 80% of the distance to be on the other tack. The purpose of this rule is to prevent you from reaching the laylines too early.

Note that this rule allows you to get progressively closer to the layline as you get closer to the windward mark and your total upwind sailing distance decreases.

Furthermore, this rule becomes less important as you near the top of the beat. As you close in on the windward mark, specific situations will play out, and depending on where the other boats are in front of you and behind you, other factors may come into play.

By following this rule you'll always leave at least 20% of the distance to each layline available to you, until you're far enough upwind that you're doing the hand-off process and looking at your final course around the mark. What are the benefits of this? Following this rule ensures that if another boat tacks in front of you, you will have room to double tack into a better lane without overstanding the windward mark. If you get an

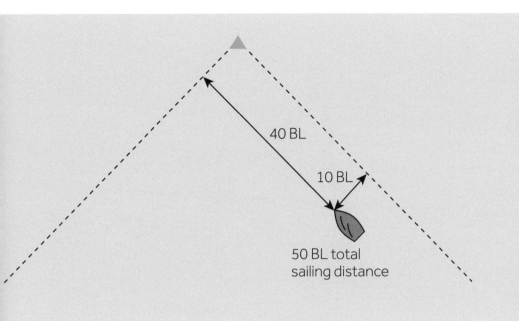

40 BL

10 BL

50 BL total
sailing distance

The 80/20 rule.

unexpected lift, this means you can take full advantage of that lift without overstanding the mark. If you hit a lull, you can tack in search of better pressure. In general, you keep your options open when you stay away from the laylines. So don't wait for that extra five degree shift, especially in shifty conditions. Drag yourself back to the middle. The takeaway from the 80/20 Rule is that you don't want to get to the laylines to the windward mark earlier than you need to.

This is a good general rule to keep in mind, but when looking deeper into boat-on-boat tactics near the laylines, it's not always so simple. A more complete tactical rule to follow is that when you're

ahead, you want to push the boats behind you to the layline. For example, by tacking on them, forcing them to sail on the tack that pushes them to the layline or else sail in your dirty air, until you eventually corner them on the layline and lead them to the mark. As the boat ahead, you always want to stay between your competition and the mark, so by cornering them on the layline, they have no opportunity to tack out and find another way to pass you. Conversely, when you're the boat behind, you want to avoid this situation of getting pushed to the layline. Instead, you want to keep your options open. By not getting to the laylines too early, you maintain some ability to tack away when a boat ahead tacks on you.

One way to reduce your

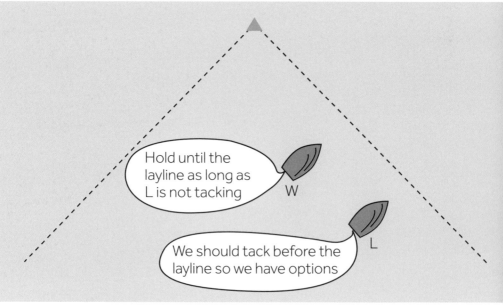

In this situation, W's goal is to push L to the right layline. W should continue on port and keep an eye on L, hoping L will continue to the layline. Then, both W and L will tack simultaneously, and W has complete control over L.

   L's goal is to not get cornered on the layline as W would like. L should tack onto starboard before the layline. If W then tacks before the layline to cover L, L has the space to do another tack onto port to clear its air without sailing past the starboard layline.

chances of getting pushed out to the layline too early is to always sail the longer tack first. When for one reason or another the windward mark is skewed incredibly far to the right or the left, you want to recognize this before the start and prioritize getting onto the longer tack. You will see big gains from doing this, especially later in the upwind. That's why during the Pre-Start Routine one of the things we did was envisage a 'middle line'[9] going upwind from the starting line and then look for whether the windward mark is skewed to one side of the middle line. If so, one tack will be longer than the other, and so one of the things we want to incorporate into our upwind strategy is sailing this longer tack first to centralize ourselves downwind of the windward mark.

   On another note, in very light wind there is a common phenomenon where the wind rises up over the fleet, so the boats in the middle, even if they are in the front row, will have significantly lighter wind than the boats on the

[9] See *Step 1: Gather Information.*

edges. One of your goals in very light wind is to get to an edge of the fleet so that you can be in better pressure, without getting to the layline too early. Sometimes in big fleets this can be difficult to do, especially if you are deep in the fleet. It is common in big fleets that the boats behind will be pushed farther and farther to the laylines as they go outside the fleet in search of clear air. Then, once they reach the corner they have no more space to clear their lane, and as soon as a boat tacks ahead of them they are destined for dirty air for the rest of the upwind. There is no great solution to this when you're deep in the fleet. I can only recommend that if you can't find clear air across the entire course, still follow the 80/20 rule. At least by staying away from the edges you can still stay in phase with the larger shifts.

Of course, to know where the laylines are in the first place you need to see the windward mark. Sometimes, however, there is fog, rain, or massive swells or waves that obscure your view of the windward mark, especially when the upwind leg is particularly long. When you can't see the windward mark at all, your best bet on the upwind is to sail equal times on starboard and port. This ensures that you'll be going up the middle of the course, and hopefully the mark will come into sight as you get closer.

I previously described imagining a 'midline' that runs straight upwind from the middle of the starting line, and then looking at the placement of the windward mark in comparison to the midline to see if it was biased to one side. This is helpful for seeing if one tack will be longer than the other. Once you've begun the upwind, however, I find it easier to envisage a new midline: the line that runs straight downwind from the windward mark. Then, at any point in the upwind, you can compare yourself to this line and know whether you are course right, course left, or in the middle. In a hectic battle on the upwind and when you have so many things you're trying to focus on at once, doing this quick check might help you realize 'I'm already on the far right and I'm only halfway up the upwind leg. I should start working back towards the middle to keep my options open.'

BE DELIBERATE WITH YOUR MODES

This topic was also covered in 'Off The Line'. To review, choose your mode according to the given situation. For the majority of the upwind you usually want to use your VMG mode as it, by definition, will get you up the course the fastest. But there are times when, because of strategic and tactical considerations, you might sail slightly higher or slightly lower than you would otherwise. For example, you may use a low mode if you want to get to one side of the course faster, if you're advanced on a pack to your leeward and you want to engage and gain control over them, or if you've overstood a layline. You might use a high mode if you're trying to survive a boat close to leeward, pinch out a boat to windward so that you can tack and cross, or if you're trying to make a tight layline. As the puffs and lulls hit, use your modes to position yourself to make gains from environmental factors as well, such as to stay connected to the edge of a puff that's to windward or to leeward of you, or to get to better pressure or current on one side of the course as quickly as possible. Overall, think of your modes as just another tool that you have at your disposal to help you with all your other tactical and strategic goals.

DUCK OR LEE BOW

Very often you'll find yourself in a situation where you're sailing upwind on port, you see that you're on a collision course with another boat on starboard, and you're presented with a choice: you can either lee bow the other boat, or you can duck them and possibly tack at a later time. A 'lee bow' is a manoeuvre in which you tack as close to leeward of your opponent as possible without fouling under the rules. This essentially means you may not cause your opponent to change course to avoid you until you have

completed your tack. With this manoeuvre you most likely put your opponent in your bad air, forcing them to tack away. How do you decide whether to lee bow or duck? There can be tactical reasons for one or the other, especially as you near laylines, but the key rule to know here is this: in light wind it is generally better to lee bow another boat, and in strong wind it is better to duck.

If you were to do a close lee bow to another boat in strong wind, nine times out of ten you would simply be rolled over by the windward boat. This happens for two reasons. First, you lose so much distance in a tack in strong wind. Second, since your area of dirty air that's projected to your windward side is much smaller in strong wind, it is very difficult to gain control over the windward boat and force them to tack away. The stronger move in heavy wind, assuming you want to tack sometime soon, is to duck the other boat first and then tack onto starboard once you've reached a safe lane. Then, as the windward boat, you are in the controlling position.

The opposite is true in light wind. In lighter conditions, not only do your tacks cost less distance, but the leeward boat has a significant advantage over the windward boat as their wind shadow extends much farther to windward. If you were to duck and tack to windward of another boat in light wind, you would always be worrying about your runway and you would never feel free to sail the boat as you would like. A good, close lee bow would put you in a much stronger position to quickly kill the boat to windward.

In general, I find that sailors, especially lower level sailors, lee bow way too often. It's all too common to watch sailors spot a starboard boat and tack, not because they would have tacked there had that starboard tacker not been there, but because they 'didn't want to duck a boat', as they'll explain to me after a race. My advice is this: don't lee bow a boat unless you have a good reason for doing so. Otherwise, you're just doing an extra tack. In fact, I would say that 70–80% of the time it's better to duck a starboard boat than lee bow them. Too many sailors don't realize that when you properly duck a boat, you're not behind them, you're even with them. As you duck their transom, remember that you get a small momentary lift, and unless they're on the layline, they have to do one more tack than you to round the windward mark.

Also, it never hurts to ask a starboard boat if you can cross. Just call out 'tack or cross!' as you approach and if they're smart they'll wave you over in most cases.

A NOTE ON BOAT SPEED: TACKING

Let's now examine how to perfect our tacks. There are three main things you can control during your tack: your sails, your weight placement, and your rate of turn. These are the things you want to focus on to improve your tacks. Each type of boat has a technique that works best for it, but the following instructions apply to virtually any non-foiling boat.

In the first half of your tack as you head up from close-hauled

The leeward lane is better in light wind because there is more turbulence reflected from the leeward boat's sail, while the windward lane is better in strong wind because the windward boat has the advantage when the opponent tacks.

Stronger position in light wind

Stronger position in heavy wind

to head to wind, make the turn slower than you might think. This is especially effective in strong wind because it lets the boat coast upwind for longer to give you some extra upwind progress, and it gives the crew more time to cross the boat. In all conditions, as you turn into the wind during your tack keep the main in tight, with the leech engaged, and have a slight leeward heel. This helps head the boat up naturally with minimal rudder, and helps keep power in the boat as you exit the tack. As you pass head to wind to begin the bear away to your new close-hauled angle, increase the rate of turn. (In dinghies, a powerful roll on the windward rail should accompany passing head to wind.) Continue turning down until you are a few degrees lower than your normal close-hauled course. Speeding up the second half of the tack, keeping the main in, and turning down to a low mode are all things that help rebuild the power in the boat after the tack, getting you back up to speed as soon as possible. In strong wind, ease the main as necessary to keep the boat flat as the crew sits out on the new windward side. Flatten out the boat once you're on your new angle. Continue on this mode to gain speed. Once you've regained good flow over the sails and good forward speed, trim in the sails again and head back up to your normal close-hauled angle.

In wavy conditions it is important to time your tack with the waves. In chop, try to tack in an area of flat water. This will help you maintain power in the boat. In large swell, time the tack so that you are turning into the wind as you go up the swell, and you're on the new tack as you're surfing down the back of the swell. The greater pressure you get as you go up the swell heels the boat over and helps you turn into the tack while maintaining speed. The next time you go sailing, try timing your tacks with the waves in this way and see the difference it makes. In big waves it will be very clear whether you have tacked at the right time or not – you will either easily reaccelerate down the back of the wave after the tack, or your bow will crash into the oncoming wave and you will lose speed.

Finally, it's important to know what distance in boat lengths each tack costs you. This depends on a few things: the wind condition, the sea state, and your class of sailing boat. Generally, as the wind increases tacks become more costly. They are more costly in choppy water than in flat water, and are usually also more so in keelboats than in light dinghies. In the 470, for example, a good tack in 20 knots of wind would cost me about 2–3 boat lengths, while a good roll tack in 5 knots would cost next to nothing. Knowing this information gives you an idea of how freely you should use your tacks. Ask yourself: given the conditions, is it practical for me to tack onto every little shift? Or do I lose so much distance in each tack that it's better to wait for the large oscillations? Should I lee bow this starboard boat, or is the distance I would lose in the tack too much? Knowing how frequently you can use your manoeuvres is a good thing to keep in the back of your mind as you consider your options.

STRATEGY IN WIND SHIFTS

We all know that wind shifts are important. After all, we read a take on them in virtually every sailing book. After a day of racing we'll exchange stories with our buddies about how 'that huge lefty before the start made me miss the pin!' or 'I went from last to first with that right shift!' But for many sailors, the wind shifts can still be the most perplexing aspect of sailing. The reality is that there's a wide range of sailors with different levels of expertise with tactics in wind shifts. There are the beginners, who figure out pretty quickly how to get their boat on the tack that points them closest to the windward mark. But for the most part, they just follow the rest of the fleet. Then there are the experienced racers. These guys do their homework before each race, know their compass numbers, time the shifts, and identify the larger patterns of the day. They probably have some

local knowledge about the venue's wind trends, and they'll be painstakingly following the weather forecasts up until the event. Finally, there are the weather pros, the grizzled meteorologists, who understand the subtleties of the sea breeze, the gradient wind, and weather systems. They seem to consistently predict the next weather event or wind shift with uncanny accuracy.

This book is not a weather book. It's not heavily focused on why the wind shifts as it does and other meteorological complexities. If you would like to learn more about the meteorology behind making high-level wind predictions (and to any sailing boat racer I highly recommend it), one of my favourite books out there is Wind Strategy by Houghton and Campbell. In this book, however, I focus on the immediate practical strategies that any sailor can get out on the water and use to help them take advantage of the wind shifts.

As with any strategic decision you'll make, the first step is gathering information. During your Racecourse Routine while you're warming up before the first race, observe the conditions and get your compass numbers.[10] Take upwind compass numbers on each tack. My personal preference is writing down the farthest-left and farthest-right compass

---

[10] Learn more in *On The Water: The Racecourse Routine*.

numbers that you see while sailing upwind for both tacks, so that during the upwind leg you can easily determine what phase of the wind you are in (whether you are headed or lifted). On dinghies it's convenient to write down your numbers on the boom with a grease pen, with your starboard numbers on the starboard side and your port numbers on the port side, so you have them there in front of you while sailing upwind. As the shift range changes throughout the day, simply write the new numbers a line down on the boom.

As a quick reminder, if a boat sailing upwind is suddenly hit with a shift and has to lower their angle to continue sailing upwind, we call that shift a 'header'. We call the opposite occurrence a 'lift'. When two boats sailing evenly upwind are hit with a shift, the boat that's closer to the direction of the shift gains. So if the wind shifts left, the left-most boat in a fleet makes

In a wind oscillating by 20 degrees, the headings in the picture above may be a boat's shift ranges that they'll write down or remember so that at any point during the race they can compare their heading to their numbers and see which phase they're in. Want to check the phase of the wind just before the start? Just sail upwind on starboard: if you're heading is 330° then there's a right shift; if it's 310° there's a left shift; and if it's 320° you're at the average angle, or no shift.

Note that, in my opinion, this is the simplest and most convenient way to record the shifts if you have a compass that tells you your boat's bearing. If you have instruments that tell you the true wind direction while sailing, then the process is much simpler.

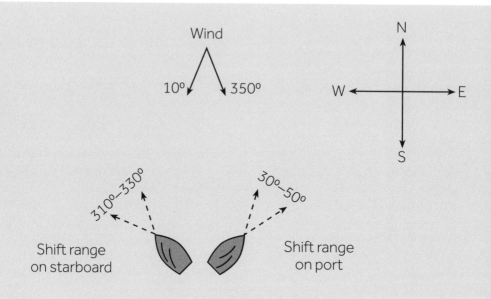

a gain. Don't believe me? Try holding your hands out in front of you, tilted with your palms facing each other, with your thumbs up, like parallel lines. Imagine these are boats. Then, as if there is a left shift, cock your wrists a bit to the left. See how the boat on the left suddenly is farther forward than the boat on the right? Now do the same thing, but with a right shift. Suddenly the right boat is farther forward over the left boat. The exact same thing happens on the racecourse. This is why you want to be on the side of the fleet that the wind shifts towards, before the shift happens.

If this doesn't make intuitive sense to you, another way of understanding wind shifts that I find very helpful is using the concept of 'ladder rungs'. Think of a ladder as horizontal lines, or rungs, extending up the upwind leg, each rung perpendicular to the wind direction. Each ladder rung signifies how close you are to the wind, and therefore how much distance you've gained upwind relative to the windward mark or to other boats. If you're a ladder rung above another boat, you're ahead of them, while if you're on the same ladder rung, you're even.

Now, let's examine what happens when the wind shifts, beginning with the situation above. As you can imagine, when the wind shifts the ladder rungs

The yellow boat looks around and anticipates a left shift, so they position themselves to the left of the fleet. When the 10° left shift hits, all the boats become headed, the yellow boat makes a gain, and they tack and easily cross the fleet.

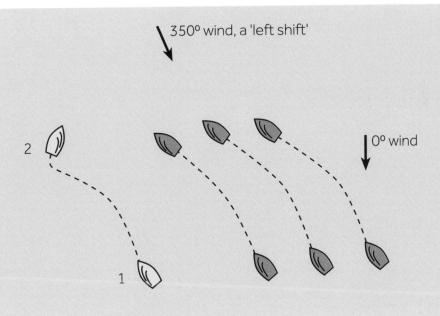

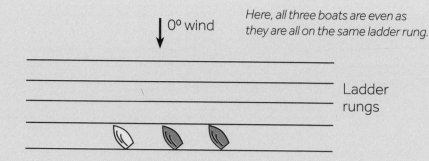

0° wind

Here, all three boats are even as they are all on the same ladder rung.

Ladder rungs

Suddenly, all the boats are hit with a 10° left shift. They've each adjusted their angle for the shift, but they have not changed position since the previous diagram. These boats were previously even, but with the left shift each boat gains ladder rungs on its opponents to windward. Note as well that the greater the separation is between two boats sailing upwind, the greater one will gain and the other will lose when both are hit by a shift. The yellow boat, for example, is now only one ladder rung ahead of its opponent directly to windward, but it is two ladder rungs ahead of its opponent furthest to windward. Assuming each boat sails the same speed, the yellow boat will continue to be ahead of the other boats until the wind shifts again and the ladder rungs shift as well.

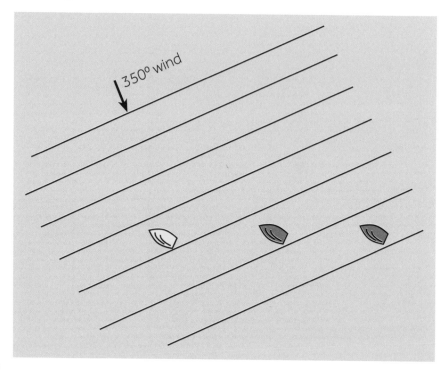

350° wind

shift with it. The effect of this is that suddenly, some boats are farther up the ladder than others, without the boats even sailing forward since the shift happened. The boats that were closer to the direction the wind shifted are now farther up the ladder than the others. See below:

Now that we've covered how boats gain or lose relative to other boats in wind shifts, let's look at how we can use the wind shifts to our advantage in the race. The purpose of knowing your compass numbers is so that at any point during the upwind you can tell whether you're headed or lifted. This makes it very easy to stay on the lifted tack – one of the first priorities in upwind racing, so that you are sailing as direct a course as possible upwind towards the windward mark. However, I view staying on the lifted tack as just the first level of proficiency in upwind strategy. Knowing your numbers and staying in phase with the wind shifts will work well enough in most local club races, but to get to the next level, you need to be able to predict what the wind will do next with some consistency. After all, the key to taking advantage of wind shifts is predicting them before they happen. Use your gathered information to make a prediction, and work your way to the side of the course where you anticipate the shift.

What does it take to make good wind predictions? Be aware of the weather events around you. Look at what the wind is doing. Look outside the boat not only at the pressure you see on the water up the course, but at the skies and the clouds. Feel how the temperature and the humidity changes throughout the day. Make your own observations and use local knowledge to fill in the gaps of your understanding. Talk to the locals – more likely than not they'll be willing to answer your questions. Gather up all the information that you can. Try to identify patterns. Ask yourself while you sail: Does increasing pressure come with a shift in one direction and decreasing pressure with an opposite shift? Does more or less cloud cover affect the direction of the breeze across the racecourse? Looking up the course, do I see more or less breeze approaching? Do I see more or less cloud cover approaching? Is there a cloud on one side of the course that might bring a shift in that direction? Is there incoming pressure on one side of the course that I want to prioritize? Patterns and observations such as these can help you predict a shift before it reaches you.

Most importantly, understand what's driving the weather. Ask yourself, what is creating the wind here? One year when I was coaching the annual 420 Midwinter Championship in Jensen Beach, Florida, one of our national-level youth events in the States, we had an interesting situation with the wind. Each day we saw a south-east wind direction (farther right than normal), 8–10 knots, with large, inconsistent oscillations. There was patchy, dark cloud cover all day drifting over us from the south and occasional thunderstorms. From my local knowledge of the venue I knew that the usual wind is a steady sea breeze out of the east. I also understood that the cloud activity from the south was an indication of the direction of the gradient wind, and given that there was a large low pressure system over Houston at the time, it made sense that we would be experiencing a strong gradient influence from the south for the duration of the regatta. Recognizing the factors at play that were driving the wind we were getting, I realized that the relatively light wind with large, inconsistent oscillations was a result of the gradient wind from the south fighting the sea breeze from the east. Most importantly, I realized that whenever we would see increased cloud cover above us and thunderstorms coming in from farther right that would signify a greater gradient influence and therefore an incoming right shift. Whenever the cloud cover decreased and we would start to see more blue sky that would indicate a greater influence from the sea breeze and an incoming left shift. To fleet racers, this knowledge is like gold.

Just by looking around us and understanding the factors driving the weather, my sailors and I knew which visual cues to look for that would indicate that the shifts were about to trend in a certain direction. In other words, we could predict the next shift with great accuracy. All we had to do was get to the left of the fleet when we anticipated a left shift, and get to the right when we anticipated a right shift. We would go on to win the championship.

With the information you gather, it's also helpful to identify what kind of day it is. Are you seeing consistent, predictable oscillations in the wind? Or is it a crazy and unpredictable day, with seemingly no pattern to the shifts and the puffs coming out of nowhere? Or do you see a persistent shift that's reliably clocking to one direction? Talk with everyone on the boat about what you see. Share your ideas with each other.

In the first type of shifty wind condition – *consistent oscillations* – your priority is to stay on the lifted tack. Usually, consistent oscillations are paired with consistent pressure. When the pressure is consistent and you can always rely on the next shift coming through, missing a shift is especially costly. Stay in phase with the wind and in sync with the fleet and wait for the others to make mistakes. When you find yourself getting close to a corner, use as much of each

Consistent oscillations	Inconsistent shifts	Persistent shifts

Types of wind shifts.

shift as possible to work back to the middle of the course. Don't wait for that extra five degrees to take you back. Keeping your options open is key. If you lose your lane, it's okay to tack away, but tack back onto the lift in the next available lane. Once again, it's not the first mistake that gets you, it's the second and the third. If you miss a shift, make sure you don't miss the next one. If you are forced to sail on a header, make sure you're really sailing your VMG mode. It's a common tendency for sailors to pinch against a header, as if it will somehow help them be affected less by the shift. All this does is slow you down. Keep your speed up and get back in phase as soon as you can.

In the second type of shifty wind condition – inconsistent shifts – it is especially important to keep your head outside the boat and look at the environment around you in order to make your best guess about the next shift. Inconsistent shifts are usually paired with fickle, inconsistent

pressure. These are the days where the wind is down to less than ten knots, where the shifts swing back and forth seemingly at random according to puffs of pressure that briefly appear in different areas across the course. In these conditions it is important to be on the lifted tack, but only if it plays into your prediction for where the next pressure will come from. Prioritizing staying in pressure is key. There is no other condition where it is more important to keep your eye on the horizon, ready to spot the next patch of breeze.

The ultimate goal in these conditions is to be on the lifted tack and in pressure, connecting the patches of pressure together as you work your way up the course. A perfect analogy for this is the game Snakes and Ladders. Tack onto a nice lift or find a patch of good pressure and you're on a ladder, making quick progress upwind. But as soon as you hit a lull or lose that favourable shift, you're on a snake, losing to the fleet around you. Now imagine all the boats in the fleet around you playing the exact same game. The less successful sailors, those who don't look outside their boat at their surroundings, will be on a ladder some of the time and on a snake some of the time. They'll just sail in whatever puff or lull happens to hit them, never proactively looking for the next pressure or shift and sailing to it. To sail at the top of the fleet in this condition you have to connect each of the ladders together, so that you're in good pressure or on the right shift for as much of the upwind as possible. While you're on one ladder – maybe a brief gust of wind or a lift – don't just take it blindly. Plan ahead. Look around for where the next ladder is coming from and use the pressure you're in now to get to it. In inconsistent conditions, sailing is like a real life game of Snakes and Ladders, and you're playing against every other boat on the course.

Finally, in the third type of shifty wind condition – a *persistent shift* – your first priority is to have a clear lane you can hold and keep working towards the persistent shift. This is one of the common closed course situations. Your goal is to lead the fleet to that side of the racecourse, continually getting headed, so that you can eventually tack and cross the fleet on a lift towards the windward mark. Typical of a closed course, the boats that get a great start heading in that direction will have an easy life staying ahead of the fleet and arriving first at the windward mark, while the boats who fall behind will have very few opportunities to recover. Understand that you'll pay a high price for losing your lane going out to that side.

One more detail to note here is that in reality, a persistent shift is rarely a continuous sweep to the right or the left. Instead, it shifts towards one side in steps, or jolts. The wind direction continues to oscillate back and forth, but the shifts in that one direction are greater and longer than the other. The net result is a persistent shift. This is important to be aware of because it means that as you're heading into the direction of the shift and you lose your lane, you'll have opportunities to tack out and come back in a strong position.

When in a shift should you tack? If you know that the headers come instantly and are short-lived, tack immediately. If, however, you've noticed that the shifts are long and slow, wait to reach the middle of the shift, or the average wind angle, before tacking. If you can see boats ahead of you up the beat, use them as wind shift indicators! Remember, any wind shift will hit them before it reaches you, so if you see boats ahead of you all make a big adjustment to their angle, you know what to expect.

As you can see, strategy in wind shifts is all about using the weather clues around you to your advantage. You don't need a PhD in meteorology to make the right predictions. All it takes is an awareness of your surroundings and an understanding of your priorities.

ENGAGE VS DISENGAGE

The concept of engaging and disengaging from the fleet is one of the fundamentals of upwind tactics. It is also quite related to the tactics of wind shifts explained above – in fact, a complete understanding of strategy and tactics in wind shifts is impossible without this concept. In almost every tactical situation you will use this concept when you gain or lose on other boats.

Engaging with another boat or a pack of boats means sailing relatively close to them, either close laterally on one side of them or directly above or below them (such as when you cross over, tack on top of, or duck behind another boat). When this happens, a boat that's ahead will stay securely ahead of a boat behind. This is because both are in the same wind conditions (pressure and phase of the shifts), so there are no outside variables that only one boat will get and take advantage of. Additionally, because the separation between the boats is

so small, when both boats are hit by a shift neither boat gains or loses much distance on the other. In essence, engaging with another boat means there is minimal lateral separation between the boats.

Disengaging is the opposite. It means separating from another boat or a pack of boats and gaining leverage on them. Leverage is a term that sailors use to refer to the lateral separation between boats. This is a powerful tool to use when you are behind, because having leverage on another boat means that when conditions change, one boat will gain significantly on the other. Take the example of a wind shift. When two boats are right next to each other, a right shift will give the boat on the right a relatively small boost forward. With a larger separation, however, even a small right shift will boost the boat on the right forward by many ladder rungs, as we saw in the previous section *Strategy in Wind Shifts*. See below how we can quantify the gain.

It doesn't have to be a shift that gives one boat an advantage, it can also be differences in pressure. Leverage increases the potential for big gains or losses because boats that are sailing far apart are more likely to experience different pressure on their side of the course. For instance, a boat on the right may get a puff of wind while the boat on the left is stuck in a lull. In this way, disengaging

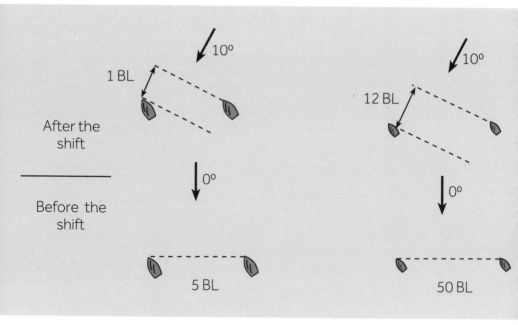

10°

1 BL

After the
shift

Before the
shift

0°

5 BL

10°

12 BL

0°

50 BL

Greater leverage gives you more opportunity to gain (or lose) from a shift or difference in pressure. In each of these examples, both boats receive a 10 degree right shift. For simplicity we will assume the boats tack through 90 degrees. In the first situation in which there is a 5 boat length separation, the boat on the right gains only 1 boat length. In the second situation the boat on the right has much more leverage on its competitor and makes a bigger gain of 12 boat lengths in the same shift.

from the other boats and gaining leverage is a powerful tool for a boat behind to make gains.

The general rule of thumb of engaging and disengaging is this: engage with other boats when you look good or when you make a gain, and disengage when you look bad or your opponents gain. When you are at a disadvantage, there is no way you will gain by sailing behind the fleet ahead of you. Tack away (unless you're on a significant lift or racecourse strategy dictates you must continue), wait for a shift or better

pressure, and have your crew keep you updated on how you look compared to the fleet. If you've made a gain on the fleet, either from finding better pressure or getting a favourable shift in your direction, that's the time to re-engage. Engaging with the fleet is like putting money in the bank. When you look good or when you make a gain, tack back towards the fleet, cross in front of them if you can, and get back in sync with the fleet. (If not, stay disengaged, maintain your leverage and keep looking for opportunities.) Once

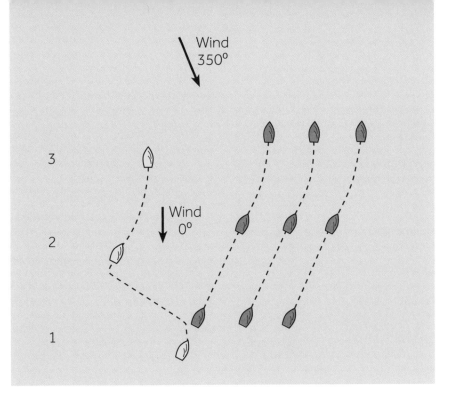

you gain the advantage, by closing up the leverage you are putting yourself securely ahead of the fleet, and you will round the top mark in front as long as you stay connected to them for the rest of the upwind.

Disengaging and re-engaging is especially important in crazy, unpredictable conditions. You know those days where the shifts seem to hit you at random, and the pressure appears and disappears without warning, turning on and shutting off the wind? Those are the kind of days where if you suddenly make a gain and look good on a large pack in the fleet, you really want to re-engage with them. When the conditions are so crazy, immediately establishing yourself ahead of other boats whenever you gain an advantage

As a boat behind, you want to disengage from the fleet so that you can gain from an opportunity that comes your way (such as a left shift as shown in the above example), and then re-engage once you make a gain.

becomes increasingly important. Disengage, make your money, but then put your money in the bank as soon as you can.

In any race, the upwind leg is the time to commit to your strategy. If it works and you look good on other boats, re-engage with them and secure yourself in the front. If not, stay disengaged, maintain your leverage and look for more opportunities. Be patient! You might go to one side of the racecourse and not look good initially, and that's okay! Unfortunately, it is typical of beginning racers to go to one side of the racecourse, look over and realize 'everyone on the other side looks so good', and then they tack to get to where those other boats are – all this does is lose all their leverage and establish themselves firmly in the back. And more often than not, by the time you get to the puff or shift that you saw a pack on the other side gain from, it will already be gone. If it's an open course and there's no one side that looks good all the time, be patient, commit to a strategy, and wait for your opportunity to come.

In an open course especially there are opportunities on both sides of the course. The game of sailing is all about using the opportunities (the cards) that you are given.

The common situation of a significantly pin favoured starting line illustrates well how fundamental the concept of engaging and disengaging is from the moment you begin the race. See the unfolding situation beginning with the image on the top right.

There was a significant 20

EXPERT TIP

A very important point I'd like to make clear here is when I say disengage with the fleet, I don't mean go all the way to a corner. Don't send it to the complete opposite side of the racecourse from the fleet. That's just gambling away your race. Instead, engage and disengage in small but frequent steps. Tack away when the fleet gets headed and boats ahead tack to cover you, and tack back to the fleet when you make a small gain from a shift or pressure. You'll repeat this process many, many times in a single upwind. And just as importantly, don't wait until you are first to re-engage with the fleet! If you were 20 boat lengths behind the leaders, and you get a shift and now you're 10 boat lengths behind, tack back to them to consolidate your gain. Too many times I see a sailor start at a disadvantage and instead of just taking a step outside the fleet to find clear air, they send it all the way to the other corner, throwing away a potentially good race.

As you may have noticed, I like to compare taking steps in the upwind to the stock market. Just as you might put your money in the stock market, make a gain, and pull your money back out to cash out your gain, a smart upwind beat is played by disengaging from the fleet, finding an opportunity to make a gain like a shift or pressure, and re-engaging with the fleet to solidify your position.

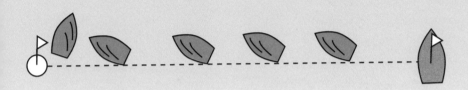

degree left shift before the start, giving the boats that started on the left a strong advantage. The boat that won the pin tacks onto port. Almost always, when the boat that wins the pin can tack and cross the fleet, they should do so, even if there is no longer a significant left shift. This makes sense, right? When you have such a strong advantage, engage with the fleet.

As soon as they can do so, all the boats in this tactically sound fleet tack onto port, as below illustration. Why would all the boats do this? One reason certainly is to get onto the left shift, but more importantly, every boat wants to disengage from the boats on their left (who are now ahead of them after this left shift) and engage with the boats on their right (who are now behind them). Each boat is maintaining as much leverage as they can on the boats to windward and ahead while staying connected to the boats to leeward and behind.

To show why this is so

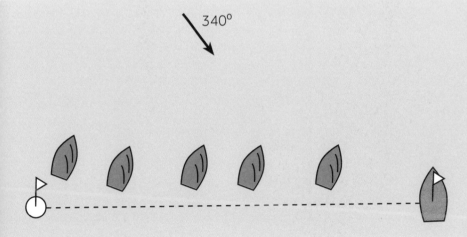

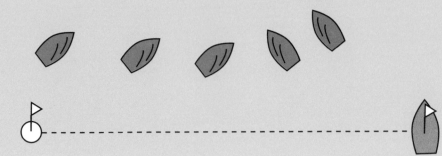

important, let's imagine the alternative. If one of the boats who started near the right side of the line were to continue on starboard, they would have to sail behind the entire rest of the fleet (essentially engaging with them). This would be a disastrous mistake, as they would be at that point directly downwind of the other boats and firmly cemented behind the fleet. Having lost of all their leverage, they have no chance to improve their position no matter what shift or pressure comes next, as above.

Suddenly, the wind swings back to the right big time. Everyone gets a header. This is exactly what the boats on the right were looking for. Because they had tacked off the line before the boats on the left could cross them and thereby maintained their leverage, the boats on the right were able to gain from this right shift that presented itself. Recognizing their advantage and hoping to consolidate their gain, the boats on the right all tack onto

starboard, as above illustration.

What happens next is the mirror image of what happened moments earlier. Now the boats on the left see their disadvantage and recognize that the boats on the right, lifted on starboard, will easily cross. Will these experienced sailors accept the loss and duck behind the right-most boats? Of course not! They all tack onto starboard in order to disengage from those boats, maintain their leverage, and get onto the new lifted tack. They know that when the next shift comes again from the left, they'll be back in the game in no time...

As you can see, when the racing is as tight as this, the battle for taking the advantage and securing your position in front continues all the way up the beat. Eventually, at the top of the course, whichever side has the last shift go their way will be first around the windward mark. Understanding this concept of engaging and disengaging with

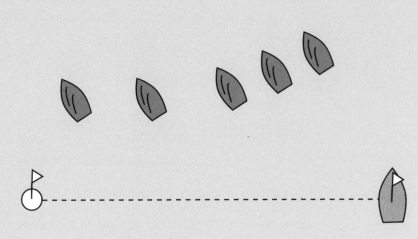

the fleet is fundamental to tactical racing upwind. If you've never heard about this before, you'll be amazed how much it will improve your performance upwind.

USING THE PUFFS

A puff is a gust of extra wind, or pressure. You can identify puffs by seeing them on the surface of the water before they reach you. They are areas of darker water – small ripples created by the puff of wind as it blows down the course. Especially in gusty conditions and flat water it's easy to see these areas of dark water as they approach you. A lull is just the opposite. It is an area with less wind, which you can identify as areas where the colour of the water looks lighter or glassy due to fewer ripples across the surface. Throughout the upwind

in most conditions we frequently encounter small variances in pressure – little puffs and lulls that last just for a second or two. We may also encounter large puffs and lulls – those large areas of pressure or holes in the wind that last for minutes. Your upwind sailing technique is incredibly important to prioritize in gusty conditions with lots of variations in pressure.

We all love to hear 'puff on!' because the puffs give us a boost forward, but there's a technique to using the puff to actually increase your boat speed. Generally, your goal in dinghies and especially in keelboats is to keep a constant heel angle upwind. This requires moving your weight, adjusting the sails, and steering in anticipation of the puffs and lulls before they hit, not in reaction when it hits you.

You want to slightly over-flatten the boat going into the puff in preparation for the increase in pressure, and be slightly heeled to leeward going out of it in preparation for the lull on the other side. To make this happen, everyone needs to lean out over the rail or sit out hard to meet the puff, maximizing your righting moment. You want to keep the boat flat throughout the entirety of the puff so that it doesn't push you sideways, but forward. If you're in overpowered conditions, ease the main appropriately and head up slightly (depending on what works best for your class of boat) before the puff hits, not after it hits, so that there is minimal change in heel angle of the boat. If a puff hits you by surprise, the boat will heel over, you'll round up and you'll slow down. See the puff ahead, make the proper adjustments, and you'll accelerate forward.

As you approach the lull on the other side, move your body weight inside the boat. If you eased the mainsheet in the puff, don't forget to trim it back in. Your goal is to maintain the boat's power in the lull, which you can do by maintaining a slight leeward heel and flow over the sails. Over-pressing the boat in a lull is one of the worst things you can do. If the team keeps too much weight to windward going into the lull and the boat heels to windward (I like to say 'sinks to windward' because the boat sinks into the water and

decelerates) you will lose a lot of height and distance forward.

As the helm, the two things you should be looking at for 80-90% of the upwind leg are the telltales on the jib and the puffs and lulls in the area of water directly in front of you. All you are doing is steering and (depending on the boat) trimming the main sheet according to the jib's telltales and the pressure you see in the moments before it hits you. If the helm and the main trimmer can't see the puffs themselves, then it's crucial that someone on the rail calls out the puffs and lulls. On a long upwind leg this may feel overly repetitive, but this is what the winners are doing. This is what it takes to win races.

One less commonly known fact about puffs is that they create a shift on either side of them. This is because as a puff glides over the water it fans out to each side. In flat water you can see this very clearly by the puff's ripples. See the diagram right.

This phenomenon is important for sailors to know because in certain conditions it can create brief but very real shifts that affect your sailing. If you are sailing into the side of a puff that is straight ahead of you, you will most likely get headed. Therefore, if you're looking to tack in the near future, just as you're entering into this puff can be a great time to tack. If a puff is coming down towards you from your windward side and you have passed across its middle, you will receive a small lift as it hits you. Recognize this as a good time to continue.

UPWIND STRATEGY IN CURRENT

Your upwind strategy in current can be distilled into three simple goals:

1 Understand what the current is doing across the racecourse and how it is changing.
2 Get to the favourable current.
3 Understand how the current changes your laylines to the windward mark.

The importance of current as a factor in your upwind strategy varies greatly depending on the venue. San Francisco Bay, for example, is notorious for having some of the strongest yet most incomprehensible currents in racing. The strategy is straightforward at max flood or max ebb when there's a 3+ knot current under the Golden Gate, but knowing where to find favourable current while everything switches at high tide or low tide is a challenge for even the most experienced locals. By contrast, other sailing locations such as those just off a coast may have little to no current at all. In other locations the effect of current is even trickier. In Biscayne Bay, for example, you have open ocean on one side of your racecourse, but the area where

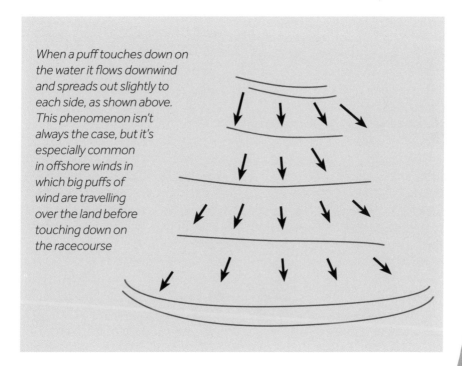

When a puff touches down on the water it flows downwind and spreads out slightly to each side, as shown above. This phenomenon isn't always the case, but it's especially common in offshore winds in which big puffs of wind are travelling over the land before touching down on the racecourse

the bay connects to the ocean is only a few feet deep, making the real source of ebb and flood the north end of the bay. You may also assume that lakes have no current, but anyone who's sailed at Rochester on Lake Ontario knows that current is a very real factor. Rivers and streams flowing into the lake, among other factors, can create significant currents that the locals will all know about.

Before you arrive at a venue to race, do some research. Find where the shallow and the deep areas of the racecourse are, and study the tides and currents. There are many resources available to you such as nautical charts of the area, a tide book, and websites with local current information, all of which I recommend looking at before a regatta. That said, the most important thing for being on top of the current in any location is gaining local knowledge. Talk to sailors who have lots of experience sailing at the venue and see if you can glean any tips and tricks – there might be trends in the current that surprise you.

In most locations with significant current, the current flows in and out of a bay according to the rise and fall of the tides. As the tide rises in the ocean, water floods into the bay to equalize the height of the water. We call this the flood tide. At some point as the tide reaches its maximum height, the flooding current slows and stops, before switching direction

and flowing out of the bay. We call this the ebb tide.

Remember, it's not the up-and-down movement of the water that sailors care about, it's the horizontal movement. Before arriving at the regatta, search out a nautical chart of the racing area and look at the depths across the race course. This is important, because depth determines the strength of the current relative to the rest of the area in a given location. In general, in shallower areas (say, less than 50 feet) the current is less strong and switches direction earlier relative to the tides. In deeper areas, the current is stronger and switches later. This is a fundamental rule that you can use to your advantage. When looking at a nautical chart, look for differences in depth across the course. If, for example, you see that one side of your racecourse is significantly shallower than the other, consider going to that side for current relief and to the other side for greater current.

Before each day of racing, look-up the times of the day's high and low tides in your tide book. These days it is most practical to use an app to find this information. This will give you at least an estimate of when the current is expected to switch. Once you get out on the water, check the actual current by dropping something that floats, like a water bottle or another floating object, next to a mark and seeing how it drifts. Watch how it moves over the course of a minute. Based on the day's tides and your own observations, make your predictions about where the favourable current will be and what will happen when the current switches at high or low tide. Think about which part of the racecourse (if any) will have advantageous current.

Once you know what the current is doing, it's easy to get to the favourable current. When one side of the course has favourable current, take any opportunities

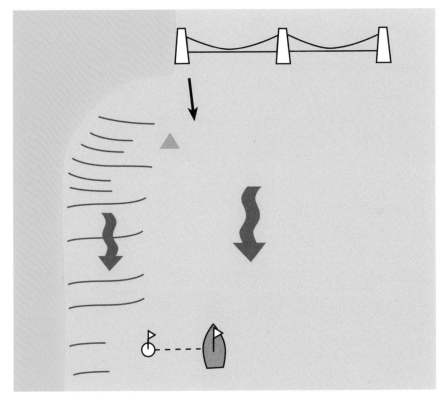

See the above example of the city-front area of San Francisco Bay. According to the charts, you know that there is shallower water on the left and a deep channel on the right. The current floods and ebbs through the Golden Gate, directly upwind. You test the current next to a mark before the first race, and you see that it is flooding strongly. You might discuss with your team: 'We are in a flood tide right now, so we want to go course left on the upwind for current relief, and sail course right on the downwind for stronger flood. However, high tide is at approximately 1pm, at which point the current will begin to switch. Let's continue to go to the left on the upwind until then, but once we start seeing an early ebb on the left this afternoon (remember, the current switches earlier in the shallower water), we need to start looking out for when the ebb on the right fills in stronger. Once the ebb in the channel is established, we'll go right on the upwind for the rest of the day so that we gain from that stronger ebb.'

to go to it. The great thing about current is that in comparison to the wind it is a bit easier to predict, so you will see great rewards by doing your homework and understanding what the current will do in the day ahead.

The final consideration for current is how it affects our laylines to the windward mark. Just as the current changes the starting Box, it changes our upwind laylines.[11]

The above diagrams show how current from each direction skews our laylines to the top mark in a different way. Understand how the current changes your laylines to the windward mark so that you know whether or not you can sail a greater distance to one side before reaching the layline, but most importantly, so that you don't overstand the mark on the other side by a significant amount.

Finally, a common misconception that some sailors have about current is that they need to sail their boat differently when they're in it. I've even heard coaches say things like 'when you're sailing upwind against the current, speed up your tacks so you spend less time with your

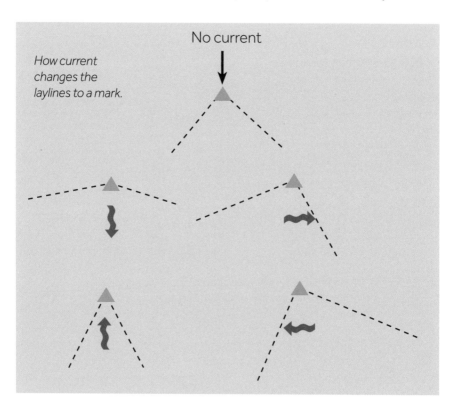

How current changes the laylines to a mark.

No current

[11] See *Starting In Current* for more information about the Starting Box and current.

bow pointed into the current'. Don't believe that kind of advice. Current has no effect on how you should sail your boat through the water. Think of the current as a conveyor belt that your boat is riding on. The orientation of your boat on that conveyor belt has no effect on how strongly the current affects your boat. I've heard Dave Perry explain this well with the example of a river: a stick floating down the river will always float down at the same speed, no matter its orientation. The stick will always be equally affected by the current of the river, whether it is pointed across the river, or parallel to its flow, or in any other direction. In the same way, current affects sailing boats equally no matter their direction. Your main priorities in current are to do your homework so that you know what it is doing and anticipate what it will do, use areas of the course with favourable current to your advantage, and be aware of how the current changes your laylines so you don't run into any trouble.

ZOOM IN AND ZOOM OUT

Sailing is a physically demanding sport, especially with dinghies, and in any sailing boat your body feels exhausted after a windy day on the water. But have you ever noticed that after a long day's racing your brain feels tired as well and your eyes feel sore? I believe this is partly because in sailing,

your focus is always changing. As a sailor, you're constantly switching your focus between zooming into your own boat to check the sails, to make sure the boat is set up to go fast, and to execute any manoeuvres; to zooming out and looking at the local area around you for the next puff, or boat-on-boat situations such as making a crucial cross; to zooming even further out, to assess the entire fleet, or to find the windward mark. In sailing, more than many other sports, we are constantly shifting between a very narrow and very broad view. It's valuable to be aware of this so that whenever you feel overwhelmed by everything going on around you, you have an idea why.

At the same time, zooming in and out is crucial to racing well. Every second you are focusing on something in your boat is a second that you are missing out on something important on the racecourse. The best teams are able to take in information on both the micro and macro levels incredibly efficiently. To this end as well as to minimize the amount that you have to switch your focus, it's best to have an active crew. After all, the crew is there to help. They should be the ones looking around with their heads outside the boat, feeding information back in about the next pressure, the distance to the layline, how you look on the rest of the fleet, and any other valuable information. The top boats all have constant communication. Work together as a team! The experience is that much better when everyone works towards a common goal.

BUILD SCENARIOS

For many sailors, it's the wind, the waves, the speed, and the sense of adventure that make sailing appeal to them. For some, it's the social aspect, the camaraderie of the sailing community. For others, it's the chess game in sailing that always brings them back.

It's a commonly heard phrase among sailors that 'the game of sailing is played 30 seconds ahead'. Personally, I prefer to say sailing is played '1–3 steps ahead', because it fits better with how we actually go about making our tactical moves. Once you know some basic strategy and tactics about where you should go on the course and how you should position yourself relative to other boats, the best way to use that knowledge effectively is to build scenarios before they happen. At any point on the upwind, and frankly the entire race, have a plan of what you would do if one of 2 or 3 scenarios were to suddenly happen. The purpose of this is so that when something happens, instead of wasting valuable time scrambling to figure out what your next right move is, you act instantly and take advantage of the situation. See the examples on the following pages.

Think of yourself building scenarios as a computer would execute a program. You are essentially coming up with a variety of If/Then statements that cover the possible situations that are most likely to happen next. Start doing this throughout your racing and you'll be amazed how it almost completely eliminates those 'What should I do?' moments of confusion in racing. Most sailors already plan scenarios ahead to an extent, but make a note to prioritize this the next time you go racing. There are many situations where you have only a brief opportunity to make a move, and by doing all the thinking ahead you'll be set to take advantage of the situation.

PLAY HIGH PERCENTAGE PLAYS

Make moves that have a high percentage of success – play high percentage plays. The key to this is making as many of your decisions as you can based on what you *know*, rather than what you think could happen. In a closed course, for example, there might be a clear bias to the right. Better pressure, more right shifts, everything points to the right winning. You find yourself mid-fleet, and think to yourself 'I'll never pass those boats ahead of me by following them!' Against all prevailing strategy, you tack, go hard left, and hope against all odds for a rogue left shift to come through and send you to the front. More often

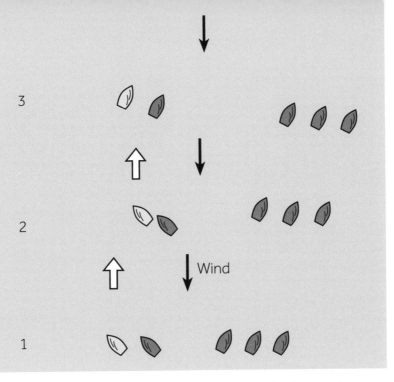

Wind

In the above situation the race has just begun. You are the yellow boat, and you look about even with the rest of the fleet. You are on a neutral shift. Most of the fleet above you suddenly tacks onto port, except for one boat directly to windward of you who is pinning you from tacking. You may plan in your mind/with your team: 'Looking ahead, if we get lifted we will want to continue on starboard. However, if we get a header we will want to tack. If the shift simply remains neutral, we want to tack soon anyway to stay connected to the rest of the fleet. However, a tack now would require ducking this windward boat which would be quite costly. Therefore, now we need to sail a high mode in order to hopefully pinch out this windward boat (or at least make them uncomfortable with their position) and force them to tack, giving us options to tack in the future. Unless conditions change, as soon as our opponent tacks we want to tack as well.'

than not, this is the fastest way to the back of the fleet. Instead, the better play is to stay in the area of the racecourse where you know there are favoured conditions, and pick off as many boats as you can one by one in small tactical situations.

From time to time the winner of a race is a boat that went the opposite direction from the fleet, 'banged a corner', took a huge gamble on one side of the course, and it paid off. You'll see this happen from time to time, but don't succumb to the temptation of gambling everything on a corner and seeing where the chips fall. That boat may win the first race by a mile, but the next time they try it they'll finish last. The message here is don't take a flier. Yes, disengage with the fleet when you need to, and go to one

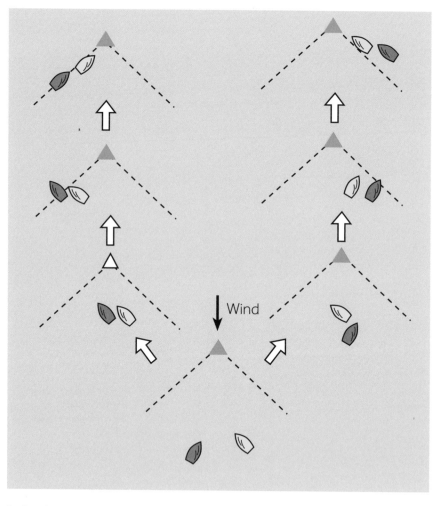

*In the above situation, the yellow boat is on starboard and slightly ahead of a
port tacker. The yellow boat has a plan for each of the two scenarios that could
happen as the port tacker approaches: 'If this port tacker ducks, we will tack almost
immediately after the duck into a position overlapped close to windward, push
them to the right layline, and tack on the layline. If the port tacker lee-bows, we will
continue, sail to the left layline, and tack on the left layline.' Either way, by planning
ahead so that it can execute its actions without delay, the yellow boat is able to
corner its opponent on the layline and lead them back to the mark.*

side if you see pressure up ahead,
anticipate a shift, or otherwise
think you might get something
there. But that doesn't mean
you need to go all the way to the
corner and gamble everything

on that side. Don't be the guy
sitting in last telling a story
about how 'I hit the right corner
the first race, and it didn't
work, so I hit the left corner the
second race, and it didn't work

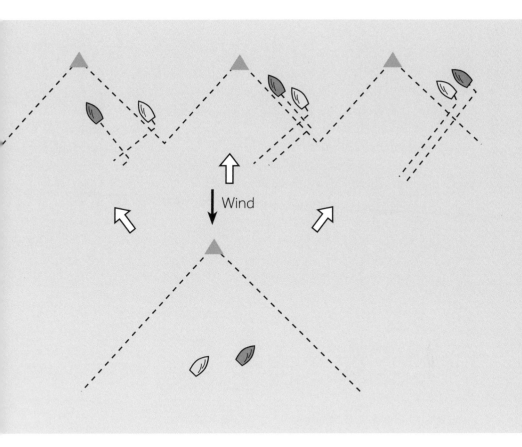

In the above situation, the yellow boat is about a boat length astern and slightly to windward of its opponent. Both boats are approaching the starboard layline to the windward mark. The yellow boat plans with its team: 'The key to taking advantage of this situation is knowing exactly where the layline is. If this opponent in front of us tacks perfectly on the layline, our only option is to duck behind him, tack a bit above the layline into clear air, and sail to the mark. If, however, this opponent tacks before what we believe the layline is, we will duck, tack onto the layline, and hopefully have an opportunity when he must tack again to make the mark. If he sails past the layline, we will follow him and tack at the exact instant he tacks, thereby taking the inside but keeping our lane clean. The further past the layline our opponent sails before he initiates the tack, the better it is for us.'

either!' When you find yourself at the back of the fleet, work your way back with small consistent gains over the duration of the race by making the right tactical and strategic calls according to the principles I've described in this chapter, not by gambling everything and hoping for a miracle. Over a score line of multiple races your consistency will put you on top.

EXPERT TIP

One of the keys to winning in tactical situations is being assertive. Sometimes you'll be in situations where there's more than one good move, or it's unclear what your next best move is. On these occasions, it's often best to be confident, quick, and assertive about your move, even if it's not the perfect play. Usually the sailor who acts immediately and assertively on a mediocre move or decision will win over a sailor who goes for a better move but with a second or two of doubt or delay. As you gain experience with building scenarios in your head, you'll find that the key to winning a tactical battle against an opponent is putting him in a position of doubt where he is unsure of what to do, while you have already planned the two or three possible scenarios in your head so you can take advantage of your opponent's moment of doubt.

IDENTIFY THE MOST IMPORTANT FACTOR

This is a big one. If there's one question to ask yourself before every single race, it's this: 'What will be the most important factor in this race?'

Racing is a constant balance of things that matter. As we've covered, there are a dozen different factors that go into every decision we make on the upwind leg. To make the decision-making process more manageable we need to have priorities. Simplify the factors. What do we need to prioritize in this race?

Let's look at a variety of examples you may encounter. If the pressure is patchy and inconsistent across the course, prioritize staying in pressure as well as playing positionally by engaging with the fleet when you look good. If the shifts are big but the pressure is quite consistent, prioritize staying on the lifted tack and focus less on the pressure. If there is a big shift before the start, prioritize getting onto the longer tack first. If it's a closed course, your first priority is getting to the favoured side in a clear lane, which also means getting a plus or equal start so that you can hold your lane in the direction you want to go. If it's a tight, crowded fleet, then staying in clear air rises up the list of priorities. If there is strong current, prioritize your position relative to the laylines. If there are consistent conditions with steady wind and steady pressure, your boat speed is a much bigger factor, so be sure to prioritize finding that perfect sail setup and maximizing your speed.

So you see how different

factors become more important in different conditions. Find the two or three factors that matter most in the race and prioritize them in your decisions about where you want to go, when you want to tack, etc. I find it helpful to visualize a list of all these factors, ordered from most important to least important. When one is more important, it goes higher on the list. As conditions change, the things on the list swap around in order of importance. Making this ordered list helps focus your thinking on what really matters in the race.

If nothing else, I hope this chapter teaches you to have a reason for every decision you make. Sail intentionally. When you decide to tack, or duck a boat, or sail to one side of the course, think about the why? Because there are so many components to upwind strategy (as I've described above) that all add up to determine your moves on the upwind, you'll make lots of mistakes. Sometimes you try something and it doesn't work out. Sometimes that pressure on one side never fills in like you expected it would, or that shift never comes. But even if your strategy doesn't work out every time, just by having a reason behind each of your moves you'll be miles ahead of the boats sailing mindlessly, without a strategy. More importantly, you'll be on the track of improving with every race. At least when you have a plan you can learn something after trying

it, even if it doesn't work out the way you'd hoped. By continuously putting in the reps, trying new things and learning from the outcomes, your strategic thinking in the upwind leg gradually becomes instinctive, and the entire upwind becomes much more manageable.

Put simply, sailing strategically is all about choosing the best option out of what is available to you. Making these decisions is very difficult, especially when you have to weigh the value of multiple strategic and tactical principles. Do I tack out of a bad lane to find clear air, or do I continue in this bad lane but sailing towards more favourable conditions? As a leader, how do I balance covering the boats behind me with sailing according to my own rhythm of the shifts and the pressure? I disengaged from the fleet and now I look slightly better, but should I tack back to consolidate my gain or should I keep going and wait for something bigger?

Sometimes, when things get too complicated during the race and you feel overwhelmed, remember that the upwind is really very simple – we have only two options, tack or continue. Then ask yourself this one simple question: What tack will take me the fastest to the next mark? Sometimes when things get overwhelming, simplifying the race with this one simple question will clear your mind, look at what really matters, and then make the right decision with the least amount of confusion.

175

Chapter 12

THE TOP MARK

I refer to the third and final stage of the upwind leg as the Top Mark area. This is the top 10–20% of the upwind that becomes especially hectic as the fleet converges at the top of the course. This stage involves getting around the windward mark in the best possible position as well as determining your initial game plan for the next leg (the hand-off).

TOP MARK TACTICS

There are a variety of approaches to the top mark. In a crowded fleet there is almost always a train of boats stacked up on the starboard layline, sailing bow to stern, all following each other around the windward mark. This phenomenon is sometimes called the 'starboard tack parade'. More rarely, when most of the fleet went to the left on the upwind, the left layline will be packed with boats. Unless you're one of the leaders, more often than not these laylines are crowded places. If you're leading the fleet, getting to the layline is a great idea if it keeps you between your main competition and the mark. However, if you're mid-fleet or deeper, my advice is to continue to follow the 80/20 Rule and keep some distance from the laylines until you're within a minute's sailing distance from the mark. The reason for this is because each of the boats in the starboard tack parade are all in each other's bad air, all sailing a fraction of their potential boat speed. Additionally,

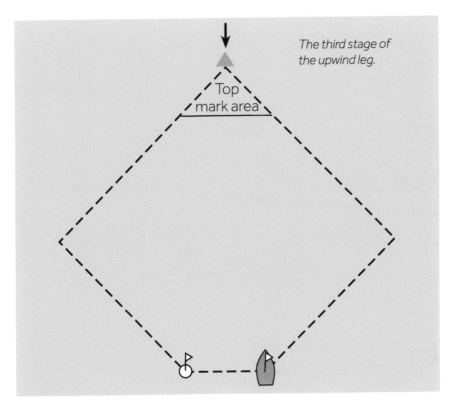

The third stage of the upwind leg.

each boat that joins the starboard tack parade tends to tack a bit higher than the boat in front of them, which in a large train of boats becomes a huge detour of extra distance. So by tacking a dozen boat lengths or so below the layline, staying in relatively clear air and sailing fast towards the mark, you are gaining distance on every boat in that train. The farther away you are from the mark, the more you will gain from taking this low lane below the train of boats on the layline. This is the exact same concept as when you're out on the road and you pass a slow group of cars in the lane next to you and merge ahead of them. When you're in the mix

of the pack, this is a great trick to gain some distance.

As you get much closer to the top mark, however, the advantage of being on the starboard layline becomes greater. As soon as you're within about a minute of rounding the mark, earlier in a more crowded fleet and later if you're in a less dense area, that's the time to start thinking about tacking into a gap on the starboard layline.

As a general rule, get to the starboard layline as soon as you see that your options to tack into a position there are about to disappear. As boats converge on the top mark the laylines become especially crowded, and as the

177

At the top mark rounding, coming in on starboard is a big advantage. The boats on port like TUR and EST have to duck boats, find a safe place to tack, and are at risk of fouling.

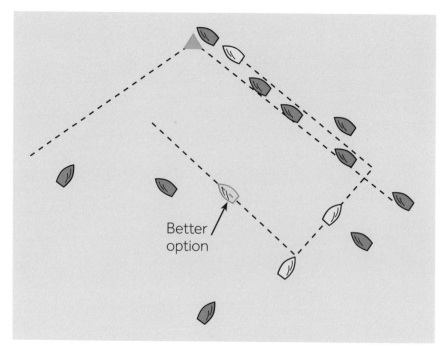

Better option

The yellow boat approaching the layline has two options. The best is not to get to the layline too early, especially since it is still relatively far from the mark. By tacking before the layline, this boat is able to sail in a lower density area and in better wind. As a result, it gains significant distance on the train of boats on the starboard layline all slowing each other down, and is able to tack into a gap close to the mark in a stronger position.

If there is no such train of boats on the layline, simply focus on approaching the windward mark from the low density side if it fits in with your upwind strategy. Doing so gives you more time in clear air.

train of boats on the starboard layline become connected bow to stern it becomes virtually impossible to sail in on port and find a gap to tack into. Tack into a gap, stay connected to the boat in front of you and you will pass any boats stuck below the layline. Any port tacker will have little chance of tacking between you and the mark.

If you're approaching th e windward mark from the left, it's very important that you view the

bottom edge of the zone (the three boat length circle) of the windward mark as your layline, not the layline to the mark itself.

Why? It has to do with the rules. The reason for this is because when you tack from port to starboard to go around the windward mark and you are within the zone, you may run into potential rules issues with RRS Rule 18. Normally, as a port tacker you're allowed to tack in front of a starboard boat, and as

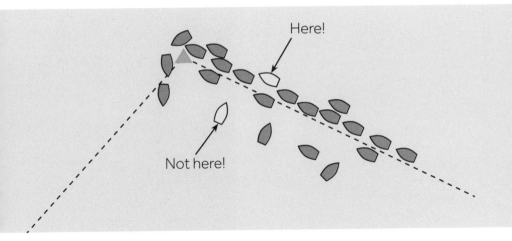

Here!

Not here!

Stay away from the laylines when you are far from the mark. As you get closer to the mark, especially in a crowded fleet, get onto the starboard layline before your options to do so disappear. Wait too long and you may become one of the boats stuck below the layline with virtually no options to round the mark without fouling other boats or ducking the fleet.

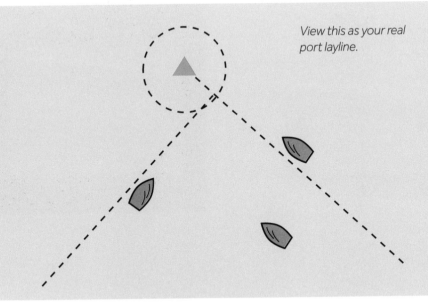

View this as your real port layline.

soon as you complete your tack you gain the right of way. Even if the starboard boat behind you has better speed and must luff up to avoid you after you have completed your tack, as the right of way boat you have every right to complete your tack in front of them. When you are in the zone to the windward mark, however, Rule 18.3 makes this an illegal move. To summarize, when you are inside the zone of the windward mark and you tack in front of or to leeward of a boat that has been on starboard and fetching the mark since entering the zone, you may not cause that boat to sail above close-hauled to avoid contact. Unless the starboard boat has well overstood the mark, you can run into trouble tacking inside of them within the zone. So many times I see sailors make this mistake when their ego doesn't allow their brain to make the right decision, and they most likely end up in the protest room with a high risk of DSQ (disqualification).

For this reason, it is always a good idea to use the edge of the zone as your left layline so that you don't run into any issues with Rule 18. It's just not worth the risk. Even if you tack below a starboard boat fetching the mark and you believe you left your opponent plenty of space, all they have to do is head up until their jib luffs slightly, say that you forced them above close-hauled, and it's up to the protest committee to decide whether or not to throw you out of the race. As the boat coming into the mark on port this is a very difficult protest to win.

As a port boat, finding a gap to round the mark is difficult enough. From the opposite perspective as a starboard boat, it is important to be aware of any port approachers so that you can prevent any boat

The optimal position here is to be on starboard and comfortably laying the mark. Approaching on port, or tacking into bad air on a tight layline, in a crowded fleet like this is difficult and high-risk.

from lee bowing you around the mark. In this situation as the starboard boat rounding the mark, I tell my sailors 'close the door'. Defending your position at the windward mark is reminiscent of defending against a port approacher during the pre-start.[12]

---

[12] See *Defending Against Sharks* to learn how to defend your leeward gap during the start.

When you see a port approacher who may try to lee bow you, bear away, ease the sails, pick up speed, and call out 'starboard!' Sail exactly on the layline to the mark, or even a bit below. Don't be afraid to point your bow below the mark! The combination of your faster speed, position on the layline giving them no room to lee bow and make the mark, and your words will almost certainly make them think 'I don't want to mess with this crazy sailor' and they'll duck below you. Then, use your new speed to pinch back up above the layline and get around the mark with good speed.

Additionally, before rounding the top mark, prepare the boat for the next leg. Make any necessary adjustments to the control lines. Ease the vang, the outhaul and

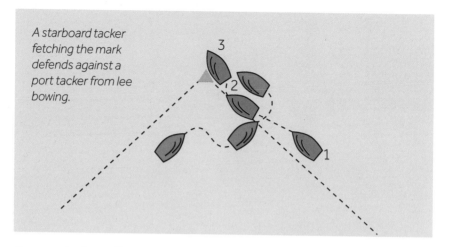

A starboard tacker fetching the mark defends against a port tacker from lee bowing.

the cunningham. Easing both the cunningham and the outhaul is important for getting the proper sail shape downwind in strong wind, as is easing the vang – forget the vang and you might very well put a bend or two in your mast, or worse!

THE DOWNWIND HAND-OFF

Your first priority at the top mark is your tactical position as we discussed above. Your second priority is to plan in advance your exit from the windward mark so that you put yourself in a strong position for the next leg. I call the process of making a plan for the next leg the 'hand-off'.

You want to round the windward mark with a plan ready for the next downwind leg. Have some ideas in your mind as you approach the top of the upwind and begin discussing your game plan with your teammates as soon as you're on the starboard

layline fetching the windward mark. Ideally, finish the downwind hand-off before the last few boat lengths of your approach. Don't wait for the last second, or wait to analyse all the information after the rounding – you want to be on top of your game ready to initiate the right call before the rounding. As a first step, find the next mark. Are you looking for a reach mark, or a downwind gate, or something else? Let's assume the next leg is a downwind. Will you hold a high mode? Will you set on a low mode and allow the boats behind you to roll over you? Will you gybe set? These are decisions that must be made *before* you round the top mark, during your hand-off process. These decisions depend on a few factors.

Most importantly, just as you want to first sail on the longer tack on the upwind, get on the longer gybe downwind. The more skewed the downwind is and the longer one of the gybes is, the more important it is that you get on the long gybe first and protect your windward lane. One way to see which is the longer gybe is with a visual inspection. This works well if you can clearly see the leeward mark or leeward gate and then see if it is offset to one side. However, an even easier way to figure this out is to think about the upwind you just completed and recall if you spent more time on starboard or port tack. If you sailed more time upwind on port tack, then starboard will be the longer gybe downwind. Therefore, do a normal set on starboard and know you might sail slightly higher around the mark if necessary to defend your windward lane. If you sailed more time upwind on starboard, then port will be the longer

gybe downwind and you should consider a gybe set.

If the gybes downwind are more or less equal in length, think about the final shift you had on the upwind and ask yourself which tack on the downwind will be the headed tack. If there was a left shift, plan to set on starboard. If there was a significant right shift, you could set on starboard but on a low mode and plan to do an early gybe. Alternatively, you could do a gybe set.

I'll go into more detail about the hand-off, the different types of sets and when you should use them in the next section, *Downwind*.

Finn fleet rounding the windward mark.

PART 4

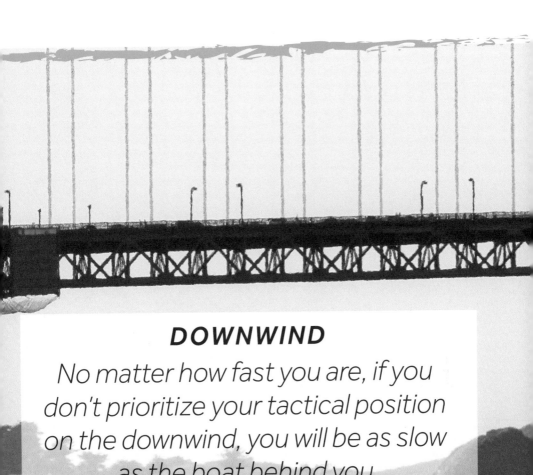

DOWNWIND

No matter how fast you are, if you don't prioritize your tactical position on the downwind, you will be as slow as the boat behind you

Chapter 13

DOWNWIND SAILING AT A GLANCE

We're around the windward mark and off to the downwind leg! After a long, tough, and potentially unstable upwind, during which the boats gain and lose from the Snakes and Ladders game of the puffs and the shifts, and where a pack on one side might look good and then suddenly the other side looks good, the top mark rounding neatly lines up all the boats and finally gives you a sense of where you stand in the fleet. There's a range of emotions sailors may be feeling: excitement from being in the first group around, frustration from rounding deep in the fleet, some stress over how to stay ahead of that pack of boats thundering down on your tail. The key to setting yourself up for success on the downwind, wherever you are in the fleet, is mastering the tactics for boat-on-boat situations, both for staying ahead of boats behind you and passing boats in front of you.

Let's break down the downwind into a few elements:

First, let's take a glance at Tactical Sailing. This is the most important section of the downwind, and we will discuss it in a moment. This involves the boat-on-boat interactions – how you sail relative to your opponents. In my philosophy, you can make the most improvement in your sailing by focusing on this element of the downwind. Tactical sailing gives you the foundation to be able to take advantage of gains you make from the other elements such as good strategy, speed, and manoeuvres.

You have to make sure your boat handling and manoeuvres are race-ready. Manoeuvres downwind are not like the upwind, where tacks are very straight forward and changing modes is quite simple. On the downwind, we have many more types of

DOWNWIND ELEMENTS TO CONSIDER				
TACTICAL SAILING	BOAT HANDLING	TECHNIQUES	BOAT SET-UP	DOWNWIND STRATEGY
• Position and speed relative to your opponents • Position near marks	• Gybes • Sets • Douses • Dynamic situations	•Relative to opponent and/or conditions •Before and after manoeuvres	•Optimizing boat speed •Preparing the boat for the next situation	•Gusts and lulls •Shifts •Currents •'S' curve •80/20 rule

manoeuvres, and they can be executed in many different ways. To this end, you need to be able to adjust your manoeuvres while they happen. Sometimes in your warm-up before the race you'll do perfect gybes, but then in the race the spinnaker collapses, or gets twisted, or the roll is wrong, or you don't reach the right exit angle, and a lot of times this is because you are changing the rhythm or the timing of the manoeuvre because you are sailing near your opponents. Everything is easy when you are sailing by yourselves, but you have to learn how to adjust your sets, gybes, or douses mid-manoeuvre in reaction to marks, laylines, boats, and other elements that are affecting you during the race.

Your Technique is something that can be tricky to master in races. When you're sailing by yourselves you can train to be as fast as you want, but when you sail against other boats the technique is actually not that smooth. You have to react all the time and adjust yourselves relative to other boats when they gybe, sail higher or lower angles, or cover your wind. Your technique also changes a little bit before and after the manoeuvres, especially when another boat does a gybe, changes their angle, or makes another move at the same time as you do a manoeuvre, and you must adjust according to their action.

Boat Set-up is all about maximizing speed. In each different condition you need to tune and adjust the sails and the setup of the boat. You have to make sure you're shifting gears as conditions change and your mode changes. Throughout the downwind you need to think about how you prepare the boat going into a manoeuvre so that the boat is set up for the exit from the manoeuvre. This might involve preparing the sheets or the centreboard for the upcoming action before it happens.

Downwind Strategy is the racecourse strategy – how you would use the environment on the racecourse to sail the fastest if you were alone on the water. One aspect of downwind strategy are the shifts, but compared to the upwind the shifts are less important. This is because you sail smaller angles downwind in most boats and in most conditions, there is less lateral separation between the boats on the downwind, and you will encounter fewer shifts during the leg as you are sailing with the wind rather than against it. What's more important, however, is the pressure – the gusts and lulls, having clear air, and a good position to stay connected to any pressure. The reason you must prioritize pressure is because on the upwind, when you sail in more pressure you sail faster but you continue to sail in the same direction; but on the downwind, when you get more pressure you sail much faster and much lower, meaning differences in pressure make a huge difference to your downwind VMG. Therefore the pressure is usually the most important factor of the downwind strategy to look out for. Make sure you're staying in pressure, and if one side has more pressure then that is one of your first priorities. Another factor is current – whether there is a strong current and whether there are differences in the current across the course – but again, because your angles are so low on the downwind the split between the fleet is not very wide and so the difference in the current from one side to the other is a bit less. Other rules such as the 'S' curve and the 80/20 rule help with optimizing our position. I will cover these later in more detail.

Once again, compared to the upwind, strategy takes a step back and tactical sailing becomes much more important on the downwind. But once you have mastered the fundamentals of downwind tactics, finding the better pressure or current, gybing on the big shifts, and playing the racecourse properly will definitely gain you places in a competitive fleet.

To perform well on the downwind you must master each of the elements listed above.

THE IMPORTANCE OF TACTICAL SAILING

Why is tactical sailing so important? It's definitely not the only element of the downwind. What might first come to mind is the strategic element: the shifts, the pressure, the current, all of which make up the racecourse strategy. In other words, how you would sail the fastest around the racecourse if you were alone.

However, luckily you are not racing alone on the racecourse; you need to react to your opponents, and so you need to think about boat-on-boat tactics. This is especially important on the downwind relative to the upwind, because as leaders you have less control over the wind and over your game plan. After all, you can't so easily stay between the next mark and your opponents as you can on the upwind. Often the boats in the back will come with a gust or pressure and they are the ones attacking, so as leaders you need to find the tricky balance between going to the edges to find clear air and staying between your opponents and the next mark (which potentially you would want to do but then you are in bad air).

It's especially true on the downwind that no matter how fast you are, if you don't have the right position, you can't execute your boat speed or strategy. Even if you have the perfect strategy with the wind and the currents, even if you have the entire racecourse figured out – no matter how fast you are, if you don't execute the three tactical stages of the downwind that I'll be discussing in this section, you will be as slow as the boat behind you. So you have to be able to execute the downwind tactics for each stage of the downwind very well. And if you do this you'll see that even if you're not very fast you will sail as if you're much faster relative to the fleet. That's why prioritizing your position on the downwind is so important.

The other elements of the downwind such as strategy and boat handling will also be covered, but these chapters are focused mostly on the tactical element of the downwind. While I know the downwind is more complicated than the boat-on-boat tactics and that big gains come from high boat speed and good strategy, I like to think that tactical sailing has its purpose – to defend your position and avoid small losses during the race. Once you have the confidence in your position and you don't need to worry about your opponents coming from behind, you will be able to free most of your focus to the strategy, speed, and progress in the race. In addition, once you are ready to defend against all types of offence from your opponents, you will have many offensive skill sets that you can use to gain on a lot of boats during the windows of opportunity that come your way. I

truly believe that if you follow the proper tactical steps you will be fast (whether you are naturally fast on the downwind or not), you will make smart decisions even in complicated situations, and you will defend your position or gain boats easily!

On the upwind, making the right strategic moves – staying in phase with the shifts, engaging and disengaging with the fleet etc – is where the biggest gains and losses are made. On the downwind, however, boat-on-boat tactics and your relative position to other boats become much more important, and having the right racecourse strategy becomes a lesser factor. This is mainly due to the difference in sailing angles on the upwind and on the downwind. Sailing upwind close-hauled, sailing boats sail a relatively shallow angle to the wind, somewhere between 40 and 45 degrees. Your modes on the upwind are also only fine adjustments in angle – one boat sailing a high mode and another on a low mode, both achieving the same VMG, generally won't have more than a 5 degree difference in their angle to the wind. What this means is that on the upwind the boats become very spread out across the course, and they are very fixed on these shallow angles.

On the downwind, however, sailing angles are much closer to where you are actually trying to go – depending on the boat, anywhere from dead downwind directly towards the leeward mark (Lasers, Optimists, Finns) to 20–30 degrees above dead downwind in boats with asymmetric kites. Additionally, on the downwind the boats have a much greater range of angles that they can play with while maintaining the same VMG. While that range is only about 5 degrees on the upwind, on the downwind one 470 could be surfing waves straight downwind and another could be planing 30 degrees higher and going much faster, and they would arrive even at the leeward mark. (This depends on the class of boat. Some boats, such as those with symmetrical kites, sail well at a greater range of downwind angles than others). What this means is that on the upwind, it is much more important to stay in phase with the shifts because our angles are so shallow and fixed. On the downwind, however, because of the lower angles and more freedom to play with them, staying perfectly in phase becomes less important. Instead, your position relative to other boats becomes much more important, and so you must focus primarily on making the right moves in the frequent boat-on-boat situations that you encounter. But before exploring these tactical situations, let's look at boat handling and technique.

Chapter 14

BOAT HANDLING AND TECHNIQUE

Boat handling and technique for fast boat speed are fundamental factors in tactical sailing. Let's take a closer look.

MODES DOWNWIND

Just as you have modes of sailing on the upwind (high mode, low mode, VMG), you have modes on the downwind.[13] The steering is just reversed: on the downwind you head up to gain speed and to sail a faster, less direct angle, and you head down to sail a slower angle that takes a more direct course towards the leeward mark. Upwind, of course, is the opposite.

Additionally, compared to the upwind, the difference in angle between downwind modes is much more extreme. As mentioned previously, while the difference between an effective high mode and low mode on the upwind is about 5 degrees at most, on the downwind two boats might be sailing 20–30 degrees apart with their angles and clock the same VMG. What makes this aspect of the downwind such fun and so awesome is it means that on the downwind your mode is one of your most important tools not just for fine-tuning your boat speed, but for positioning yourselves where you want to be. You could sail high over the top of a pack in front of you, for example, or sail low to separate from a windward boat, without

really compromising your VMG. In essence, you choose your modes at any time throughout the downwind in order to position the boat as you want according to your strategy and tactics. Later chapters are dedicated to knowing what that proper position relative to other boats and the racecourse should be. For now, let's focus on how you sail your different modes.

In your class of boat and in a given condition on the racecourse (strength of wind, sea state), you'll usually be able to go out sailing and find your VMG angle. It's the angle downwind that feels comfortable, stable, and fast. Not too high and not too low. Remember, similar to the upwind, your downwind angle is a balance between heading high for more speed and more power,

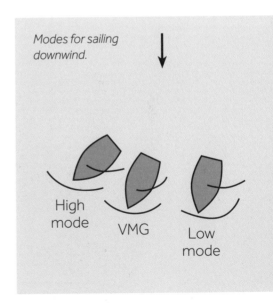

Modes for sailing downwind.

High mode

VMG

Low mode

---

[13] See *Off The Line* to learn more about upwind modes and curving.

and heading low for a more direct route to the leeward mark. Your VMG angle is the average angle that strikes the perfect balance between high and low to take you downwind as fast as possible. It's also important to note that it changes according to the wind strength. In contrast to the upwind in which your angles are relatively fixed in all conditions, on the downwind in very light wind you'll sail much higher (10–15 degrees, depending on the boat) than you would in moderate conditions in order to get the power you need to keep the boat moving forward.

505 boats racing downwind on San Francisco Bay.

In strong wind you'll sail much lower (10–15 degrees lower) than in moderate conditions because you no longer need that higher angle to stay powered up and on a plane.

As you learned from the upwind, however, holding your VMG angle dead straight is not fast. That might work in an imaginary world of perfectly flat water and perfectly consistent wind, but in the real world there are waves, variations in pressure, and gusts and lulls, all of which require you to change your mode, your sail trim, and your crew weight position. Curving, subtly heading up and down according to the wind, the waves, and the speed of the boat, is the fastest

way of sailing in these real world conditions. Let's first cover how and when we use these different modes downwind.

The high mode is all about speed and power. To transition to a high mode, create some leeward heel in the boat, trim in the sails (especially the main) and the boat will head up naturally with minimal use of the rudder (remember, heel the boat right to go left, and vice versa). Trim in the sails to suit the higher angle, easing out the spinnaker guy and trimming the sheet, and in stronger conditions add some vang to get more return at the top of the main. Keep the boat flat or with a slight leeward heel, but avoid windward heel at all costs. Pump the main a few times, press the boat (in strong wind, crew weight must shift to windward as you head up in order to keep the boat flat), and the boat will accelerate forward. Remember that the high mode is only effective if it makes you sail much faster (a reason why it works best in light displacement, planing boats that sail relatively high angles anyway). In very light wind you should feel the spinnaker fill, more power in the sails, more flow over the foils, and the apparent wind direction moves forward; once this is established, you can head down based on your feeling of the boat, when you feel you have the speed to head down. In strong wind, when you

head to a high mode and press the boat you should feel the boat take off: the bow pops out of the water, the boat feels powerful, there's a big wake and white water everywhere, and you are ripping it over the waves. If you are heading up and not accelerating forward, something is wrong. Check your sail trim, or maybe you are heading too high for the condition.

When do you want to sail on a high mode? Whenever you need more speed or power in the boat. For example, in very light wind you sail very high angles anyway because you need the extra power to keep the boat moving forward through the water. Additionally, if you see that you can pass waves downwind if you go to a high mode, do it! You're passing other boats who are still trying to surf the waves. And in any condition, when you see some big motorboat chop rolling towards you, have someone call it out and head up five or ten degrees before it hits you to power through it without losing speed. At any other time that you lose speed, or your sails lose some pressure, move to a slightly higher mode to rebuild your speed.

One other advantage of the high mode is that it moves your apparent wind angle further forward. For fast planing boats this is a huge factor. Skiff sailors, for example, are experts of what we call 'apparent wind sailing', which involves building up boat speed on the downwind leg before bearing

away to their lower VMG angle. The idea behind this is that when you head up to a higher angle downwind, the boat goes much faster (again, this depends on the boat). With this extra speed your apparent wind angle shifts forward. This new apparent wind angle acts as your own private header, allowing you to bear away again to a lower angle while going much faster. Interesting concept, right? Apparent wind sailing is most applicable to fast boats with asymmetrical kites such as 49er skiffs and certain keelboats, but it's a good concept for any sailor to generally understand.

The low mode is all about taking your speed down and using it to take a more direct course to the leeward mark. When you're heading up, you're looking for more power. When you're heading down to a low mode, it's because you have a surplus of power that can be better used for sailing a low angle. To transition to a low mode, the boat must be sailing fast, and it must be flat. Any leeward heel will force you to use significant rudder. In cases where you are heading down to an extreme low mode or essentially dead downwind, also called sailing by-the-lee, a small roll to windward actually helps you head down and build pressure in the sails (you might do this to make a mark, surf down a wave, etc). The sails must also be eased, depending on how low you are heading. Even if you are still 10–20 degrees above dead downwind, it is incredibly important that the main is eased all the way out against the shrouds, especially in slower boats that sail lower angles, and the spinnaker must rotate to windward. In all conditions the vang must be significantly eased as well. Crew weight should be to windward. Windward heel is not a problem. In fact, it can actually help the boat stay balanced on a low angle with minimal rudder. Make the bear-away smooth by properly easing the sails and heeling the boat so that minimal rudder is used and you should find that you lose very little speed but sail a much more direct angle to the mark.

When do you want to sail on a low mode? Most commonly, you use the low mode when you are trying to surf waves. This happens generally in medium wind conditions, when the boat is moving fast enough that you can catch waves, but not so fast that you are consistently passing waves.

Waves or not, the critical point about soaking low is that you want to head down with the *speed*, not with the pressure. Knowing how much you can head down and the optimal length of time you can stay low before heading back up requires having a good feel for the boat, something that takes months to acquire and years of experience, really, to master. So keep at it! The more hours you put in on the water, the better you'll

get to know your boat – when it needs more power, when it can be sailed lower – and your boat speed will be on an upward trend.

That said, when the wind becomes very strong, and the boat is planing and you are going faster than the waves, you might reach a point in boat speed where you recognize that you are passing waves. Soaking low to try to surf the waves is no longer worth it. At this point, it is incredibly important to make the adjustment to heating it up, sailing a higher mode, gaining more speed, getting on a plane, and committing to passing waves. In these conditions the apparent wind factor is huge. In any boat that's fast enough to pass waves downwind in big breeze, head higher, get going much faster, and bear away again using your apparent wind. Trust me, the boats that make this critical adjustment will make huge gains over the boats that don't.

I have described above the times when you would switch to either a high mode or a low mode in order to sail the fastest down the racecourse if there were no other boats around you. A lot of the time, however, you are choosing your modes based on the position you want to have relative to the other boats – keeping clear air, setting yourselves up for the next manoeuvre, taking the inside at a mark, etc. We will dive into this in later sections.

A NOTE ON BOAT SPEED: CURVING DOWNWIND

Just as on the upwind, curving is an incredibly important element of downwind boat speed, perhaps even more so since the wider range of angles allow for huge adjustments up and down. Once again, if you were to hold one fixed angle on the entire downwind you would be very slow. Downwind speed is all about curving up and down between slight (and sometimes extreme) high modes and low modes according to the waves and the speed of the boat.

Remember the basic rule to using curving to produce great boat speed?

In flat water this rule is quite simple to follow. Just adjust your mode according to the speed of your boat. Use a gust to gain speed, and use that speed to soak low. As you begin to lose speed from sailing on a lower angle or from the gust dying out, head up again to build speed and repeat the cycle again. This is the perpetual cycle of curving that drives your downwind boat speed. This might all sound like a lot of work, but trust me, as you gain experience and time doing this it will become a natural, effortless habit whenever you sail downwind. It does, however, take a lot of communication and coordination between the helm and the crew. It also requires constant steering and constant trimming and easing of the sails. I always say that on the downwind, the spinnaker trimmer is steering the boat rather than the skipper. As they are the one who can feel the pressure in the kite, they should be constantly communicating with the skipper things like 'light pressure, head up 10 degrees' or 'good pressure, bear away 10'. It takes a good team and good communication to sail the boat fast, and this is no more true than when flying the kite on the downwind.

Note as well that it's not just either a high mode or low mode that you sail on – it's a range between the extreme high mode and extreme low mode that you can play with as you choose. Sailors become attuned to this more and more

THE KEY RULE TO CURVING

On the upwind, when you feel fast, head slightly higher, trim in the sails, and flatten the boat. When you feel slow, head down slightly, ease the sails, and create more leeward heel. On the downwind, when you feel fast, flatten the boat, head down slightly, and ease the sails. When you feel slow, create some leeward heel, head up slightly, and trim in the sails.

as their boat speed improves. Sometimes, especially in flat water and consistent pressure, subtle curving of just 5 or 10 degrees is all it takes to be fast in the puffs and lulls. In other conditions you might make macro changes to your angle, such as heading up 20 or 30 degrees and pumping the main to build a plane, and then using that plane to catch a big wave and heading way down. It all depends on the conditions.

In most venues and most wind conditions, however, there are waves. Firstly, when there are waves, I can't stress enough how important it is to identify whether or not you can surf them. Analyse the sea state. Are the waves short and choppy, or are they long and smooth like ocean swell? What direction are they coming from? Are they aligned with the wind? How big are they? Are they surfable, or are they more of an annoying distraction? If you can't surf the waves, either because they are too small or because the wind is too light, sail as if the water were flat. Curve up and down according to your speed and find a rhythm that works.

Let's now look at the technique for surfing the waves. (Again, this applies to some boats more than others. Some boats are too slow to generally surf waves. Others sail such high angles in all conditions that surfing waves is not really a focus. Other boats surf waves very well.) Build speed, and as a helm, watch the waves on your

windward side. As a wave passes under you, wait until your bow is tucked into its trough with its peak just ahead of you, and just as the next wave behind you begins to lift up your stern, forcefully pump the sails, press the boat to windward by shifting bodyweight, and soak low in the direction of the wave. In a keelboat, all you can really do is initiate surfing from your boat's momentum, which makes timing your peak boat speed from your curving with the arrival of the waves even more important. Once on the wave, maximize your gain! You know that feeling when you're surfing a wave and you can sense when it's just about to pass

EXPERT TIP

In fact, here's a simple rule I like to follow that helps me surf a wave as long as possible: as long as you are faster than the wave in the initial part of surfing, keep heading down. If you're the same speed as the wave, stay on course. But as soon as you're getting slower than the wave, start heading up. By developing the ability to head up on the right timing before the boat loses momentum, you'll be able to surf the same wave again and again. All it requires is a very good feel for the boat.

under you? Ride the wave as long as you can, but anticipate when you are about to fall off the wave and *before* that happens, head up to rebuild power and repeat the process.

If you can catch waves, time your curving to help you do so. Curving and surfing waves is all about having the right timing. To catch waves, match your moments of high boat speed with the brief opportunities to catch each wave so that you have the best chance of initiating surfing. After all, speed is your friend. Just think about normal surfing on a surf board – the faster you can paddle, the easier it is to catch waves. When you feel slow, go on a high mode, accelerate forward, and look for the next opportunity

The continuous cycle of curving downwind in waves.

to catch a wave.

How well you can surf the waves depends a lot on the wind direction relative to the wave direction. Usually the waves come from roughly the same direction as the wind, but as the wind oscillates back and forth we see situations where the directions of the wind and the waves are no longer aligned. Other times the wind may die and then come from a different direction while the direction of the waves remains constant. You'll notice at these times that it's much easier to surf the waves on one tack than on the other, because the wind angle allows you to sail at a lower angle on one tack that better aligns you with the waves. My advice when this happens is to prioritize sailing on the tack on which it's easier to surf the waves. If you notice this trend before others and gybe onto the correct tack, you'll jump away from the fleet.

What this usually also means is that your fastest mode of sailing is different on each tack downwind. For example, let's say there's medium wind and a significant left shift. Now, on starboard tack you have a header, which aligns you well with the waves. The waves are now much easier to catch, so you realize that your fastest mode downwind is relatively low because you are trying to catch as many waves as possible. Once you gybe, however, you are on a new tack and lifted, which makes catching waves virtually impossible.

Understanding that you cannot surf the waves any more, you realize that now your fastest mode downwind is to sail a small high mode so that you can power over the waves, and so you adjust to sailing a higher, more powerful mode.

As you can see, the wind direction relative to the waves greatly determines whether or not we can surf the waves. In an oscillating breeze, this actually makes the waves your greatest tool for determining what shift you have on the downwind, even more so than your compass. Is it easier to surf waves on this tack versus the other? If yes, you're headed, and if not, you're lifted. You can see this just by looking at the angle of your bow to the waves in front of you. Using this information, get on the headed tack if you can. It's true, as I mentioned before, that staying in pressure and having a good tactical position are both generally more important than sailing according to the shifts on the downwind, but all other things being equal, getting onto the headed tack will help you surf more waves and make those small speed gains.

If you are consistently faster than the waves, head up to a hotter angle to power over them. Think of waves as ladder rungs of the racecourse. When you're trying to surf waves, you can only go as fast as the wave itself. But if you're passing waves, you're passing ladder rungs on the

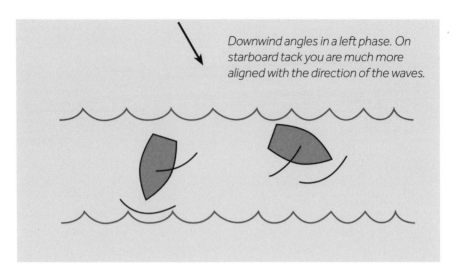

Downwind angles in a left phase. On starboard tack you are much more aligned with the direction of the waves.

downwind and you're making huge gains on the boats that aren't.

GYBING

Recognizing that every boat gybes differently, let's look at some of the basic principles of gybing that apply to all racing boats:

1 Begin the gybe at full speed, surfing a wave if possible
2 Minimize your turn
3 Know your exit angle

First of all, when gybing in all conditions speed is your friend. Have you ever tried to gybe in strong wind but the boat feels heavy and slow in the water, you've headed dead downwind and you're pulling on the mainsheet but the boom just doesn't want to come over? Then, the bow dives into the next wave, the sails load up even more with the pressure, and you get that feeling that something bad is about to happen? This is the

product of trying to gybe with low speed. There's lots of pressure in the sails, the boat is nose diving into the waves, it feels unstable and unbalanced, and the boat is difficult to steer. If you try to gybe from low speed in light wind you will lose at least a few boat lengths of distance, as you have to head up to a very high angle after the gybe to rebuild your speed – in strong wind this sort of gybe will most likely end in a broach or a capsize. So, before you even begin your gybe, first build high boat speed by even heading up to a small high mode, doing a few pumps and getting on a wave. When you gybe while surfing down a wave you'll be amazed at how little pressure there is in the sails, how responsive the helm feels, and consequently, how easy it is to gybe.

Your goal in the gybe is to minimize the turn. Once you have high boat speed, use that speed to head down a few degrees to slightly below your VMG angle, on a wave if possible, while maintaining your speed. From there, begin a steady turn through the gybe, pressing the windward side of the boat, rotating or flipping the kite, flipping the main, flattening the boat after the roll and accelerating forward with a pump on the main, whatever specific techniques your boat requires. As you steer to your new angle, head up according to your speed. If you successfully maintained high boat speed throughout the gybe, you may be able to complete the gybe on your VMG angle on the new tack. If you lost some speed you will need to head to a higher angle to rebuild that speed before dropping down to your VMG angle – the amount you must head up is in proportion to the amount of speed that you lost. Complete the gybe and the exchange of all the lines and sheets between crew members, rebuild high boat speed, do a few pumps on the main, and reassess your position. If you made a mistake – you lost the kite, or did a crash gybe, or otherwise lost all your speed – then you must pay the price of heading up to a higher angle to rebuild the flow.

Finally, depending on your boat speed, the sea state and the wind condition, know your exit angle. In medium and strong wind conditions your goal is to gybe to a relatively low mode, surfing a wave throughout the gybe if possible and maintaining high boat speed

so that you can gybe to your VMG angle without the need to head up to rebuild your speed. In very light wind, recognize that you are (in most boats) sailing much higher angles downwind already, so your goal is to actually make that giant turn from high angle to high angle as quickly but also as smoothly as possible while maintaining as much power in the boat as you can, with open sails, constant leeward heel, and smooth movements in the boat.

As you might imagine, the first step of executing successful gybes is perfecting it when you are sailing alone. When you are sailing in the open sea by yourselves it is easier to do a perfect gybe, and if you train hard you will have very successful gybes. But in a race, the tactical element of the gybe comes into play. When you are sailing in the mix of the fleet, you need to have different types of gybes in your toolbox: gybe from high mode to low mode, gybe from low mode to high mode, gybe from low mode to low mode, gybe from high mode to high mode. You have to adjust the type of gybe you are doing, sometimes while you are gybing. Let's say you begin a gybe and the boat behind you syncs a gybe above you to cover your air – you'll have to change the exit mode of the gybe to either a high mode to clear your air to windward, or soak low deeply in the exit of the gybe to build some separation and find clear air on the leeward side. How you adjust your gybes, or your other manoeuvres such as sets and douses, depends on the actions of your opponents. To have successful manoeuvres in any situation in the race, we have to achieve the level of being able to adjust our sets, gybes, or douses mid-manoeuvre according to other boats and other variables in the race.

DYNAMIC SITUATIONS

Whenever an opponent engages with you, you have an opportunity to defend or attack. This is what I call a 'dynamic situation', and you will engage in many dynamic situations throughout a given downwind as either the leader or as the boat behind. These situations require you to be ready at any time to change your type of sailing, whether it's attacking in the window of an opportunity or defending against the attacking action of the opponent.

Making the right moves in dynamic situations is all about thinking ahead and knowing how you want to position yourself now so that you have a strong position in later parts of the downwind. For example, if you know you want to stay on one tack for a long time you'll be sure to defend against any attacking boats heading up to roll you to windward. If you know

that you will be gybing shortly, you'll use all your speed to soak low, almost to the point of the boat behind you rolling over you, so that you can gybe to a clear lane. As you near the zone of a leeward mark, you'll put yourself in an overlapped position with another boat to take the inside.

New situations develop all the time, and even when you and other boats are just sailing straight and not making any moves on each other, just by sailing across the course your tactical priorities are changing. A good example of this is when you cross the midline, the imaginary line running straight upwind from the leeward mark that divides the racecourse in half.[14] Just by sailing on starboard with another boat and crossing the midline from the left to the right side of the course (looking downwind), your priorities change completely. Now, as the outside boat (the boat on the right) or as the boat ahead, you are starting to think about finding a time to gybe, while before you were more focused on boat speed and keeping clear air.

While keeping high boat speed is generally assumed to be the first priority, in some tactical dynamic situations you actually want to slow the boat down in order to maintain a favourable position relative to another boat – when you're in a

---

[14] See *Step 1: Gather Information* and *The 80/20 Rule* to learn more about the midline.

When sailing downwind you are always thinking about your relative position to other boats, to maintain clear air, have freedom to gybe, proactively position yourself for the next situation, etc.

sandwich between two or more other boats on either side of you, for example. In my philosophy, being in a sandwich is never a good position. To escape from a sandwich or to prevent becoming trapped between two boats ahead of you, you actually want to slow down. Instead of sailing forward into the bad air of the next boat, you want to slow down a bit, keep your bow free, and stay in clear air, so that you keep control over the boats behind you, and when an opportunity to gybe out of that sandwich comes your way you can take it.

These are examples of how your tactical priorities are constantly changing, and so you must continually ask yourselves how you can position your boat to take advantage of the next event in the race, whether that's a long starboard or port, a gybe, or a leeward mark rounding. It's all about looking ahead and anticipating what your position will be in the minutes ahead. Manoeuvre your boat now into the position that will give you the best chance of success further down the leg.

HALF AN ANGLE

The Half an Angle rule is an extremely important concept to remember in both the downwind and the reach legs. Following this rule helps you defend, as a leader, against a boat behind you trying to roll over you.

A boat rolls over you on the downwind when they head up behind you, get between the wind and your sails, sail fast while blocking all your wind, and gain the advantage. It is quite clear that in most situations (unless, for example, you're about to gybe, you're making separation on an extreme low mode, or you're about to round a mark) you want to prevent boats from rolling over you on the downwind. The opponent's sails block all of your air, you lose the pressure in our sails completely, and they end up coming even with you on the windward side and will likely pass you. When you get rolled like this, you not only lose one boat and a lot of distance, but you also lose all your options. You can no longer head up for better pressure, position, or speed without sailing into the shade of the windward boat. Depending on the position, the windward boat may force you to sail low and slow, allowing for more boats from behind to roll you over. All it takes sometimes, especially on the reach, is for one boat to roll you over, and then as you sit there with no pressure, a train of windward boats all connected bow to stern rolls over you, choking all your air and leaving no opportunity to regain your lane. For these reasons, it is incredibly important that you protect your windward lane, in most situations on the downwind and especially on the reach. Here, the Half an Angle rule is a big help.

The Half an Angle rule says that when a boat following behind you heads up to roll over you, head up by half of the angle that they headed up. This strikes a good balance between heading up enough so that you defend your clear air, but also continuing to go forward and separate while your opponent loses distance by sailing high.

Half an angle, however, is just a guideline. In some situations you need to head up much higher, actually matching their angle, in order not to get rolled, while in other situations you only need to head up very little. How much you actually head up depends on three things:

1 Your distance to the next mark

Remember, on the downwind the boats behind have the advantage because they can use their shade of bad air as a weapon to slow down the boats ahead of them. As a boat ahead, understand where another boat's area of bad air is and do not allow that boat to roll over you or put you in their bad air, except in specific situations.

When an attacking boat behind you heads up to roll over you, head up by half of their angle.

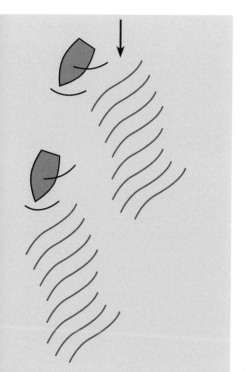

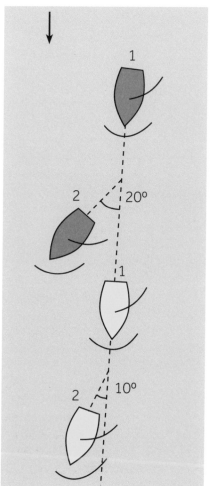

2 Your distance from the boat behind you

3 Your relative speed

The closer you are to the next mark, the less you need to head up in response to an attacking boat. Why? Well, assuming you already have the position you want, such as the inside position at the mark, the less it matters whether another boat rolls you over. You're so close to the mark that whether or not they block your wind, you'll still be ahead of them at the mark because you have the inside position. As you approach a leeward mark or a reach mark, the Half an Angle rule becomes less and less relevant, so you can sail closer to your VMG angle. Once you're already in the zone (the three boat lengths circle) of the mark, Half an Angle does not apply at all because the rounding order is already fixed. If you're far from the next mark, however, you want to be sure that you protect your windward lane at all costs, so that you're in a clear lane for all the distance left to sail.

The less distance between you and the boat behind you, the more you must head up to defend your windward side. The more distance there is between you, the less you should head up. This makes sense, right? Imagine you've just rounded the windward mark onto the downwind with a boat on your tail, and that boat suddenly steers higher to try to roll over you. With only a boat length

or two of separation, you've pretty much got to match their angle, wait for them to give up, and then bear away yourself. But if there's ten boat lengths between you and your opponent heads up, you're not so worried about them putting you in the shade and rolling over you, so only head up a small amount, and prioritize making separation as they lose distance on their higher angle.

Finally, when a boat behind heads up to try to roll you over, look at your relative speed. Now that they've headed up, is your opponent going much faster than you? If so, head up more, not only to defend your windward lane, but maybe that higher angle is actually faster downwind. Conversely, if your opponent heads up and does not gain much speed forward, don't head up so much. Do what you need to do to defend your lane, but if the high mode is obviously not working, don't spend more time than you need to sailing high.

For experienced sailors this Half an Angle rule is already something that they naturally do, even if they've never seen it described specifically in a book as it is here. For beginners, take note of this rule and remember what factors to weigh whenever a boat behind you tries to roll over you. It will come naturally with experience, but as with all the information in this book, reading it here will give you a head start on developing this skill and your improvement will be much faster.

Chapter 15

DOWNWIND DISTRIBUTION

Let's now look at each area of the downwind leg more closely. Like the upwind, I like to divide the downwind into three different stages.

THE FIRST STAGE: 'TOP ROUNDING' (FIRST 5%)

The first stage of the downwind is the Top Rounding. In this stage of the downwind you should focus mostly on your tactical position relative to your opponents and on your boat handling. The tactical element here is a bigger focus than the strategic element. Going into the top rounding you should have a game plan for the downwind and for the type of mark rounding/set you will do. This plan must be made prior to rounding the mark, a process I call the hand-off.[15] Your goal in this stage is to have the right position relative to your opponents so you can focus on your boat speed, technique, and prevent any unnecessary fights in the next stage, which is the majority of downwind.

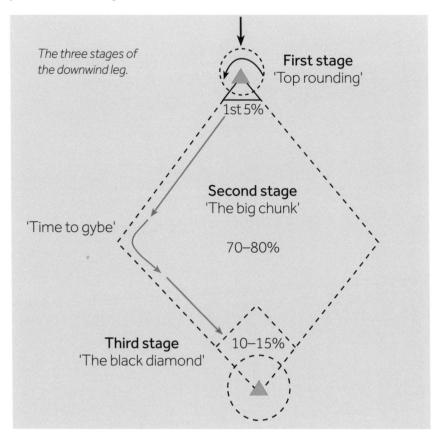

The three stages of the downwind leg.

First stage
'Top rounding'

1st 5%

Second stage
'The big chunk'

70–80%

'Time to gybe'

Third stage
'The black diamond'

10–15%

---

[15] See *The Top Mark* to learn more about the 'handoff'.

THE SECOND STAGE: 'THE BIG CHUNK' (70-80%)

I call the second stage the Big Chunk. This makes up the majority of the downwind, and it is dedicated to high boat speed and strategy. This part of the downwind is the part that becomes more strategic, and less tactical. Any fight with another boat, tactical sailing, or wrong decision-making is most likely an outcome of mistakes in the prior stage.

This stage is mainly the time to execute your strategy and boat speed: curving, surfing waves, getting to more pressure, sailing on the headed tack, getting to favourable current, etc. However, there are tactical elements that you must also keep in mind in order to have the optimal position relative to the other boats. Within this middle stage is also the 'Time to Gybe', another situation where you must prioritize your relative position.

THE THIRD STAGE: 'THE BLACK DIAMOND' (LAST 10-15%)

I call the final stage of the downwind the Black Diamond. This is the diamond-shaped area created by the laylines to the leeward mark on the last 10–15% of the downwind. This stage of the downwind becomes tactical sailing

again – your relative position to other boats is everything. I like to think that this is the most critical area of the downwind. Naturally, this area has a tendency to merge the entire fleet into one very small crowded area. This is where big gains and losses are made. One small mistake can cause a loss of many boats, distance, control of the situation, and a bad energy or rhythm that can send you into a negative spiral for the rest of the race. On the other hand, make a good move at the mark and you can pass many boats as you turn back upwind.

As you approach the leeward mark(s) you must do another hand-off to prepare yourself for the next leg. (In most racecourses the next leg is an upwind or a reach.) The upwind hand-off involves choosing a leeward gate mark and making an initial game plan for the next upwind. In terms of rounding the mark, ask yourself: Are we coming in at an advantage or a disadvantage towards the mark? Are the sailing rules in the upcoming situation advantageous to us or not? What can I do to get an inside overlap on the boats ahead and break overlap with the boats behind going into the zone? What will happen in this rounding and what is my best option? In the area of the Black Diamond, if you know how to read the situation and predict what scenarios will play out in the next 30 seconds, you will have an opportunity to gain significantly.

Chapter 16

THE FIRST STAGE: 'TOP ROUNDING'

The Top Rounding is the very first stage of the downwind, approximately the first 5%. Although this may seem like only a very brief part of the downwind, there is a lot more going on in this stage than simply turning downwind. This stage includes bearing away around the windward mark, setting the spinnaker (if applicable), and most importantly, positioning yourself relative to the boats around you according to the plan you make during the hand-off.

In this stage of the downwind you should focus mostly on your tactical position relative to your opponents and on your boat handling. This is such a crowded and hectic area that there is not much else you could effectively focus on. Where are my opponents? How do I want to position myself around my opponents? The tactical element here is a bigger focus than the strategic element. For this moment you can actually put the strategy – the shifts, the pressure – in the back of your mind and only focus on the boat-on-boat. Your end goal in this stage is to have the right position relative to your opponents so you can focus on your boat speed, technique, and prevent any unnecessary fights in the next stage, which is the majority of downwind. To this end, going into the top rounding you should have a game plan for the downwind and for the type of mark rounding/set you will do. In other words, you need to know ahead how you want to position yourself relative to other boats. I call the process of making this plan for the next leg the 'hand-off'.

The top rounding is the first stage of the downwind.

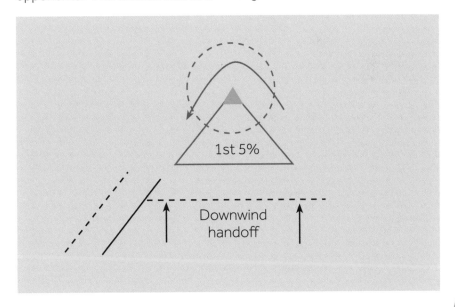

1st 5%

Downwind handoff

THE DOWNWIND HAND-OFF

The hand-off must be done before rounding the windward mark, usually at some point while you are sailing on the starboard layline fetching the mark. After all, if you were to round the mark and *then* start asking yourself 'Where is the next mark?' 'Where is the next pressure?' 'How do I want to position myself?' the outcome might well be disastrous. So be sure you have this discussion with your team before the rounding.

Here are some questions to discuss with your team that will determine your game plan:

✳ First, find the next mark. Are you looking for a reach mark, or a downwind gate, or something else? Let's assume the next leg is a downwind. Where is the leeward mark? Is it biased to the right, or to the left?

✳ Is the downwind skewed to one side? In other words, is one tack downwind longer than the other? This may be due to the placement of the leeward mark, or a wind shift. One way to see which is the longer gybe is with a visual inspection. This works well if you can clearly see the leeward mark. However, an even easier way to figure this out is to think about the previous upwind and recall if you spent more time on starboard or port tack. If you sailed more time upwind on port, then starboard will be the longer tack downwind. If you sailed more time on starboard, then port will be longer on the downwind.

✳ What is the phase of the shift right now? What is the headed tack on the downwind?

✳ What is the racecourse strategy? Is one side of the downwind favoured? Look around you at the clouds and the pressure on the water. Where is the next pressure? Does one side have favourable current? What side was winning on the upwind?

✳ Where is the fleet in front of you? Did they all set on starboard, or did they all gybe set? Are the boats spread out or are they all following the leader? If they are all going in one direction, is there a good reason?

Once you have gathered this information about the downwind, it's time to make a game plan. Ask yourself: What is my plan for the first part of the downwind? Where do I want to position myself? When rounding the windward mark, I like to break down the rounding into four basic types of sets: High Mode Set, Optimum VMG Set, Low Mode Set, and Gybe Set. You must decide which type of set you will do during your hand-off so that you know exactly what the plan is when you round the mark. Each one is ideal for a certain situation as I will soon

Finn sailors round the windward mark to a short reach to the offset mark.

By this time you should have a plan for your downwind, and this is a great time to make sure your plan is still optimal and correct.

explain. For now, the tactical and strategic principles to know for the first part of the downwind are these:

1 Get on the longer tack downwind first. The more skewed the downwind is (say, 80% on starboard and 20% on port) the more important it is that you get onto the longer tack immediately and protect your windward lane.

2 Get on the headed tack. If there was a significant wind shift before the rounding, one tack will be a much more direct course to the leeward mark while the other tack will take you sideways.

3 Go to the favoured side. Look for whether one side has more pressure or favourable current.

Finally, in addition to our tactical position, I'd like to touch on the proper boat handling and technique for bearing away around the windward mark. The main goal here is to maintain high boat speed. All too often I see sailors ripping upwind, but then they round the mark and when they go to set the kite, all the sailors' heads go into the boat and the boat just stops. They float downwind, and only when the kite is up their boat starts sailing again. Yes, you have to set the kite when you round the mark, but that doesn't mean everyone in the boat needs

to only think about hoisting the kite as fast as possible. You need to prioritize high boat speed around the mark. As you bear away, the boat should be as flat as possible. In the 470 and many other dinghies, a small amount of windward heel actually helps the boat bear away around the mark with minimal use of the rudder and maintain its speed. Trying to bear away with leeward heel is very slow. In fact, for many boats such as skiffs and large keelboats in strong wind, it is physically impossible for the boat to bear away if there is any leeward heel. The sails of course must be eased, the jib may be eased at the same rate as the main, if not slightly ahead. Be sure that all sail controls – vang, cunningham, backstay, etc – are adjusted before the mark. Once you are on a downwind, the crew may work on hoisting the kite but the helm must maintain high boat speed. Make sure the main is powered up, stay on a fast angle, make sure no boat behind you is covering your air, surf a wave if you can. As a coach watching races from the outside I see how sometimes one boat might take one or two seconds longer to hoist their kite than the others, but they actually achieve a better result around the mark because they have a better technique of maintaining their speed and position.

There are four basic types of sets you can choose from when rounding the mark, which we will cover now. The key is choosing which one to do in a given situation.

SET 1: HIGH MODE

The first type of set is the high mode set. Think of this as the set for a 'long starboard'. When there is a big left shift or the course is very skewed, starboard tack can be much longer than port on the downwind. A significant shift, strong current or out of place mark can make the downwind 80–90% on starboard, or in some cases even 100%. You will experience races where you can make the leeward mark after the top rounding without gybing. In these situations, in addition to holding on starboard, you want to be in the windward position with full control over your opponents

and avoid fights with any boats behind you. Let's first think from the perspective of the boat ahead. To prevent any boats behind you being tempted to take you to a fight (this is when a boat behind you heads up to try to roll over you), stay on a high mode around the mark. Even continue upwind for a half boat length after the mark if you have a boat on your tail. Your opponents will think 'What is this crazy sailor doing, they are not going in the right direction', and they will head down and make some separation on your leeward side. Then you can bear away in a strong windward position and trap your opponent who is now overlapped to leeward of you, and then you are comfortably pressing down on them for the long 90% starboard. This way you avoid tempting any

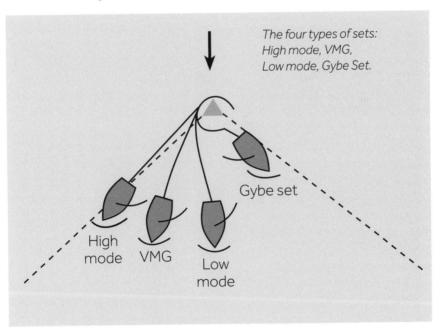

The four types of sets:
High mode, VMG,
Low mode, Gybe Set.

Gybe set

High
mode VMG
Low
mode

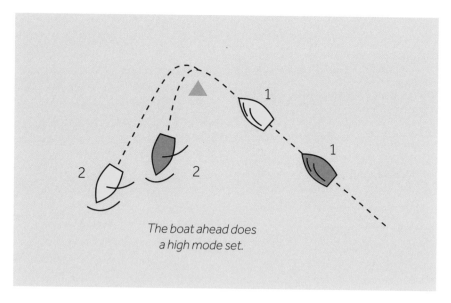

*The boat ahead does
a high mode set.*

boats to head up on you around the mark, so you can press low, force your opponents to go on a low angle, and avoid a gybe or a long port tack towards the end of the downwind.

As the boat ahead, you need to protect your windward side from any boats behind you heading high. If a boat does try to roll you, you must head up to defend against them. This high mode fight is necessary to protect your lane – the problem is that it slows both you and your opponent down, meaning other boats are gaining distance and potentially passing both of you. The goal, therefore, is to prevent these fights from happening in the first place. Especially if you know there is an aggressive boat behind you who you suspect will try to roll you on the set, stay extra high around the top mark. By taking those few extra boat lengths to go

extra high, the boat behind won't be tempted to try to roll you, and you'll have the strong windward position. 'Lose a few feet in the beginning and gain dozens of boats in the long run.'

Let's now switch our perspective. As a boat behind, if you see that the boat ahead of you is not staying high and doesn't seem aware of the boats behind them, try to roll over them! The closer you are behind them, the easier this is to do. Just know that they will most likely head up to defend from your attack, so it's important to decisively secure the windward position. Don't just point your bow a few feet above their stern with the plan of slowly rolling them, because when they head up to defend you will be forced to either give up or engage in a costly fight. Instead, head up hard before they can react, so that you end up a full boat length to windward of

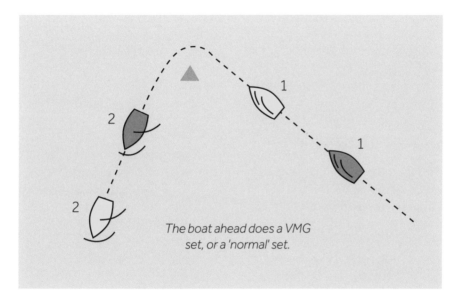

The boat ahead does a VMG set, or a 'normal' set.

them while they're still setting the kite. (Remember, prioritize your position over quickly setting the spinnaker.) Don't even give them a hope of heading up to defend. Then, they will soak low to make a separation and you can press down on them for the rest of the long starboard.

As both the leader and the follower, establish the position you want early and decisively so that you don't have to fight for it later.

SET 2: OPTIMUM VMG

This second type of set is the Optimum VMG set. Think of this as how you would set if you were racing alone – you would round the mark and set the kite on your best VMG angle, not too high and not too low. This is the most common set that we use.

You use this set when: you want to continue on starboard and

the downwind is square. You would like to have slight control over the boats behind you. You want to continue for quite some time, without any fights, but potentially you might want to gybe in the near future. Finally, you want to avoid any bad air from the boats behind you. To do this, you round the mark on an average downwind angle and position yourself somewhere between directly ahead of the bow of the boat behind you and a few feet to windward of their line. This position slightly to windward ensures that you have clear air and avoids tempting the boat behind to head up on you, while still keeping access to gybe.

This set is the most common because you use it when you want to keep your options open. When there is no very clear strategy you don't know how long you will continue on starboard or how early you will gybe, so you want to maintain some flexibility. With this set you can continue on starboard sailing fast in clear air, but you also have access to gybe onto port and reconnect with the middle of the downwind.

SET 3: LOW MODE

The third type of set is the low mode set. You use this set when you want to continue on starboard around the mark, but you most likely want to gybe in the near future. To do this, you want to round the mark onto a low angle downwind, sometimes even by-the-lee in boats with symmetrical kites. Maintain speed around the mark as best you can and have the best set possible, aiming to sail forward and mostly lower than the opponents. You don't want to be rolled right away going around the mark (maybe a bit after it's okay, but know that you're then committed to an early gybe), but you do want to have access

to gybe onto port. You want to position yourself somewhere between directly ahead of the bow of the boat behind you and to leeward of their line.

One common situation when you would do this low mode set is when there is a big left shift making starboard tack headed downwind, but the leeward mark is more biased to the left of the downwind. You would want to stay on starboard at the beginning of the downwind to use some of the left shift, but as soon as the wind shifts back right you want to have access to gybe so that you can be the first bow going to the left-hand side of the downwind (looking downwind, of course).

Another time you might use the low mode set is when the leeward mark is slightly biased to the left or when there is some left strategy, but the starboard layline to the windward mark behind you is very crowded with many boats. You still want to go left, but

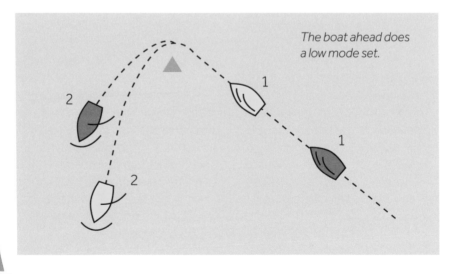

The boat ahead does a low mode set.

you would rather not do a gybe set, because you want to avoid the traffic and the cone of very bad air created by the fleet still sailing upwind. Also, most boats on average lose 1–2 boat lengths of distance with a gybe set. By setting low on starboard and planning to do an early gybe once you set the kite and sail some distance from the mark, you are staying in better wind and gaining distance forward on boats who did a gybe set.

SET 4: GYBE SET

The fourth type of set is the gybe set. We use this set when there is a big advantage to the left side of the downwind (looking downwind). This may be a large right shift, or current flowing across the course, or the leeward mark may be very far left, making the downwind leg 80–100% on port tack. There may be much more pressure on the left looking downwind. Whatever the reason is for the big left-side advantage, we want to get onto port tack as quickly as possible, be in the windward position with full control over our opponents, and avoid fights with any boats behind us. You want full control over your opponents on port tack, so you can press low on your opponents and avoid a gybe at the end of the downwind or a long starboard tack. You might have noticed the idea here is essentially the same as the high mode set on starboard. The only difference is that we are first gybing onto port tack before setting the kite and defending the position.

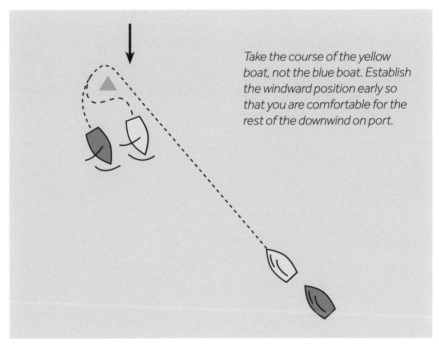

Take the course of the yellow boat, not the blue boat. Establish the windward position early so that you are comfortable for the rest of the downwind on port.

One thing to keep in mind here is that even if you execute a perfect gybe set, you still lose about 1–2 boat lengths of distance. So make sure you are sure that you have a good reason to gybe, because doing so must give you back these 1–2 boat lengths and even more.

To execute the gybe set, continue to bear away around the mark so that you gybe onto port tack. It is very important that you are the inside boat at the mark so that you have the windward position after you complete the gybe. Finish the gybe on a high mode (before you even hoist the kite) to gain some speed, height and pressure. After all, most likely there is a wind shadow from the boats sailing upwind on the starboard layline. Most importantly, however, make a tight turn around the mark and stay high so that you trap your opponents to your leeward side. Although you may lose some distance here initially, you are now securely in the windward position and you have the entire downwind on port to press down on your opponents. Remember, 'lose a few feet at the beginning and gain dozens of boat lengths in the long run'.

REASSESS

Now that you've completed the top rounding, you should be more relaxed and have a comfortable position. Once you have space around you, time and a clear mind, look around and reassess your position, your surroundings and the next leg. Did anything change? In particular, look at:

❋ Your position relative to your opponents

❋ Your speed and angle relative to your opponents

❋ Where the mark is relative to you and your opponents

✳ Where the next pressure is

✳ The phase of the shift

Conditions on the racecourse can change quickly, so you must be able to reassess the conditions and adapt your plan if necessary. You may now be in a different shift than when you rounded the mark. In an offshore wind especially, the side of the course where the next pressure is coming from

A fleet rounds a mark and sets the kites for the downwind. The boats follow a variety of strategies, some staying high, some going low, and some gybing.

can change very quickly. From here you can decide whether to continue or gybe. Continue to look at the marks ahead of you, the fleet around you and the pressure behind you. You are now on the Big Chunk.

225

Chapter 17

THE SECOND STAGE: 'THE BIG CHUNK'

I call the second stage of the downwind the Big Chunk. This makes up the majority of the downwind, and it is dedicated to high boat speed and strategy. This part of the downwind is the part that becomes more strategic, and less tactical. Any fight with another boat, tactical sailing, or wrong decision-making is most likely an outcome of mistakes in the previous stage.

One of the topics in sailing strategy is how we sail the course. Let's first zoom out for a moment to look at the big picture of the downwind. Our downwind tracking should more or less resemble the letter 'S'. I call this the 'S Curve'. There are a lot of different approaches to how the downwind should look, but the S curve is a way I like to visualize the path of a boat racing downwind.

As you can see from these S curves, there are many different ways a boat may choose to sail the downwind. There is no one correct S curve. What is common in each of these S curves, however, is that following the top rounding, each boat is doing only 2–3 gybes. On average, you should do only

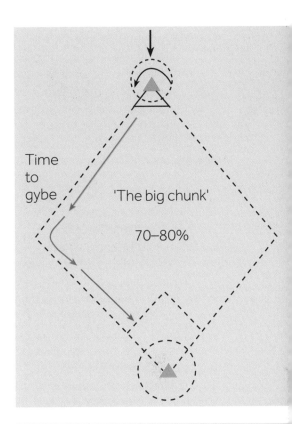

Our downwind tracking should look roughly like an S curve. You can see how each of the four S curves in this diagram correspond with different ways one might sail the downwind. For example, staying high and gybing late, or sailing low and gybing early, etc.

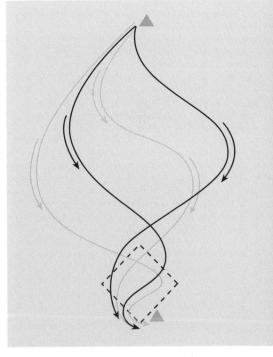

2–3 gybes on the downwind until you reach the Black Diamond (at which point things become much more hectic and you may need to do more gybes to optimize your position for the mark rounding). Obviously, the number of gybes may change with the conditions – light vs strong wind, shifty vs steady. You may do one or two more gybes in some situations, and sometimes you may only do one gybe, but in general the S Curve is the type of tracking I would like to see in the downwind as a coach. If you are doing more than 2–3 gybes in a downwind before you reach the bottom Black Diamond, something is most likely wrong. Think about where you can reduce your gybes along the way.

The S curve, of course, will look different for different types of boats, but it is still a great way to visualize the downwind in any boat and understand how many gybes you should do. For skiffs, asymmetric kites and other boats

that sail high angles, their S curves will be much wider. For Lasers, Finns, and other boats that sail very low angles, their S curves will be much narrower, but there will still be a clear S curve in their downwind tracking.

Let's now look at the laylines downwind. Remember the '80/20 Rule' from the upwind chapter? This rule applies on the downwind as well! It asks that you always leave at least 20% of the layline available to you at all times. In other words, avoid sailing all the way to a layline and having your course to the mark be 100% on one tack. Always have your course to the mark at least 20% on one tack and no more than 80% on the other tack (the 80/20 ratio).

You leave this extra distance so that you avoid getting caught on the layline, just as you do on the upwind. Just as boats will tack on you on the upwind and push you to the layline, boats behind you will gybe on you on the downwind, and

you want to have the space to take another step towards the layline to get out of this situation if needed. In addition, on the downwind you have a greater variety of angles, so if a boat gybes on you and you both end up soaking low you may actually end up over the layline. That is why it is so important to leave this space before the layline available to you, especially in a crowded fleet where clear air is difficult to find.

Again, the Big Chunk is mainly the time to execute your strategy and boat speed: curving, surfing waves, getting to pressure, sailing on the headed tack, getting to favourable current, etc. However, there are tactical elements that you must also keep in mind in order to have an optimal position relative to the other boats. For one, you must find the tricky balance of going to the outside of the fleet to get clear air and going back into the middle to stay between the boats behind you

The timing of the gybe and the position after the gybe are some of the most important elements of downwind tactics.

and the next mark. On the upwind leg this is easy because the boats ahead have the advantage of clear air. To stay ahead of a pack of boats, simply position yourself directly upwind of them. Then they have no leverage on you, and are likely losing distance by sailing in your bad air. On the downwind we have the opposite situation. As a leader, you are vulnerable to the bad air from the pack behind you. In a big fleet, especially in the top 50% of the downwind, the entire middle of the course often has a wind shadow created by the fleet above. By sailing high and on the outside of the fleet you will have better air, but you also lose control over the fleet. They may get a gust of wind or a shift that you don't get and come strong, or other boats may gybe on you when you

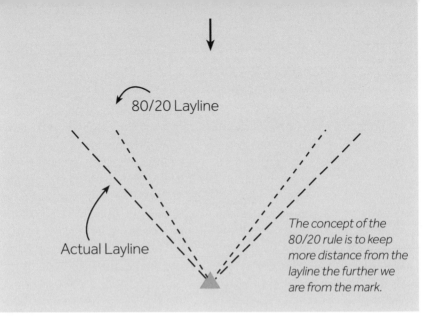

80/20 Layline

Actual Layline

The concept of the 80/20 rule is to keep more distance from the layline the further we are from the mark.

gybe to go back to the middle. On the other hand, position yourself too much downwind of a crowded pack and you will not be able to execute your optimal boat speed. This is the tricky situation you have as leaders that makes your positioning downwind so important.

To have a successful downwind as a boat in front, then, you must have a very good awareness of where there is clear air and of the laylines to the leeward mark. On the first half of the downwind it is almost always a good idea to be on an edge of the fleet, but as it comes time to gybe back in, look for gaps in the fleet of boats behind you and find those lanes of good pressure that you can take back to the middle. Sail clean – the most important thing is that you don't get caught with a boat or pack of boats all sitting on you and slowing you down. Understand where the layline is so that you know whether you must gybe

soon to avoid getting caught on the layline, or if you can continue farther and make more separation from the fleet. Conversely, as a boat behind, recognize that you have the advantage of better pressure and clearer air. Recognize that you can pass a pack in front of you if you have a better position, so look for those opportunities. Catch a few boats here or there when they gybe on the layline. Take advantage of mistakes made by the boats in front of you.

Another way I like to look at my position is with the middle line. On the downwind leg, this is the imaginary line going straight upwind from the leeward mark or gate. If the course is square, this is the line between the leeward mark and the windward mark. It is important to pay attention to this line because you can use it to understand your priorities in a given position.

When you are on a tack and on a side of the downwind such

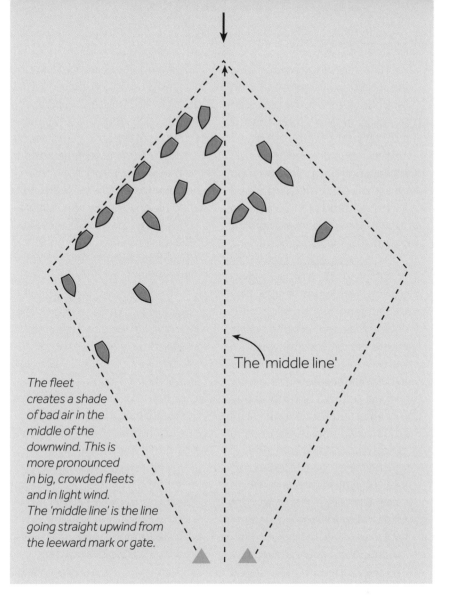

The 'middle line'

The fleet creates a shade of bad air in the middle of the downwind. This is more pronounced in big, crowded fleets and in light wind. The 'middle line' is the line going straight upwind from the leeward mark or gate.

that you are sailing *towards* the middle line, don't think too much about any upcoming gybes or tactical manoeuvres. Focus on sailing fast. You have a long distance before the next layline, so prioritize executing optimum boat speed over thinking ahead about your position.

Once we cross the middle line and are then sailing *away* from it, especially in the later

phase of the downwind that is naturally more crowded, we have to consider and prioritize more our relative position to our opponents. Realize that now that you have passed the middle line, any distance you sail forward brings you closer and closer to the layline to the leeward mark. This is the time to start looking at your position and be thinking about how you want to be positioned relative to the fleet for the upcoming gybe.

TIME TO GYBE

Within the Big Chunk is a key tactical moment (or rather, a range of time) which I call 'Time to Gybe'. This moment comes actually a few times during the downwind. Looking at the big picture, each of the 2–3 turns in the S Curve is a time to gybe. This is essentially a time in the downwind (usually when you are approaching a layline) where you will need to gybe in the near future. It's a critical point in the downwind where you must prioritize your relative position.

'Time to gybe'

'Time to Gybe' is how I refer to the brief range of time in which you need to gybe, usually because you are approaching a layline (pictured above) or for another tactical or strategic reason.

When you see that you will have to gybe soon, look at your relative position to your opponents and think about whether continuing to the layline is bad for you or good for you. Will you get caught on the gybe? Or are you pushing other boats to the layline? If you are not in a good position, gybe early and perhaps pay a small price now for a better position in the second half of the downwind.

Once we cross the middle line and are then sailing away from it, we are approaching the time to gybe, so we have to start to consider and prioritize our relative position to our opponents more. Chances are you're sailing on the edge of a pack of other boats. (Stay on the edges of packs of boats. Avoid being in the middle of a pack, or as I call it, 'in the

sandwich'. Being in the sandwich is never a good thing!) At this point ask yourself: Am I the outside or the inside boat relative to the middle of the course?

The basic principle is that as the inside boat and/or as the boat that is more in the back of the pack, your goal is to push your opponents all the way to the layline, and beyond if possible. If and when they gybe, you want to gybe on top of them and position yourself to windward of them, essentially catching them on the gybe. That way you are in the controlling position and sitting on them for the next long tack downwind. Do this successfully and you have the potential to make gains and likely pass the boats in front of you.

As a boat more on the outside

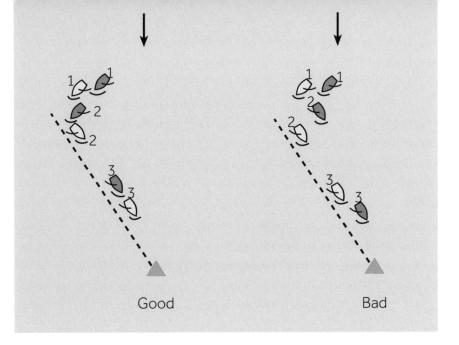

Good   Bad

Before we continue, what does it mean to get 'caught' on the gybe? This is when you gybe (most commonly you are on or close to the layline, although this can happen at any area of the downwind) and a boat or pack of boats on your tail sync a gybe on top of you, directly to windward, blocking your wind with their sails and giving you bad air. Getting caught on the gybe is incredibly costly, because for the rest of the downwind the boat to windward will be pressing down on you, and only once they have rolled you will you be free from their bad air and sailing fast again. As you can see, getting caught on the gybe can cost you many boat lengths of lost distance.

As the boat ahead, the only two methods of escaping your opponent's bad air once they catch you on the gybe are: sailing on a very low angle to create a lateral separation (not a good option if you are already on the layline); or, heading to a very high angle to cross through your opponent's bad air and position yourself in front of their bow, in clear air – a manoeuvre I call the 'cross'.

and/or in the front, your goal is not to get caught on the layline, but rather initiate the gybe back into the middle of the course in clear air, sailing fast. Since you want to be in a clear lane sailing back into the middle, you usually want to gybe before the boats behind you gybe (unless a significant portion of the pack behind you is gybing very early and you want to continue to make some separation). Usually you want to

initiate this gybe slightly before you are actually on the layline, before too many of the boats in the pack behind you are thinking about gybing, so that you have the best chance of being the first bow leading back into the middle without other boats gybing on top of you.

Especially as a boat in front, you will need some time to be aware of (or create) opportunities to have the freedom to gybe when you want. This is why having a strong awareness of how far you are from the middle line, how close you are to the laylines, and whether you have access to gybe helps you prepare for the upcoming gybe and the next steps ahead. Then, you have the time to really optimize your position before you gybe – maybe soak low to leeward of the boats on your tail so that you have access to gybe, and look for a good wave to surf during the gybe. Communicate with your team: 'Gybing on the next good wave.' It may take a few seconds to find that great wave to gybe on, but if you have a boat or pack of boats on your tail it can make all the difference. Sometimes that extra one or two boat lengths boost from gybing while surfing down a wave is all you need to cross that pack on port and successfully reconnect with the middle.

In general, when it's 'time to gybe', I recommend prioritizing the next tack/leg of the downwind over the perfect position now. Let's say you're sailing on starboard, approaching the right layline to the leeward mark: don't just sail all the way to the layline or even over it, gybe, and put yourself in the position where the pack behind you is gybing on top of you and then covering you for the entire rest of the downwind. Even if there are boats to leeward of you blocking you from making an easy gybe, don't fall into this trap. Instead, gybe onto port a little bit

> **EXPERT TIP**
> *I often like to think from the perspective of my opponents. I ask myself, what would I do if I were in their position? Understand that while you are pushing an outside boat to the layline, they will eventually try to gybe. When they do, you have to be ready for it.*

before the layline, duck behind a few starboard tackers, and be the first bow onto port tack, sailing fast in a clear lane. You'll pay this small price early on, but you'll soon see the pack of boats you ducked all gybe on or over the layline, all sailing in each other's bad air, and you have the entire rest of the downwind to squeeze down on them and put yourself in front before the leeward mark. Pay a small price earlier for a better position on the next tack.

Let's now look at a number of tactical situations you will commonly encounter on the Big Chunk.

No 1: On starboard, left side of the downwind, and to the right of your opponents This is quite an optimal situation. You have not crossed the midline, meaning that there is not yet any impending urgency to gybe. All you have to do is take advantage of every

We have to think ahead and proactively position ourselves for the 'time to gybe' moment of the downwind. This is especially true when we are closely leading a pack of boats.

opportunity (shift, gust of wind, surfing a wave, good relative speed, opponent's mistake, etc) to soak low and press down on your opponents towards the left layline (looking downwind). The more that you and your opponents sail a lower mode, the more you reduce the distance you'll have to sail on

port tack to get to the leeward mark, and the easier your life will be during the mark rounding.

No 2: On starboard, middle of the downwind, and to the right of your opponents Now that you have crossed the middle line, this is the stage when you want to

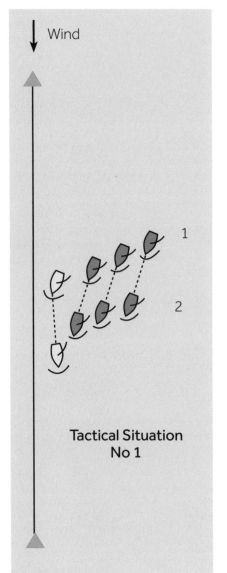

Tactical Situation
No 1

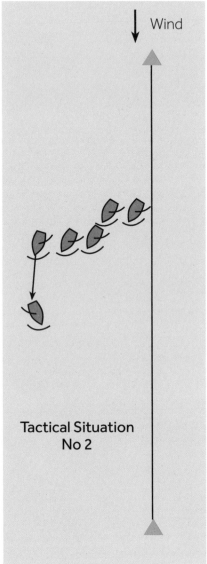

Tactical Situation
No 2

start thinking about your tactical position and take proactive steps for better positioning. The most important thing to understand here is that from this point on, any distance you sail forward brings you closer to the right layline, and there is a higher chance that you will get caught on the gybe. If you were to continue as you are, you would eventually end up on the right layline as an outside boat and you would be in a difficult position when it's time to gybe. Therefore, try to reposition yourself to the left-hand side of your opponents. Wait for an opportunity to gybe onto port (a gust, a long wave to gybe on, opening in the pack, lack of attention by your opponents) and cross to the left side of your opponents. This doesn't mean you are necessarily committing to the left-hand side of the downwind. All strategy being equal, you can always gybe back to starboard in the leeward position, and then you have the advantage to potentially push/lock your opponents on the right layline.

No 3: On starboard, right side of the downwind, and to the right of your opponents This situation is really bad! You are nearing the right layline, you are locked on the right-hand side of the downwind, and you have a long way to sail on port tack. You must try to gybe onto port in any way possible (while abiding by the Racing Rules of Sailing). Your goal is to gybe without getting caught

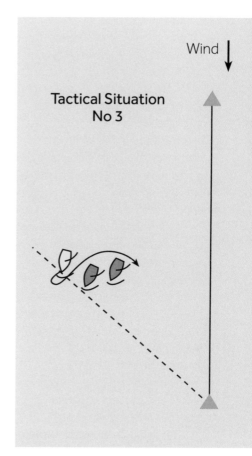

Tactical Situation No 3

Wind

on the gybe. The optimal option is to use any opportunity (gust, surfing a long wave, relative boat speed advantage, opponents are fighting or arguing) to sail lower than your opponents to leeward, to the point that you are on your opponents' bowline or even lower and in front so that you have free access to gybe and cross. There are other manoeuvres you can use at the high level, such as a 'surprise gybe' or 'fake gybe', in order to throw off your opponents and make this critical cross. If this cross is not possible, you must do a rough manoeuvre to gybe and duck behind the boats that are holding you (pictured above).

If you are successful with either of those options, you have the first bow to the left and everything is great. If you failed and got caught on the gybe, your goal is to sail on a high mode once the other boats have rolled you, pushing your opponents to the left layline (or rolling over them if they don't defend) and potentially have some more opportunities later on. Sometimes, if you had a more successful gybe than your opponent, you can soak low during the gybe and open a window of air between you and your opponent and use it for better relative boat speed (hopefully the opponent will get stuck with other boats to windward of him). Anyhow, you don't want to end up in the position where the windward boats are pressing down on you on the layline.

No 4: On starboard, right side of the downwind, and to the left of your opponents We now look from the perspective of the leeward position in a pack of boats on the right-hand side of the downwind. This is quite an optimal situation which you would like to maintain as long as possible. Try to push and lock the entire pack all the way to the layline, even a bit over the layline. Do this by sticking your bow to the leeward side of the stern of the next boat, so they cannot gybe. (It is very important that you close the gap

in this way to prevent the windward boat from escaping.) Hopefully this boat is holding the boat to windward of them from gybing, who is holding the boat above them from gybing, and then you are pushing the entire pack to the layline and you choose when to gybe. On starboard, consider your options and build scenarios – what would you do if the other boats try to gybe early before the layline, or duck behind you, or are gybing and crossing? If you successfully push the pack to the layline, great! Then gybe when you are on or slightly past the layline. The rest

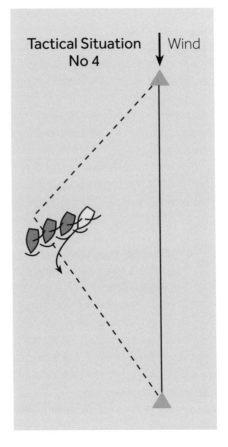

Tactical Situation No 4   Wind

of the pack is now over the layline and behind you (remember, they cannot gybe until you gybe), and you will easily lead them back to the leeward mark. If instead the pack is able to freely gybe in front of you, then you sync a gybe to windward of them when they gybe, so that you have the clear air and you are pressing down on the pack with your shade of bad air for the rest of the downwind.

No 5: On starboard, in the middle of the pack This is a bad position! You never want to be in the middle of a pack, or in the sandwich. It's better to be on the edge of a pack. For one, when you're in the sandwich you can't execute optimum boat speed. There will always be a boat to windward or to leeward blocking some of your air or messing with you, and you won't be able to curve or sail on the angles that you'd like. You won't be able to achieve your optimal VMG. Even if you are faster than the boats around you, you might surf a nice wave or get a gust and push forward a boat

length but then you'll be dragged back in line with your opponents by the pack's bad air that you just plunged into. As a result, you will only be as fast as the slowest boat in the pack.

Secondly, by sailing in the sandwich you can never win from any weather changes or other strategic factors. If the right side has a gust and the right-most boats in the pack are winning, you are not there. And if the left side has a gust or a shift and the left-most boats are winning, you are not there either! Avoid the sandwich and stay on the outside of the packs.

No 6: On port, left side of the downwind, and to the left of your opponents This given situation is very similar to situation No 3, but this time you are doing a gybe to starboard. Since starboard has the right of way over port, you have much more flexibility to control the timing of the gybe, because all you have to do is flip the boom to the other side of the boat and you have the right of way. (Of course,

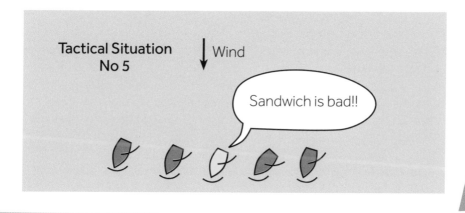

Tactical Situation No 5

Wind

Sandwich is bad!!

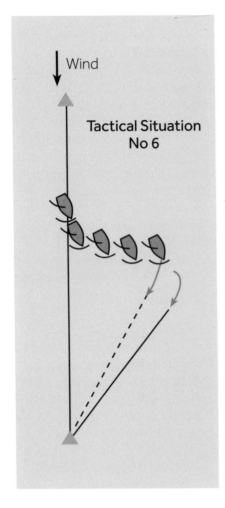

Wind

**Tactical Situation
No 6**

have clear air after you gybe. My recommendation is that you make use of your variety of modes and angles on the downwind to achieve this goal. Look at how you are positioned relative to your opponents and identify if it would be easier to keep clear air by either: (1) gybing to a high mode and sailing high to cross and break through the bad air of the boats that gybe on you, or (2) gybing to a low mode and sailing very low to make some separation from the windward boats (pictured above). If you plan on gybing to a high mode in order to keep clear air, soak low on port and optimize your position before the gybe as you sail towards the layline. Then, gybe on the layline or even a bit over the layline, so that you punch out from the pack on a direct course to the zone of the leeward mark. If you plan on gybing to a low mode in order to keep clear air, gybe a bit before the layline so that you have room to soak low and separate from your opponents without overstanding the leeward mark (pictured above).

For each of the above tactical situations when you are on starboard tack, there is a corresponding situation on port tack. The big difference, as you see in this situation, is that you are gybing onto starboard. This gives you more flexibility rules-wise, and the timing of the gybe is easier and depends mostly on you. Other than that, all the same tactical ideas apply.

you must give the other boats room to keep clear according to Rule 15.) As the left-most boat in this situation, getting caught on the gybe is the greatest threat. In this situation, as soon as you gybe and gain the right of way over the rest of the pack, the most likely outcome is that your opponents will all gybe on you. Before you gybe you must anticipate this outcome ahead and make a plan for how to approach it. Obviously, the greatest priority is that you

Chapter 18

THE THIRD STAGE: 'THE BLACK DIAMOND'

I am from Israel. It is the desert – there is not much skiing. Ever since I moved to the United States I began skiing in the winters, and I always looked at the black diamond runs and thought they were way too difficult for me. Slowly I realized that they are doable, but are definitely a challenge – just like the bottom stage of the downwind, hence the name.

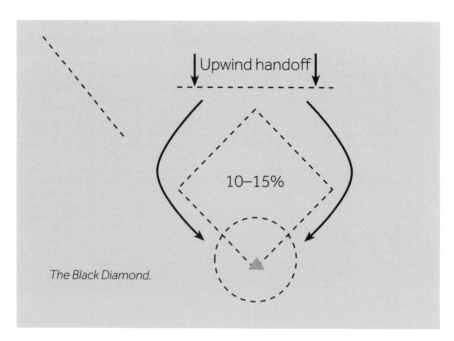

Upwind handoff

10–15%

The Black Diamond.

I call the final stage of the downwind the Black Diamond. This is the diamond-shaped area created by the laylines to the leeward mark on the last 10–15% of the downwind. Previously in the Big Chunk we focused mainly on executing high boat speed and your strategy. However, as you near the bottom of the downwind and start thinking about the leeward rounding, this is where you have to prioritize your tactical position. This stage of the downwind becomes tactical sailing again – your position relative to other boats is everything.

More specifically, the Black Diamond begins about 300–500 feet away from the mark (farther for bigger boats), where you really start thinking about your positioning for rounding the mark on the inside, and it ends

at the zone of the leeward mark. (Inside the zone the main focus is boat handling for the douse and rounding). You can think of this more simply as the last minute to half a minute of the downwind. The exact size of the Black Diamond varies of course with the size of the boat, the size of the fleet, the conditions, etc.

I like to think that this is the most critical area of the downwind. Naturally, this area has a tendency to merge the entire fleet into one very small crowded space. This is where big gains and losses are made. One small mistake can cause a loss of many boats, distance, control of the situation, and a defeatist attitude or rhythm that can send you into a negative spiral for the rest of the race. I have seen my sailors who are doing an amazing race at the front of the fleet suddenly make one mistake at the leeward rounding, losing maybe 3–5 boats, and then they are done for the race, all the time trying to recover from this one mistake. Needless to say, mistakes in this area can be very costly. On the other hand, make a good move at the mark and you can pass many boats as you turn back upwind.

In the area of the Black Diamond, if you know how to read the situation and predict what scenarios will play out in the next 30 seconds, you are coming with a strong advantage and you will gain significantly. This is a very important skill and ability to have on the water. The situation here is extremely complicated. There are a lot of parameters that are changing all the time, even without you doing anything. There are a lot of manoeuvres, boats gybing all the time, packs of boats fighting for overlap – endless possible scenarios that could happen. Keeping track of it all, anticipating what will happen next, and positioning yourself accordingly is a very important skill with big consequences in the race.

For you to really make use of the following tactical steps for this final area of the downwind, you must be confident with your boat handling. You should have a strong gybing technique from and to a variety of angles, dousing the kite, and rounding a leeward mark to an upwind. You should also be relatively comfortable with close-quarters action with other boats, as the leeward mark is almost always very crowded. The more comfortable you are with your technique and boat handling, the more you'll gain from these tactical steps. But even if your boat handling is not the best – maybe your gybes aren't always perfect, or you mistime the douse – having the right position will give you an edge over the boats around you and you'll see that even if you're slow, you'll sail as if you were much faster.

THE UPWIND HAND-OFF

Whatever your skill set may be, your first step before going into the Black Diamond is to do the hand-off to the next leg. The Black Diamond is a very intense, hectic area of boat-on-boat tactical sailing. Similar to the Top Rounding, we must do our hand-off to the next leg before we're entering this high-action area. The only difference now is that you're doing the hand-off to an upwind – you want to make an initial game plan that puts you in the best possible tactical and strategic position for the next upwind leg. Discuss with your team:

✳ Where is the leeward mark? Is it a single mark, or a gate?

✳ Which gate mark is favoured (closer to the wind)?

* Is the next leg skewed? Is one tack upwind significantly longer than the other?

* What is the phase of the shift right now? Which is the lifted tack on the upwind?

* What is the racecourse strategy? Is one side of the upwind favoured? Look around you at the clouds and the pressure on the water. Where is the next pressure? Does one side have favourable current? What side was winning on the downwind?

* Where is the fleet in front of me? Did they all round one gate? Are they all on one tack? Are the boats spread out or are they all following the leader? If they all chose the same gate, is there a good reason?

* Based on how I am positioned right now, is it easier for me to round one gate than the other?

Then, using this information, make a basic game plan including whether you want to tack or continue after the rounding, and generally where you want to go on the racecourse. If you have a leeward gate, the following are the general principles you should bear in mind when choosing which gate mark to round. I cannot give you an exact formula for making the perfect decision, given the multitude of factors that go into the seemingly simple choice of

picking a gate mark. You'll have to weigh all these factors and think about which ones are more or less important in a given situation.

GO TO THE GATE THAT IS:

1 Favoured (farther upwind than the other one). The gates being set unevenly, or the final wind shift before you round, can make one of them favoured. Remember, the price of going to the unfavoured gate is often higher than you think – you not only have extra sailing distance downwind to get to that gate, but also a lot of extra distance to sail upwind.

2 Up current (a bigger factor in light wind and strong current, a smaller factor in strong wind and weak current).

3 Better aligned with your strategy (takes you to better pressure, current, etc).

4 Less crowded.

5 Easier to round as the inside boat, based on your current position. Usually, if you are on the left of the downwind it is easier to go to the left gate, and if you are on the right it's easier to go to the right gate.

If you have a single mark (in most cases rounded to port), the most important thing to think about is which tack (starboard or port) you want to get on first after the rounding. You should decide early on whether you want to continue around the mark or do an early tack. Which tack aligns with your strategy, such as taking you to better current or pressure? Which tack is the lifted tack? Which tack is the longer tack upwind? On which tack will you have more clear air from boats in front of you? Whether you have a single mark or a gate, use these factors to plan your rounding.

APPROACHING THE MARK

As you approach the mark, remember that the closer you are to the mark, the less important the 80/20 rule is. Just as you can almost disregard the 80/20 rule at the very top of the upwind, you can do the same when you are at the bottom of the downwind. The determining factor is whether or not you can maintain inside overlap with your opponent given the distance you have to the zone. For example, if you are only a few boat lengths from the zone of the leeward mark, don't be afraid to gybe on the layline. Even if a boat rolls you over, you will still have the inside overlap at the leeward mark.

If you are far from the mark, however, follow the 80/20 Rule and gybe a bit before the layline. This leaves you room to do another step outside or perhaps soak low to separate from another boat that gybes on you, so that you can still come in strong to the mark. Put simply, the shorter the distance to the mark, the later you should gybe relative to the layline. When you are farther away from

the mark, you want to gybe before the layline so that if opponents gybe on top of you, you can hold the lane on a low mode until the zone.

On another note, try to avoid the middle of the black diamond. This area is very crowded because the fleet gets very congested just above the mark or between the gates. Don't be there! There is less pressure over there because the fleet blocks a lot of the wind, you will need to do a lot of manoeuvres, you aren't set up to be the inside boat, and you don't want to be in the middle of the pack. Instead, aim your downwind during the Big Chunk to the top of the Black Diamond, and from there actually go outside again to a layline and come back to the mark 'strong and hot'. What this means is that you come into the mark from the outside on a fast, slightly high angle. This way, while everyone else in the pack is slow and floating downwind, you stay in good pressure, sailing fast, with good flow, outside the pack, and you will probably have the inside position at the mark. This is an area where you can make huge gains and potentially pass an entire traffic jam of boats by sailing on the inside.

This is definitely the best way to approach a leeward mark or gate, and you'll see this in the example situations I run through later in this chapter. Another reason it is so powerful is that it avoids a very common but harmful tendency sailors have when they come to the leeward mark, and I want you to be aware of it: it's called the 'mark magnet'. Ever heard of it before? Even if you haven't, you'll probably be familiar with what I mean. There is a tendency for sailors, as they approach the leeward mark, to sail a lower and lower angle in order to make the mark. They approach the mark from far away, thinking they're on the layline, and as they close in to the mark they realize they're above the layline but they stubbornly point lower and lower

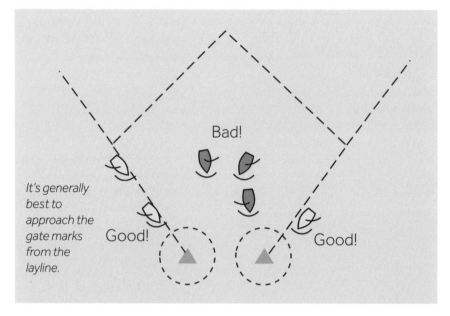

Bad!

Good!

Good!

It's generally best to approach the gate marks from the layline.

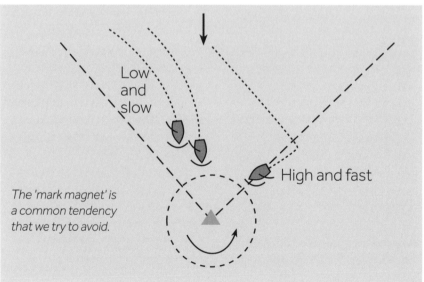

Low and slow

High and fast

The 'mark magnet' is a common tendency that we try to avoid.

to make the mark, slowing almost to a stop but refusing to do those two extra gybes. This is very slow and you lose a lot of distance doing this! Sailors probably prefer this option out of laziness, but the better option is almost always to sail fast on your VMG angle and do those two extra gybes. When you sail in the middle of the black diamond in the mix of all the boats it is very difficult to gybe on the perfect layline, so the mark magnet is almost unavoidable. By coming from the outside you avoid this trap and keep high boat speed all the time.

INSIDE OVERLAP

As you manoeuvre with other boats in the Black Diamond, your goal is to be the inside boat rounding the mark. To achieve this, then, your real goal is to be the inside boat at the zone (the three boat length circle around the mark which determines the rounding order under the RRS). I like to ask myself a series of questions to help achieve the best position while approaching the zone.

First, what would I try to do if I were the other boat? Again, thinking from the perspective of your opponents is an incredibly important skill all around the racecourse, but it is especially true in the Black Diamond. You have to be ready for any potential moves your opponents may make, and the best way to anticipate what will happen in the near future is to put yourself in the head of your opponent.

Second, am I coming in at an advantage or a disadvantage towards the mark? In other words, do I want to maintain the situation, or do I want to change the situation? This is the point at which you assess your positioning for the rounding. When you have the advantage going towards the mark and you are looking to maintain the situation, I like to think of this as being on defence. (For example, you are clear ahead of another boat going towards the mark and you need to make sure they don't get an inside overlap.) When you are at a disadvantage, I think of this as being on offence. (For example, you are a boat behind and you want to create an overlap.) You have to distinguish between whether you are defending your position or attacking your opponent's position.

Third, what is the upcoming manoeuvre and how am I preparing for it? It is common for the manoeuvres in this area to be very complicated. Sometimes you are doing a double gybe, or a gybe and a gybe and a douse, or a gybe to a reach... The boat handling here is very difficult, so you need to think about how you can simplify these manoeuvres and prepare for them. Call out to your team what the plan is for the upcoming manoeuvre before it happens!

THE DYNAMICS OF THE ROUNDING

As a final note, I'd like to touch on the proper technique for actually rounding the leeward mark. When rounding in a crowd of boats you are usually making quite a sharp turn, going from a downwind to an upwind in a very narrow area. When making this turn you want to use as little rudder as possible, meaning you must use your other controls – heel of the boat and sail trim – to steer the boat into the wind. Going around the

Lasers at a leeward gate.

mark you should have a constant leeward heel. This is what naturally heads the boat up. Maintain this leeward heel until you are at your upwind angle, at which point you can powerfully flatten the boat to accelerate forward. As you head up, the sails should be gradually trimmed in, the main coming in at a slightly faster rate than the jib (the same as when we accelerate off the start line). The mainsheet can be actually slightly over-trimmed throughout the turn

relative to your angle. In dinghies this is easy to do. Big keelboats sometimes simply don't have the manpower to trim in the sails as quickly as they would ideally like as the boat heads up around the mark. In this situation, prioritize trimming in the main over the jib. If one sail is going to flap, better the jib than the main. The main plays a very big role in helping the boat pivot upwind and for holding height after the rounding, so it is important that we keep the main engaged throughout the turn.

As you finish the turn upwind, prioritize height over speed! Chances are that there is a line of boats in front of you that all rounded the same mark, each in each other's bad air. Assuming there's no plan to tack soon, you must survive this lane as best you can. Just like when using your high mode to survive a difficult lane off the start, you must dig for as much height as possible after a crowded rounding so that you hold your lane and sail in the best air possible. As the pack thins out – boats tack away, other boats lose their lane – you can work back to

your VMG mode.

In terms of positioning, you always want to round the mark 'wide and tight'. Approach the mark wide so that when you turn back upwind you pass the mark tight. As you approach the mark from the downwind, don't aim directly at the mark – aim for a point about a boat length inside it. Just remember, if you are the inside boat entering the zone with other boats overlapped outside of you, you have the right of way. Don't let your opponents intimidate you into approaching the mark right next to it, thereby having a bad rounding. Position yourself with a wider gap as I've described above, be vocal, or do whatever else you need to do to approach the mark with a wide gap so that when you turn upwind you pass just to leeward of the mark – not a boat length or more to leeward of it.

We have tendency to push the douse as late as possible. If it's not necessary to gain the inside overlap, it's recommended to douse a bit earlier than you think and prep the boat for a quality rounding and a good lane to start the next leg.

As a boat ahead, make sure you do a proper wide and tight rounding so that any boat behind you stays behind you. Give them no option but to follow your stern or go to your leeward side. If they can squeeze in to windward of you at the rounding, they may end up in a controlling position where they can prevent you from tacking. Alternatively, as a boat behind, watch the rounding of the boat in front of you. If they botch the rounding, that's free space for you to take. Wait for the boat in front of you or inside you to potentially make a mistake so that you can do a proper wide and tight rounding

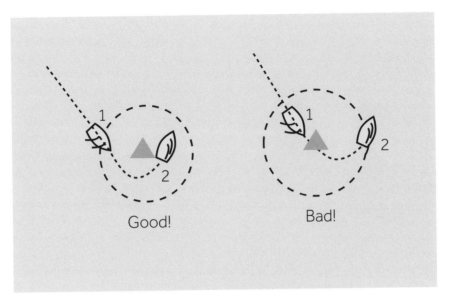

Round the mark 'wide and tight' whenever possible.
Notice that as he approaches downwind the sailor must aim
about a boat length inside the mark, NOT directly at the mark.

and end up to windward of them.

Finally, and perhaps most importantly, avoid the pinwheel at all costs. Sometimes you will come into the zone as an outside boat. There may be one boat overlapped inside you entitled to mark room, or an entire pack. The worst thing you can do here is stay overlapped to leeward and round on the outside of them. We call this the pinwheel. Fall into this trap and you'll be in very bad air and you'll have little option to tack. In short, this is the quickest way to the back of the fleet. Instead, when you are the outside boat slow down (over trim the sails, do a bunch of big turns back and forth) to break the overlap and round with your bow directly behind your opponent's stern, doing a proper

wide and tight rounding. You lost a couple boats on the rounding, but you are in relatively clear air, sailing fast, you'll pass any boats that got trapped on the outside of the pinwheel, and you have options to work with.

This is how you must round the leeward mark 99% of the time. In rare situations it may work to round on the outside of another boat, but only if no other boats rounded closely ahead of you that would give you bad air, and you are 100% sure that you are forward enough that you would round with your bow ahead of your opponent.

Let's now look at some common tactical situations you will often encounter in the Black Diamond. This is not an exhaustive list – there are endless situations –

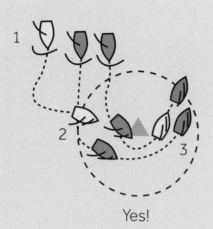
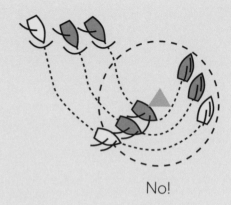

Yes! No!

Avoid the pinwheel at all costs! Notice that although in your racing you may enter the zone as the outside boat somewhat often, you should virtually always end up rounding right next to the mark. I like to teach this to my younger sailors by having a rule in practice races that they must be able to reach out with their hand and touch the mark when they're rounding.

but I believe these will be the most helpful for teaching you the tactics for rounding leeward marks. The following situations assume you are rounding a leeward mark to port. I will cover each boat's perspective in each situation.

No 1: Approaching on port tack to the left layline As the boat on the left (looking downwind), look at how far away you are from the layline and from the mark. See illustration No 1, part 1. Currently you are the inside boat. Your goal, of course, is to have the inside position with your opponent when you enter the three boat length zone of the mark. The rule to follow here is that as much as your distance to sail to the mark

on starboard tack is shorter, you will gybe to starboard later. The determining factor is whether or not you can maintain an inside overlap with your opponent to the zone once you gybe. If you are only a few boat lengths away from the zone, you should gybe on the layline, because even if your opponent catches you on the gybe and begins to roll over you, you will still have the inside overlap going into the zone.

On the other hand, if you are far from the mark, you want to gybe slightly before the layline so that if your opponent gybes on top of you, you can hold your lane until the zone. See illustration No 1, part 2. (If you were to gybe on the layline, your opponent could

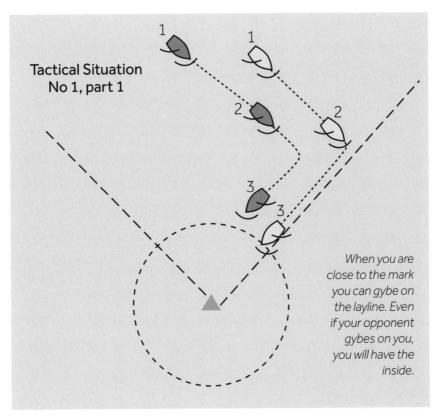

Tactical Situation No 1, part 1

When you are close to the mark you can gybe on the layline. Even if your opponent gybes on you, you will have the inside.

easily gybe on top of you, roll you, and break the overlap before reaching the zone.) This is why it is important to gybe earlier than the layline. By leaving this extra distance before the layline, if your opponent gybes on you then you can sail on a low angle to clear your air. You just need to remember to gybe early enough so that if your opponent soaks low on you and you are forced to sail low as well, you will not over-lay the mark. Then, even if your opponent does soak low on you, you will still both end up to the right of the mark, and as long as you maintain the overlap you will have the inside.

If, instead, you are the other boat positioned on the right, you are now on the outside and a bit behind, so you are clearly at the disadvantage. See illustration No 1, part 3. Your goal, therefore, is to take advantage of any mistake by your opponent. If you are only a few boat lengths outside the zone, you will most likely not have a chance to pass your opponent unless they make a major error. For example, if they gybe before the layline to the zone, you can duck their stern, gybe on the layline, and then when they are gybing back you have the inside overlap to the mark. You must be ready to take advantage of any mistake your opponent

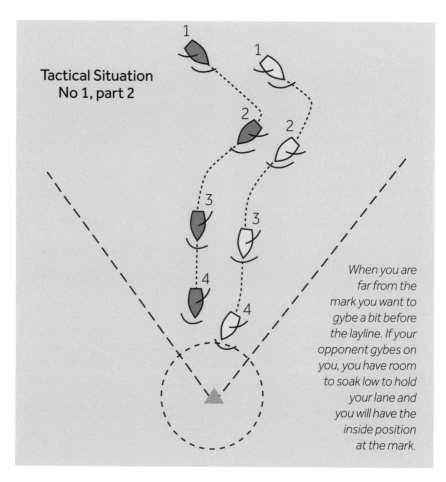

Tactical Situation No 1, part 2

When you are far from the mark you want to gybe a bit before the layline. If your opponent gybes on you, you have room to soak low to hold your lane and you will have the inside position at the mark.

may make. If your opponent is a good sailor and gives you no free opportunities, you must stop fighting for the inside and instead focus on your boat handling. You need to recognize the point when your best option is to change tactics, stay behind your opponent for now, and prioritize the rounding (wide and tight with your bow directly behind their stern) in order to open your options and give yourself the best chance of passing them on the next leg.

If you are far from the mark,

you have a better possibility of passing your opponent, even if you are slightly behind. Sailing on port, you want to wait for the boat on the left to initiate the gybe. In particular, you want to see if your opponent sails all the way to the layline before gybing. If they do, you want to gybe directly on top of them if not a little bit to the right of them. Your goal here is to put them in your bad air and be positioned slightly to their right so that their only option of escaping your bad air is to soak low. As they go to a low mode to

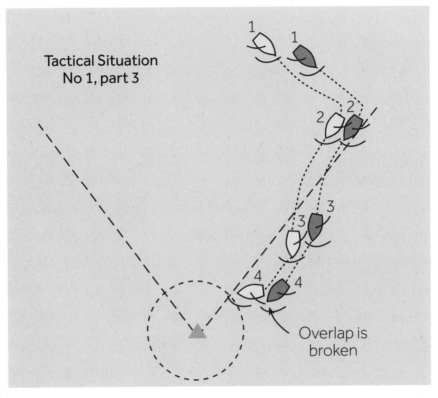

Tactical Situation
No 1, part 3

Overlap is
broken

try to free their air, you want to head low as well and press down as much as you can on your opponent – sail low whenever your opponent heads lower, or sometimes by you heading lower they will naturally head lower as well even though they technically have the right of way – with the goal of pushing you and your opponent as far to the left and over the layline as possible. Work as low as you can for the entire sailing distance towards the zone, hopefully making slow and steady progress. Then, when you are close to entering the zone, you will have hopefully overstood the layline by a couple of boat lengths and you can head up suddenly and

powerfully, breaking the overlap with your opponent, and enter the zone clear ahead. See the above illustration.

NO 2: APPROACHING ON STARBOARD TACK TO THE RIGHT LAYLINE As the boat on the right, you are the outside boat to the mark and a little bit ahead. See illustration No 2, part 1. You don't want to stay here, because then both boats will sail to the layline and gybe and you'll be behind your opponent, so you need to initiate a manoeuvre earlier to get the inside. The problem with your position here is that you cannot gybe and cross your opponent. Gybing and

The bottommost boat is in trouble, as it is about to be pinwheeled and will be in a very bad leeward lane.

ducking them is your only option. You need to initiate high mode sailing – breaking the overlap, building high pressure and flow, and making a bigger gap for the gybe. Then, before the layline, you need to gybe and duck your opponent.

Let's think for a second from your opponent's perspective: if you were in their position as the inside boat, you would hope to push the outside boat all the way to the layline so that you could gybe securely ahead of them towards the mark. So by gybing earlier, you are presenting our opponent with a challenge. You are putting the pressure on

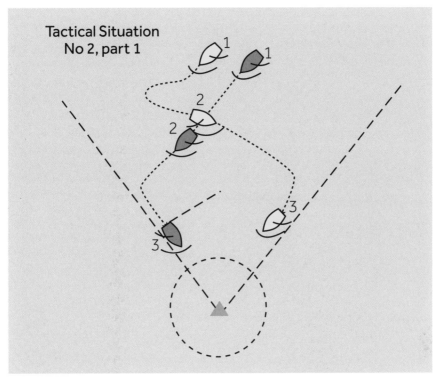

Tactical Situation
No 2, part 1

As the outside boat, gybe early and give your opponent a doubt of what to do. Hopefully they will continue and give you the left-hand side, giving you an easy inside overlap. If they gybe with you, you both now have two more gybes to make before the mark, which means more chances for your opponent to make a mistake or give up on the inside.

your opponent and giving him a question of what the right move is: 'Should I gybe with this boat, or should I continue to the layline? What should I do?' Just by giving your opponent a doubt, you already have the advantage. If your opponent continues on starboard, you are now the inside boat. All you need to do is maintain the inside position to the mark. If your opponent gybes with you, there are now two more gybes to make before the mark, which increases the chance of your opponent

making a mistake, or maybe giving up on the left-hand side.

In general, whenever you can give your opponent a doubt of what is the right move, you have the advantage. Don't just give up on the situation and continue all the way to the layline as the outside boat. That's exactly what your opponent wants you to do. Take the initiative, make a manoeuvre to take the inside, and see how your opponent reacts. In other words, give them opportunities to make mistakes.

In this situation, if they don't gybe with you before the layline, you will duck, stay to the left of them, and as they approach the mark on port you'll have an easy inside overlap. Put pressure on other sailors and you'll be surprised how many easy points you'll gain from sailors who don't really know how to defend their position.

If instead in this situation you are the boat positioned on the left, you are the inside boat to the mark, so you want to maintain this position all the way until the layline. See illustration No 2, part 2. To do this, close the gap on your opponent. You want to keep your bow close to the leeward side of your opponent with your bow overlapped with their stern if possible so they cannot gybe. Don't be afraid to lose a couple of boat lengths to do this. I call this position 'bow to stern', another one of my cue words that are incredibly helpful for team communication. Your tactician should be able to call out 'bow to stern with the windward boat!' and you'll know what he means. You also want to keep high pressure in the boat – centreboard lower, slightly hotter angle. In this position, you are preventing your opponent from gybing and the boat is powered up in case you need to gybe to protect the inside.

Connecting your bow to your opponent's stern is a very strong position here. They cannot gybe in front of you, and they would have to head high and make a very difficult manoeuvre to gybe and duck you. If you are successfully locking your opponent from gybing, then great! You'll push them all the way to the right layline and gybe on your own terms. You'll easily have the inside position at the zone. If your opponent does manage to gybe, you need to gybe with them to protect the inside. See illustration No 2, part 3. You don't want to allow your opponent to roll you, but you also want to prevent a costly fight on a high mode. You should head high to protect your lane and to discourage your opponent from trying to roll you. When you are securely ahead and this is less of a threat, you should take every opportunity that you can to make your opponent and yourself soak low towards the mark.

Most of the time when racing you are not sailing with just one other boat. There is usually the fleet around you, and if you are engaging with one boat in one area, you may be losing an entire pack of boats in another. In this situation, however, my tip is to gybe with your opponent to protect the inside of the mark even at the cost of potentially losing other boats. First protect what is in your control, and don't take other unnecessary risks. Staying ahead of this one boat is a sure thing if you make the right moves; staying ahead of another pack on the other side of the course is most likely not. Protect the situation that is in your control.

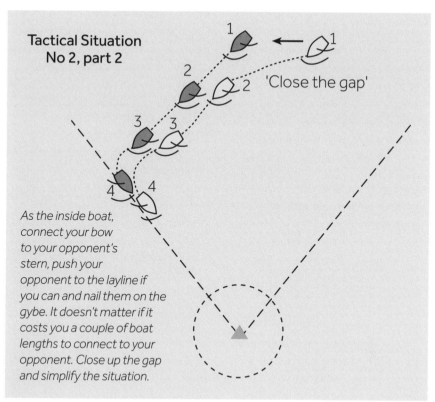

Tactical Situation No 2, part 2

'Close the gap'

As the inside boat, connect your bow to your opponent's stern, push your opponent to the layline if you can and nail them on the gybe. It doesn't matter if it costs you a couple of boat lengths to connect to your opponent. Close up the gap and simplify the situation.

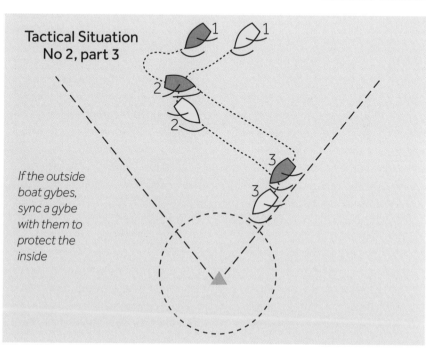

Tactical Situation No 2, part 3

If the outside boat gybes, sync a gybe with them to protect the inside

The only situation where I might go back on this advice is if you gybe with your opponent and they are taking you to a costly high mode fight. Think about how much distance you are losing on another pack of boats by continuing with this fight. Think about how much longer the race is, how many remaining upwinds and downwinds you still have to pass this boat, and whether it's actually worth it to fight with this one boat now and risk losing the fleet.

No 3: On opposite tacks, on the left layline

Two boats are approaching the Black Diamond on opposite tacks. In this example we are on the left layline, although this situation could happen in any area across the course. See illustration No 3, part 1.

As the boat on the right (port tack), you are about even with the boat on the left, who is on starboard tack and on the layline. In this position you are the outside boat, so you want to establish an inside overlap before reaching the mark. You should aim to duck your opponent very closely and gybe immediately after ducking such that you end up in a position close to leeward of them and overlapped with their stern.

Now read that again and visualize this manoeuvre. It may sound like a tough one to pull off, but I assure you it is quite possible if you master the proper technique. To do this, duck your opponent 'wide and tight', just like we do at the leeward mark. Head up early, before you reach their stern, and head down later so that while you are ducking their stern you are already on a downwind VMG angle or even lower. Make the duck as close as you safely can (leave only inches to spare) and continue to bear away in one continuous motion, rolling into a perfect gybe just after you duck. If you execute this proper ducking technique and a successful gybe, there is a very good chance that you will end up with your bow overlapped to leeward of your opponent. The combination of you having greater speed than your opponent from sailing a high mode and you blocking your opponent's wind for a few seconds as you duck them, forcing them to head up slightly to regain speed and pressure, makes it very likely that you will finish the manoeuvre with a solid overlap. Having forced your opponent to head up slightly to regain their speed, they should now be slightly above their optimum layline to the mark, leaving you positioned perfectly on the layline. Connect your bow to their stern and maintain the overlap to the zone.

If instead you are the other boat positioned on the left (starboard tack), you are currently the inside boat and you want to defend your inside position from your opponent on the right. You also have the right of way as the starboard boat. See illustration No 3, part 2. You need to first see your opponent ahead of time coming on port. Once they're close (within a few boat lengths), head up significantly before they start to duck you, aiming straight at them, somewhere between their mid-boat and stern. Head up just enough that you give your opponent a second of

doubt of what they should do: 'Did something change? Should I steer higher still to duck this boat? Or should I gybe? Maybe I'm crossing them now and I can just continue?' The timing here is everything. Head up early enough that your opponent must react to you (after all, you are a starboard boat speeding at them), but late enough that it comes as a surprise.

Duck your opponent wide and tight, and immediately roll into a perfect gybe. Execute this well and you will finish the manoeuvre to leeward and overlapped with their stern. Now focus on your boat speed so that you maintain the overlap all the way to the zone (this is easier to do with boats that sail lower angles such as symmetric kites and most dinghies).

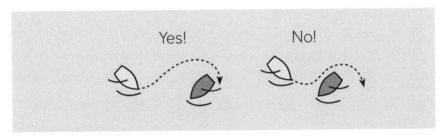

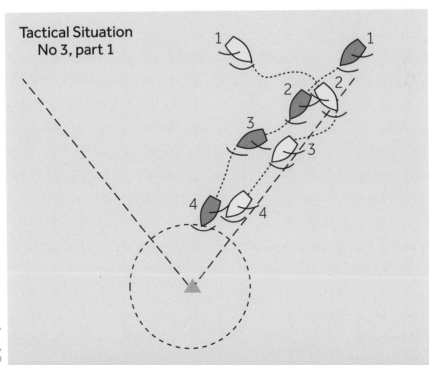

Tactical Situation No 3, part 1

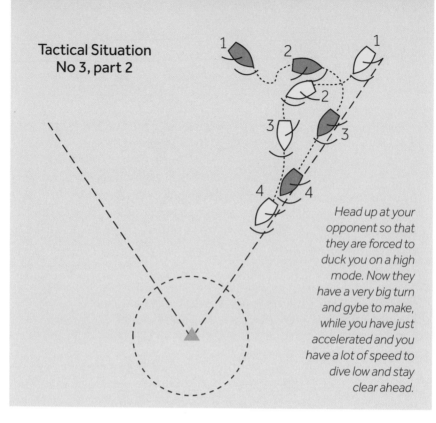

Tactical Situation
No 3, part 2

Head up at your opponent so that they are forced to duck you on a high mode. Now they have a very big turn and gybe to make, while you have just accelerated and you have a lot of speed to dive low and stay clear ahead.

The point of doing this is to cause your opponent to do a rushed, low-quality manoeuvre. If your opponent heads higher to duck you, they will be ducking you on a high mode. If you headed up enough to really put pressure on your opponent, they will actually be sailing almost parallel to you on a reach when they duck you, not wide and tight as they would prefer. This is good for you, because now they have no chance of completing a big turn and successful gybe that gives them an inside overlap. Most likely they will be at least one boat length behind, and now you have the speed to dive low, position yourself in front of their bow, and be clear ahead at the zone.

If your manoeuvre of heading up was really perfect (timing and angle), your opponent will not be able to head up and duck, and they will be forced to do a last second and low-quality gybe. See illustration No 3, part 3. They'll likely lose the kite, lose their speed, and have to head up to a high angle after the gybe to regain pressure and flow. This is perfect for you, because now you have the speed forward and the slight gap above the layline to head down, soak low, and make some separation from your opponent without pointing too far below the mark. In this situation you are now sailing low and fast and your opponent is sailing high and slow, so you'll easily have enough separation to hold this lane and stay inside and ahead when you

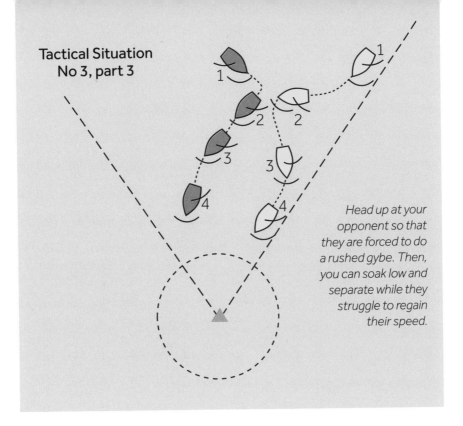

Tactical Situation No 3, part 3

Head up at your opponent so that they are forced to do a rushed gybe. Then, you can soak low and separate while they struggle to regain their speed.

reach the zone.

As you can see, in these tactical situations you need to have a plan. Build scenarios as discussed in the upwind.[16] When you have a plan, your chance to have a successful execution goes up. But when you are just reacting to what other boats are doing, then everything is happening very fast and most likely you'll miss the opportunity to defend your position. That's when you lose control of these tactical situations. Sail according to your own plan, on your own terms, not in unplanned reaction to what another boat is doing. You want to be the initiator. You want to have the plan, take the initiative, and either be the boat

attacking or in control. That's why we are looking at these common situations – this is how you learn to look at your tactical options, understand what your plan is, and initiate the next move.

No 4: Approaching the mark on port tack on the right layline

As the boat behind, you are on port tack on the right layline to the mark and about half a boat length directly behind the stern of your opponent. See illustration No 4, part 1. If you were to continue as you are, you would round the mark behind your opponent, so you want to change the situation. In other words, you are the attacking boat, and your goal is

---

[16] See *Build Scenarios.*

to get an inside overlap before the zone. You should connect your bow to the stern of your opponent, getting as close to them as possible, and suddenly head up 20–30 degrees to try to surprise them and roll over them. (Remember, most likely you only have one chance to catch them unaware, so time it carefully. Pick a moment when they are slow, fell off a wave, the spinnaker luffed for a second so they cannot head up, they don't see you, etc. Conversely, your boat must be ready: centreboard down, guy ready to be eased and sheet trimmed, main in, etc.)

Two scenarios might happen: (1) your opponent doesn't see your attack or gives up on you, and you successfully roll them and win the inside. (2) they see you, head up to defend, and you are on a high mode on a fight. See illustration No 4, part 2. This scenario is more complicated. You don't want to lose too much distance by continuing this fight for too long, but you want to sail long enough so that your opponent is pushed above the layline and will have to now gybe to get to the mark. If both boats are above the layline, you now have a situation similar to the first one and you might have another chance to pass your opponent on those two gybes. Alternatively, you can sometimes push your opponent above the layline and force them to do two

extra gybes, while you suddenly dive to an extreme low mode and make the mark.

If instead in this situation you are the other boat, you are about half a boat length clear ahead of your opponent. See illustration No 4, part 3. You want to maintain this position all the way to the zone and prevent your opponent from taking you to a fight. To do this, especially earlier on, sail a little bit above the bow line or heading of your opponent to discourage them from trying to roll over you. This way there are fewer chances that your opponent will attack and you have a better position to windward to react if they do so. Focus mostly on your relative position to your opponent here, more so than on curving and optimum boat speed. Even head up and slow down a bit, let your opponent feel like he is gaining speed on you to leeward and invite them to go to your leeward side. Then he is trapped on the outside, he cannot easily head up behind your stern to roll you, and he cannot head you up higher than the mark under Rule 17, Proper Course.

If your opponent is attacking anyway, use the Half an Angle Rule to defend your lane.[17] As you near the three boat lengths zone, it is super important that you do not allow your opponent to become overlapped on the windward side. Especially as the helm of the boat

[17] Refer to *Boathandling And Technique* to learn about the Half an Angle Rule.

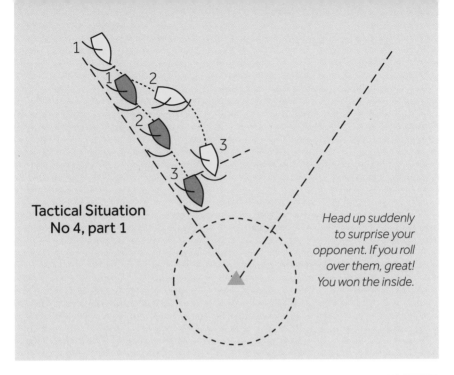

Tactical Situation
No 4, part 1

*Head up suddenly
to surprise your
opponent. If you roll
over them, great!
You won the inside.*

*If they defend, continue the fight long enough that you are both
above the layline, and you may have another chance to pass them in
the two gybes before the mark, as covered in situation No 1. Another
option, shown above, is to actually force your opponent over the
layline while you still make the mark. Although you are the outside
boat and you must round wide to give your opponent room, they may
struggle with doing two extra gybes right before the mark, have a bad
rounding, and you will likely finish the rounding ahead.*

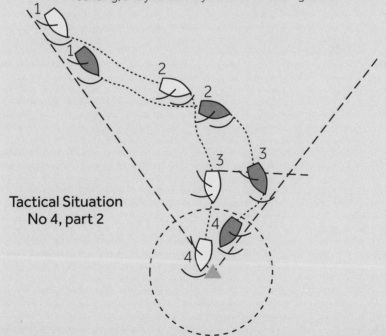

Tactical Situation
No 4, part 2

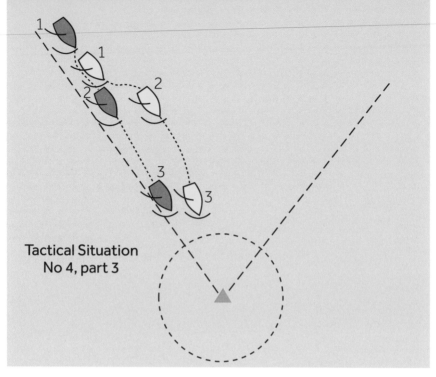

Tactical Situation No 4, part 3

Right now your opponent behind has its 'bow free'. They can head up and down, take you to a fight, or play with you all the way to the mark. You want to head up slightly and actually slow down, inviting your opponent to your leeward side, so that they become trapped to leeward. Then, they can no longer head up and you have them trapped all the way to the mark.

ahead, you will be spending a lot of your time looking backwards at your opponent so that you have the right relative position and you are ready to react to any attack they may make. You should be ready with your boat setup: centreboard low, spinnaker guy ready to be eased, main sheet ready to be trimmed in. As soon as your opponent heads up to roll you, you want to see it and respond. If your opponent pushes you above the layline and you do need to gybe before the mark, gybe as late as possible, on the layline or even a bit later, so that your opponent has no option to take the inside. Look back to the

first tactical situation for how to position yourself in this scenario.

No 5: Approaching the mark on starboard tack on the left layline
This situation is quite similar to the previous situation, except that the inside position at the mark is now the leeward side of your opponent instead of the windward side.

As the boat behind, your two options for passing your opponent are: (1) surprise your opponent by heading high, rolling over them, and breaking the overlap before the zone, or (2) establish an overlap to leeward of your opponent's stern going into the zone. See illustration No 5, part 1.

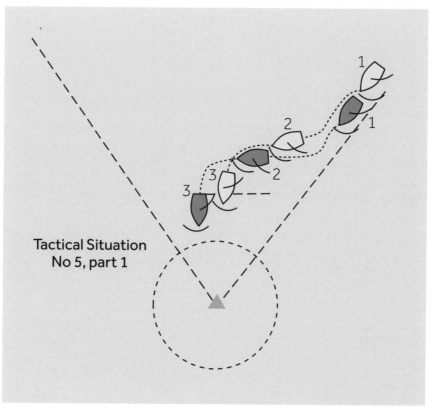

Tactical Situation
No 5, part 1

Both boats are on the layline. As the boat behind, try to roll your opponent. Most likely they will defend against you and head higher as well. Keep playing with them and gaining distance. Keep pushing them above the layline to the zone, but keep your bow free. Then, you have the position on their stern to either soak low and get the inside (shown above) or lock them from gybing to the mark.

Since both boats in this example are on the layline and sailing their VMG angle, holding an inside overlap with your opponent will be difficult. Remember, it's much easier to hold an overlapped position to leeward of another boat when both boats are sailing lower angles. For this reason, the boats are under the layline and you will both need to sail a low mode at some point to get to the mark, connecting your bow to their

stern now and putting yourself in position to establish an overlap later may be the best option.

On the other hand, if the boats are on the layline or slightly over it, I suggest first trying to roll your opponent. As in the previous situation, you will probably only have one chance to catch your opponent unaware. Go for this attempt early, when you are far from the mark so that you would have time to completely roll over them and break the overlap before the zone. If you successfully roll them, great! Make sure you put them in your bad air, press low over them as much as possible, ideally a bit over the layline, and head up to break the overlap just before the zone. If they do defend against you, keep playing with them, heading up and down, forcing them to defend against your attacks. Keep your bow free. Continue sailing high and pushing your opponent towards the right layline. Your goal is to push them as far to the right as you can so that on your own timing, when you have a moment of good speed or a wave, you can suddenly soak low to leeward of them, and now we have a situation like No 2 which we covered previously. You have a chance to overlap with your opponent's stern as both boats head down into the zone, or you can lock your opponent from gybing and push them out to the right.

If instead in this situation you are the boat ahead, your goal is to keep your opponent behind you. See illustration No 5, part 2.

Keep your stern in front of your opponent's bow. If they do become overlapped to leeward of you, push them as far to the left as you can. Then, when you are just about to enter the zone, you have room to head up sharply, surprising your opponent before they can react, and break the overlap before the zone.

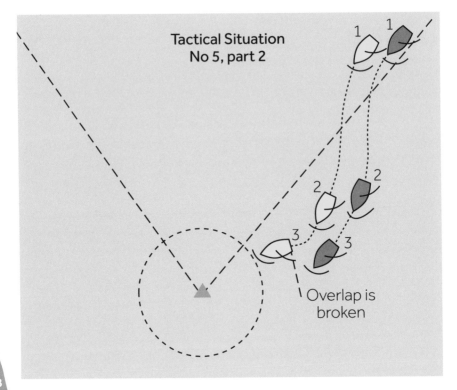

Tactical Situation
No 5, part 2

Overlap is broken

Stay between your opponent and the mark. This is very similar to situation No 4. If your opponent heads higher, protect your lane according to the Half Angle Rule. If your opponent bears away behind you, bear away as well so that you keep your stern in front of their bow and they do not become overlapped to leeward. When you are close to the zone it is okay to let your opponent roll you because you'll be the inside boat. The difference here from the previous situation is that it is super important to prevent your opponent from getting overlapped to leeward of you.

That said, let's look at the situation if your opponent does become overlapped to leeward of you. They now gain the right of way and may head you no higher than your proper course towards the mark. With that in mind, your best option is to soak as low as possible – sail low whenever your opponent heads lower, or sometimes by you heading lower they will head lower as well to avoid you – with the goal of pushing you and your opponent as far to the left and over the layline as possible. Make this your priority for the entire sailing distance towards the zone. Then, just before you enter the zone, head up suddenly and powerfully, breaking the overlap with your opponent, and enter the zone clear ahead.

When you do this, show your opponent that you are clear ahead! Be assertive and vocal,

and don't give them any doubt that you have broken the overlap. As a sailor in competition I would actually swing my hand across my stern to show clearly to my opponent, the jury and other witnesses/opponents around that there is no overlap. By being assertive on the water it is less likely that your opponent will illegally barge in between you and the mark or take you to the protest room.

No 6: On opposite tacks, far from the mark In this situation, both boats are on opposite tacks, on the left side of the downwind near the left layline, and quite far away from the mark. The boat on starboard is a couple of boat lengths ahead of the boat on port. This situation is similar to the third situation, except that we are far from the mark so we are not yet optimizing our inside position for the mark rounding.

As the boat on the right (port tack), you will try to gybe exactly on top of your opponent, blocking their air, so that they will have to change course. By doing this you are forcing a response from your opponent; a new situation is established. You just want to put pressure on your opponent and hopefully they will react badly to it.

If instead you are the boat on the left (starboard tack), see the port tacker coming and make sure you have good speed and flow. If they gybe on you, be ready to either: (1) head aggressively low to avoid their wind shadow and separate from your opponent, (2) head up a lot to cross through their wind shadow and find clear air to front of them, or (3) do a quick gybe to avoid sailing a long time in an uncomfortable lane. The key is for your action to be sharp, immediate and assertive. You and your team have to see the scenario ahead and be ready for it. Any doubt or stalling will put you in a long-lasting situation without control and in a bad lane/position.

I'd like to end here with a note on balancing risk with reward. I have just shown you how to maximize your chances of passing boats in a lot of situations, but even if you are doing everything

right, it doesn't always work out the way you want. You may do a successful manoeuvre to pass a boat, but maybe they don't give you room when they should, or they barge in at the mark, or you round on the outside and don't have the best outcome of the rounding, and then the door opens for a lot of other unfavourable situations. Other times you may be fighting with a single boat while losing a lot of distance on the rest of the fleet. In situations like these you have to ask yourself if continuing this fight with the other boat is really the smartest action to take. When I'm unsure whether I want to engage in a situation I ask myself:

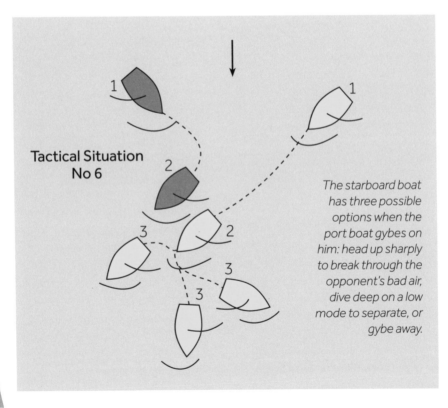

Tactical Situation No 6

The starboard boat has three possible options when the port boat gybes on him: head up sharply to break through the opponent's bad air, dive deep on a low mode to separate, or gybe away.

What part of the race am I in? Am I rounding to a reach to the finish? Or am I rounding to another upwind? In that case I have at least two or three more legs to pass this boat. Maybe, instead of continuing the fight to pass this boat, my priority now is to have a perfect mark rounding right behind her stern. While she's so focused on being the inside boat, I will focus on getting onto the lifted tack on the upwind.

Consider if the fight is worth risking the fleet. Understand there are a lot of opportunities around the racecourse – don't try to win everything in one moment. Play the game of sailing 'boat by boat, leg by leg, race by race'. Maybe you lost this small fight, but you still have another leg to pass this boat. Your focus now is on the rounding and setting yourselves up for the next opportunity.

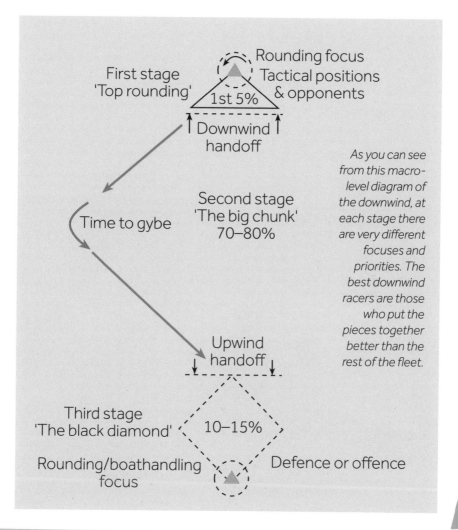

Rounding focus
Tactical positions & opponents

First stage
'Top rounding'
1st 5%

Downwind handoff

Second stage
'The big chunk'
70–80%

Time to gybe

Upwind handoff

Third stage
'The black diamond'
10–15%

Rounding/boathandling focus

Defence or offence

As you can see from this macro-level diagram of the downwind, at each stage there are very different focuses and priorities. The best downwind racers are those who put the pieces together better than the rest of the fleet.

PART 5

REACH

The reach is the most exciting leg of the race — it's also where you can typically gain or lose the most places

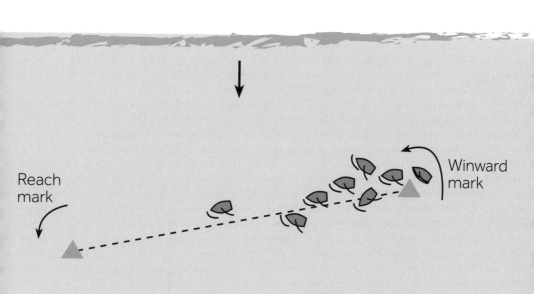

Reach mark

Winward mark

The reach leg is every sailor's favourite part of the race. It's where you bear away to that full-power angle, get up on a plane, thunder down the waves, clock those high speed numbers, and unleash the boat's full potential. It's the time during the race when you can forget about all the complex tactics and strategy – just put up the kite, point to the mark and send it! Right? Not necessarily. Boat speed is just one aspect of the reach. The other is boat-on-boat tactics which is still incredibly important, even on the relatively simple reach leg.

The reach leg has huge potential for big gains and big losses. It's quite similar to the Black Diamond in this way. The main way that places change on the reach is by one boat rolling another. We've all heard the horror

This is the reach leg. Usually the reach leg follows an upwind leg, as shown above. We see reach legs on trapezoid courses, triangle courses, and even on other race courses that commonly have a reach to the finish. 120 degrees off the wind is a standard angle for the reach.

stories: perhaps you've rounded the windward mark to the reach leg and you bear away to set the spinnaker. It's a tight angle to the next mark, and the boats behind you are holding high. The kite is finally up, but by the time you head up again the boats that were on your tail are now above you, already blocking your wind. The train of boats rolls over the top of you, one by one, as you struggle to regain your lane.

Looking from the other perspective, in a crowded fleet

you could pass a lot of boats by taking the high lane and rolling boats that get trapped on the low lane, sometimes gaining as many as 10–15 boats just on the reach. If you usually sail at the top of the fleet and in a race you find yourself in the back – maybe you had a bad start, or made some mistakes on the upwind – the reach is usually where you'll have the greatest chance of gaining back a lot of places in the race.

The hand-off to the reach leg, of course, should come before the top rounding. The strategy on the reach is relatively simple compared to an upwind or downwind, so there is less we need to think about. The main pieces of information we want to gather are these:

❉ Where is the reach mark? Is it high, low, or a normal angle?

❉ How strong is the wind? How about the shift? How high or low an angle can we sail in this wind? Is there anything else unusual about the conditions that may affect the reach?

❉ What are the boats ahead of us doing? Are they pointing to the reach mark, or pointing above it, or struggling to make the mark? Did they or did they not set their spinnakers?

❉ Will we have a big pack of boats directly behind us when we round, or will we have open space behind us?

First, consider whether the reach is tight or low (sailors also say 'open'). The higher the reach mark is set and the stronger the wind is, the tighter the reach will be. The lower the reach mark is and the lighter the wind is, the more open the reach will be. This is true for any boat sailing with a spinnaker, because they must sail progressively lower angles as they become overpowered with the kite.

With this information, make an initial plan for the reach. Do you want to set the kite immediately after rounding the mark, or do you want to wait? Or do you want to set at all? Do you want to continue heading high after the mark to build some height to windward or do you want to head low immediately after rounding the mark? The general rule here is that if the reach is low, head down to the mark and set immediately. If the reach is tight, continue heading high after rounding the mark and be patient to set.

Now that we have the initial game plan, let's look at the dynamics of the reach. I've organized this part into three steps to follow during the reach leg, plus an initial note on boat speed:

1 Protect the windward lane
2 Go to your fastest angle and set
3 Sail fast and clean

Chapter 19

A NOTE ON BOAT SPEED: REACHING

Let's first look at the proper technique for being fast on the reach. Just like the upwind and downwind, your three main boat speed factors are your sail trim, heel angle, and heading.

On the reach, your boat should either be flat or have a bit of leeward heel. Windward heel must be avoided at all costs. Just like the upwind, crew weight must be brought to windward to press the boat when a gust hits, and weight must be brought back to leeward when a lull hits. In most boats your fastest mode is to maintain a slight leeward heel throughout the reach. Keep this heel angle consistent – any rocking back and forth is slow. The most important thing about heel angle is that you do not allow a lull in the wind to cause a windward heel. Windward heel slows the boat down, kills all the flow over the sails, and causes the boat to slide sideways.

If you were sailing in an imaginary environment with perfectly flat water and perfectly consistent wind, you would simply point the boat in the direction of the reach mark, trim the sails correctly, and you'd be sailing your fastest VMG towards the mark. The real world, however, is not like that. There are variations in the pressure (puffs and lulls) and in the waves. Having great boat speed on the reach is all about making constant adjustments so that you're always sailing your correct mode

In both light wind and strong wind, head low in the gusts and high in the lulls. Don't fight the gust on a high mode – use the gust for speed forward. Don't sail low in the lull and lose all your speed – head up in the lull to maintain the pressure in the boat. Your track on the reach should show such curving. You'll know you're doing a good job when, throughout the gusts, the lulls, and the curving up and down, the heel angle of the boat stays steady and the boat maintains a consistent plane.

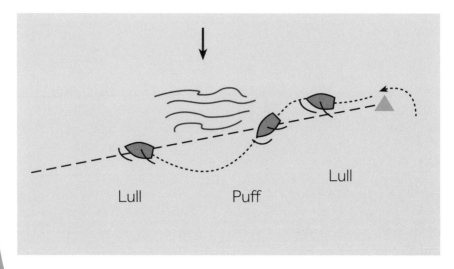

Lull   Puff   Lull

according to the pressure and the feel of the boat.

For the helm: the biggest factor for boat speed on the reach is your heading. As with the downwind, you actually have a very big range of angles on the reach: high mode, low mode, and VMG mode. On the reach you must do very frequent steering changes up and down, especially as the wind gets stronger and gustier. Here's how to steer on the reach: whenever the boat feels fast or you're about to enter a gust, bear away. Whenever the boat feels slow or you're about to enter a lull, head up. The key here is to change your angle *before* the gust or lull hits, or more importantly, *before* the gust or lull causes the boat to change its heel angle by either heeling over to leeward or sinking to windward. I like to think of this as steering according to the power in the boat. A higher angle, of course, is more powered up, while a lower angle is less powered up. Head low in the gusts and high in the lulls to maintain a constant amount of power in the boat. Do this well and you'll find that your boat keeps a very consistent heel angle and maintains its speed and plane very well.

For the main trimmer: on the upwind you are used to mostly trimming and easing the main in order to keep the boat flat. As described above, however, on the reach the angle is the primary tool for maintaining the power in the boat. Ideally, if the helm is doing a good job of curving according to the pressure, the range of the main sheet adjustment should be very small. Any trimming and easing of the main should be for fine-tuning the amount of power in the boat. The steering should be used for making the big adjustments in the gusts and lulls.

The main sheet is just one of the primary controls on the reach – the other is the vang. On all boats, the vang is an incredibly important control line when reaching. As a main trimmer you must be very conscious about the shape of the leech, and the vang is your primary control for this. In light wind, adjust the vang and mainsheet based on proper sail shape, keeping the leech of the main a bit more open than you would have it on the upwind. The vang should be relatively eased so that the top of the main is open to promote air flow. As the power in the boat increases, trim in the vang to close the leech further for maximum power.

In strong wind, the vang becomes critically important. Opening and closing the leech controls the amount of power in the sail, so you must adjust the vang as the boat becomes overpowered. (Remember, the boat becomes more overpowered on the reach as the wind becomes stronger and as the reach angle becomes tighter.) As you become overpowered, ease the vang to reduce the power in the sail. On bigger boats in a strong breeze, it's a good idea to have someone ready to release the vang at all times in order to dump all the power in the sail if the boat is about to broach.

If the reach is low you can usually keep a lot of vang on to stay powered up, even in strong wind. It's mostly when you are overpowered and struggling to make the mark on a tight angle that easing out the vang is a big help. Have you ever sailed on a reach completely overpowered, struggling to make the mark, boat heeling way over, and the mainsail is almost completely eased and flapping? This is very slow because the main is (1) creating drag by flapping, (2) closing the slot with the spinnaker, and (3) creating an unmanageable amount of heel. In other words, the main is acting like a brake. To fix this, make sure the vang is significantly eased! This creates an incredible amount of twist in the sail, opening up the top of the leech and depowering the boat. This in turn allows you to actually trim in the main sheet and the boom quite far while leaving the top of the sail very open, thereby reducing the drag and opening the slot without adding much power. This is the fastest way to go when overpowered on a tight reach.

For the kite trimmer: keep the luff blinking. This means keep the kite trimmed in just enough that its edge does not collapse. Ease the kite out just until the luff of the kite starts to fold inward, at which point trim in again and repeat. Ideally the kite should be constantly blinking in this way. The frequent angle changes that you have on the reach require almost constant trimming and easing of the kite.

If your boat reaches with both a kite and a jib flying, the jib is not a huge factor. Just make sure the jib is not over trimmed. The jib should be eased enough that it's luff is on the verge of flapping.

For the boat to be fast, everyone on the team must be coordinated with each other. The kite must be trimmed according to the helm's heading. The main must be trimmed according to the heading and the heel of the boat. And the helm must steer according to their own feeling of the boat, a crew member calling out the puffs and lulls, and to the feedback from the trimmers about the pressure in the kite. Practice the reach like you would any other angle and you'll be amazed at the results once the team acts in perfect harmony.

Chapter 20

3 STEPS TO SUCCESS

This massive offset leg before the downwind is almost like a reach leg.

STEP 1: PROTECT THE WINDWARD LANE

When you round the windward mark to the reach, your first priority is to *protect the windward lane*. You do not want to allow any boat to roll you, so you must stay on the high lane relative to the fleet around you and make sure no boat behind you is threatening to roll over you. I tell my sailors all the time that when you begin the reach, the first priority is the position and the second priority is the spinnaker. It's unfortunately

all too common to see a boat round the windward mark, and everyone in that boat puts their heads down and works on hoisting the kite. They might get their kite up fast, but by the time they look outside their boat again they're far to leeward of the rest of the fleet and they've already been rolled by five boats. Adding an extra sail doesn't help if it means you end up with a train of boats above you blocking your wind! In general, the helm's job is to look at the big picture while staying high and fast to protect the windward lane, while

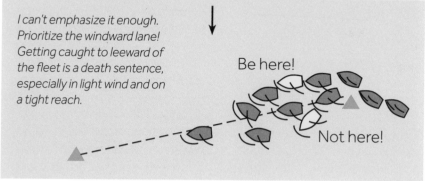

I can't emphasize it enough. Prioritize the windward lane! Getting caught to leeward of the fleet is a death sentence, especially in light wind and on a tight reach.

Be here!

Not here!

the crew prepares the kite. Then, once you've built your height to windward, you may briefly bear away to hoist the kite when you can do so without getting passed to windward.

I guarantee that if you take the windward lane, every time you will either hold your place or pass boats. And if you do get passed by a boat to leeward, understand that it's an incredibly rare occurrence. Taking the low lane is a high risk move. It's like sailing to a corner on the upwind. It might work for a sailor once and they may gain a few boats, but the next time they try it they'll be rolled by the entire fleet and finish last. Take the windward lane every time. The windward lane is the 'high percentage play' on the reach leg and it can lead to big gains as well.

Looking even closer, I've found over years of experience that simply by taking the high lane, you'll pass 2–3 boats on every reach on average. (These are usually the unfortunate boats who got trapped on the low lane.) If you are especially fast on the reach that number will be even more. This of course depends on many factors – how crowded the fleet is, the level of the fleet, whether the reach is tight. But that is a significant and reliable gain. Over a series of 10 races that's 20–30 points!

Furthermore, understand that it's enough for just one boat to roll you for you to have a very big loss. On the reach, especially when the reach is tight, the tendency of the fleet is to sail as a 'train' of boats, each boat bow to stern in a long line. All it takes is for you to lose concentration for a moment and allow one boat to roll you, and then the next boat will connect to that boat's stern and roll you as well, and the next boat, and so on. When you are trapped in such

bad air, 10–20 boats may roll over you before a gap opens and you can regain your lane. I can't emphasize it enough. Protect the windward lane.

Staying high is especially important at the beginning of the reach and during the set. But even after you set the kite you must continue to protect your windward side for the entirety of the reach. That said, you also don't want to get stuck in any costly fights. In other words, you don't want to head up more than you have to, because you don't want to sail extra distance. The first step to protecting your windward lane without sailing more distance than you need to is to position your boat high initially, so that you prevent any boat on your tail from being tempted to roll you. The next step is to follow the Half an Angle Rule. This rule was outlined in the *Downwind* section, but it is perhaps even more useful on the reach. To briefly summarize, see box right.

I highly recommend using the Half an Angle Rule to protect your windward lane for the entirety of the reach.

If there is one thing you take away from this chapter, it is to protect the windward lane. It is by far the easiest way to prevent any losses, while almost always giving you the opportunity to pass other boats as well. It is the first and most fundamental step to sailing the reach.

The Half an Angle Rule helps you defend against a boat behind you trying to roll over you. This rule says that when a boat following behind you heads up to roll over you, head up by half of the angle that they headed up. However, this amount is only a rough guideline. How much you actually head up depends on three things:

1 Your distance to the next mark
2 Your distance from the boat behind you
3 Your relative speed

See *Boat Handling and Technique* in the *Downwind* section for more information.

STEP 2: GO TO YOUR FASTEST ANGLE AND SET

Your second priority when you begin the reach, after ensuring you have a safe position on the windward lane, is to go to your fastest angle and reach maximum boat speed. This is, of course, a lower angle than your close-hauled angle from the upwind. Put the bow down, ease the jib, flatten out the boat, and the boat should take off. When you round the windward mark the boat should accelerate. If you are bearing away and not accelerating most likely something is wrong.

Once you have high boat speed under two sails, consider setting the spinnaker. Understand that there are situations where it is better not to hoist the kite. This may be counter-intuitive to newer sailors, but adding another sail does not always make you go faster. You may choose not to set the kite when either the reach leg is too tight or when the wind is too strong. In the 470, my teammate and I had a rule that if we were planing on the reach with two sails, there was no need to set the spinnaker. Note that I don't mean when the boat is just starting to surf waves, I'm talking about reaching full power towards the mark, passing waves, and ripping it. In that situation, adding the kite would only slow us down, because with the extra sail the boat would become overpowered and the main would be flapping, creating extra drag.

If you choose to set, first prepare the kite – spinnaker pole, tack line, sheets, etc. The crew can do this while the helm holds the angle. Then, reassess how tight or open the reach is. If the reach mark is high and you don't think you'll make the mark from where you are, be patient, continue on a high mode, and climb high to build some height before setting. Most boats have to bear away for the set. Take into account the height you'll lose when you bear away.

If the mark is low, go for a more immediate set.

Before you actually hoist, look behind you at the boats on your tail. As soon as you see them going for the hoist, you probably should too if you're happy with your windward lane. But if they are not going for the hoist, understand that if you bear away to set they will stay high and roll you. Do this only if you're absolutely sure you will be able to end up in front of them again once you add the spinnaker. Otherwise, continue to climb high until you reach a point where after bearing away briefly to hoist you will still have the windward lane.

Remember, in every scenario protect the windward lane!

STEP 3: SAIL FAST AND CLEAN

Once the kite is up, your goal is to maximize boat speed and not get caught up with other boats.

As you're sailing towards the reach mark, don't be afraid to head above and below the mark. Remember, on the reach you are usually not sailing on a fixed angle, but rather you are curving up and down according to the gusts and lulls. Despite this, many sailors are afraid of heading below the mark – they point to the mark on their low mode and above the mark on their high mode. The net result is that they end up sailing a lot of extra distance. Their course on the reach is an arc rather than a line. To reduce this tendency, be sure that you are pointing above

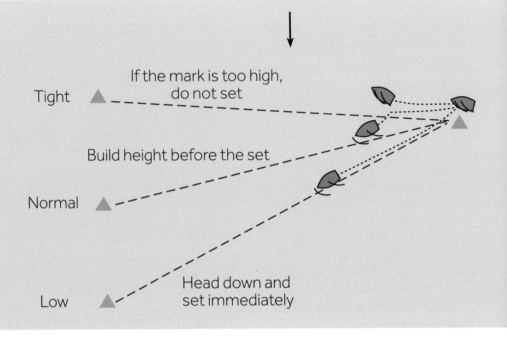

Tight — If the mark is too high, do not set

Build height before the set

Normal

Low — Head down and set immediately

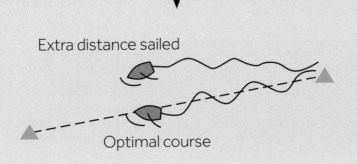

Extra distance sailed

Optimal course

the mark on your high mode and below the mark on your low mode. Your net progress will be towards the mark.

It's easy to sail the reach leg when you are alone. The boats around you when you're racing add another element to the game. If you are fast on the reach, maximize your gain by sailing fast and clean for as much of the reach as possible, without getting caught up with other boats. When there's a slow boat ahead of you, you'll have to roll them to pass them. Your goal is to roll them quickly and easily without getting caught up in a costly fight. To this end, wait for the right timing – a moment when your opponent is unaware of you, they slow down, luff their kite, head lower, fall off a wave, etc – and head up with a sharp manoeuvre before they can react. Ideally, roll over them with at least a boat length of separation. This reduces the chance that they'll defend against you. Maintain high boat speed and pass each boat one by one.

Sometimes you'll see a group of boats fighting ahead of you. A neat trick here is to connect your bow to the stern of the windward-

The line between the windward mark and the reach mark is called the 'rhumb line'. Don't be afraid to curve above and below this line as shown by the bottom boat. The top boat is an example of the common mistake many sailors make: sailing higher than necessary on the reach, even when there are no boats behind to defend against.

most boat if you think that boat will win. If so, when it rolls over its competition, you're just behind it passing all the same boats.

If you are a bit slow on the reach, your number one priority is not to allow any boat to pass you on your windward side. Stay on the high lane and use the Half an Angle rule to defend your windward position. If someone does try to roll you, you are the leeward boat, meaning you can head an opponent up all the way to head-to-wind if necessary. Do not let any boat catch you unawares, and do not let any boat pass you to windward. Make it clear to the boats behind you that their only way to pass you is to leeward.

Before you round, do a hand-off to the next leg. That was a brief moment of high speed insanity. Now you're off to the rest of the race.

PART 6

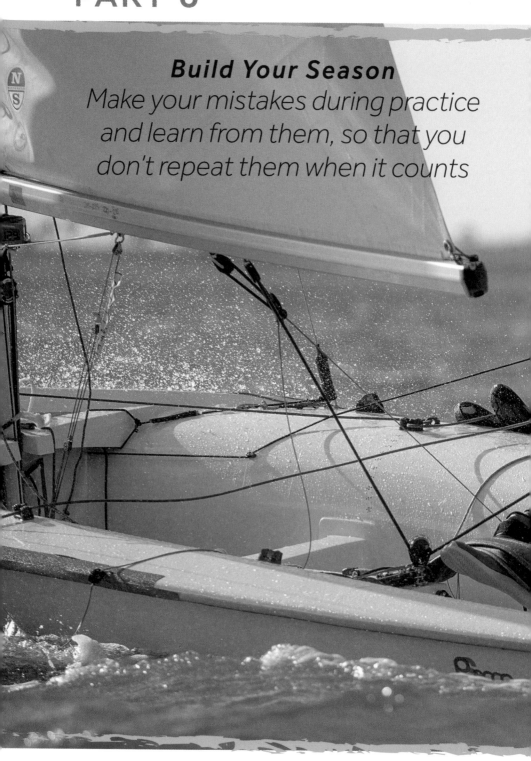

Build Your Season
*Make your mistakes during practice
and learn from them, so that you
don't repeat them when it counts*

Chapter 21

PLANNING YOUR SCHEDULE AND PRACTICE

In the following chapters we will explore how to build a proper training plan that you can follow in order to direct your journey of learning and improvement in racing. It's often said that a championship is won even before the first day of racing. It is important to do everything you can to prepare yourselves away from competitions so that you come to regattas at peak performance.

Practice makes perfect, and although you can never achieve perfection, you can get close to it and reduce your mistakes to the point that they are almost non-existent. At the highest levels of the sport, sailing is a game of mistakes. In a tight, competitive fleet in which everyone has strong boat speed and tactical prowess, any boat will have a high price to pay for tacking onto the wrong shift or losing the kite through a gybe. Those who make the most mistakes will quickly fall to the bottom, while whoever makes the fewest mistakes will score the most consistent results and after a few races find themselves at the top of the fleet. Your training time is the best time to iron out those mistakes. That is why a proper practice routine and an effective training plan is so critical to your success. Make your mistakes during practice and learn from them, so that you don't make any when it counts.

The first step towards building a successful season is looking at your regatta schedule and identifying when you need to be at your peak performance. This will be different for every sailor, every team, and every class of boat, depending on the time of year that your most important championship or group of events takes place.

For example, for much of the youth sailing in the United States, the largest events in various classes such as the Club 420, International 420, and others take place during the summer months. In order to perform well at these summer events, such as the annual Youth Championship, youth sailors and coaches must plan their training in the year before these events to ensure that they cover the proper range of skills. The focuses of training are myriad and range from boat speed, to boat handling and manoeuvres, to starts, to racecourse strategy, to boat on boat tactics, to fitness, and even boat equipment setup. With the sheer number of skills that sailors can (and should) practice, it is imperative that before your season you plan carefully which specific skills you will focus on and when your training schedule will account for each one, so that by the time of the major regatta you have mastered the range of

skills that you had selected to improve on.

Apart from sailing skills, don't neglect your athletic fitness. A huge factor to your sailing success, especially in strong wind, is your fitness and nutrition plan. Your gym training schedule should mirror your sailing training schedule in the months up to the event, such that your sailing abilities and your fitness are both at peak performance on Day One of the regatta or season that you are preparing for.

The balance between fitness training and sailing training on the water is, of course, specific to each boat. The training schedule of a competitive laser sailor, for example, will typically have a greater component of land-based fitness training than most keelboat teams. However, fitness and proper nutrition have grown increasingly important in all classes, especially in the Olympic classes, over the past few years as the competition has grown and rule changes in some classes have permitted pumping and kinetics in greater wind ranges. Even in less physical boats, physical fitness is important for being able to focus and make quick and sharp decisions throughout an entire day of racing without getting tired. Although fitness may hold less importance in some boats, overlook a proper fitness plan and you will face one more disadvantage on the racecourse.

So, what should your training

schedule look like? The greatest piece of advice I can give to the intermediate or advanced sailor looking to take their sailing to the next level is to 'divide and conquer'. Divide your training schedule into phases over the course of the year, so that you can focus separately on specific aspects of racing throughout your training period.

During my career as a 470 Olympian and World Champion, for example, my training schedule in Israel followed this same advice. We began our training season with straight-line boat speed – learning how to sail fast in every wind and weather condition in a straight line, spending hours figuring out exactly how much to adjust the rudder or move in and out of the boat, until we had virtually mastered our skills. We spent almost a month focusing only on this straight-line boat speed, until it became automatic. After that, we focused solely on boat handling manoeuvres – tacking or gybing hundreds of times upwind and downwind in every wind condition and sea state. Then we began sailing short courses, individually breaking down the different parts of the course such as rounding marks, sets, and douses, for another month. As we mastered our speed and boat handling skills, we began putting it all together on a real racecourse, adding more boats to the mix and developing our boat-on-boat tactics. Only at this point,

after having mastered our boat handling skills, did we choose to put an emphasis on starting drills, given that the start is one of the most complex areas of racing in the sense that it incorporates all aspects of boat handling, fleet management, and racecourse strategy. Then we sailed longer racecourses and focused on assessing the racecourse and on fleet management. In the final weeks before a regatta, we refined our boat speed down to the smallest detail, making sure we had the perfect rig settings and sail shape, and keeping track of the positions of all our sail controls.

There are a few main reasons behind dividing your training into specific phases. First, it ensures that you have the fundamentals down before you continue with your training. Think of the steps of your training process as a series of building blocks. Each phase of your improvement is a new building block that you add to your previous skills. I strongly believe, for example, that a sailor needs to have their straight line speed as an automatic skill before they begin working on their manoeuvres such as tacks and gybes. Training in phases ensures that you master the fundamental skills before you progress to more complex areas of focus.

Second, by focusing your training on specific skills for a period of time, you can take a deeper dive into each skill set and master each one to a greater degree than you would by occasionally encountering them during practice. For example, if you decided to target windward mark roundings as an area for improvement, you would improve your skills much more by dedicating a few days of practice specifically to mark roundings – rounding a mark from close-hauled to downwind, setting the spinnaker, gybing, dousing the spinnaker, and sailing upwind back to the top mark to repeat the drill – rather than by only occasionally encountering them during practice races.

Third, individually practising specific skills allows you to tailor your training to improving the aspects of sailing that you know you need to work on. Rather than sailing around a racecourse and superficially practising a range of skills, dividing your training into phases allows you to dedicate more time to working on the skills that you know you need to improve on. If you struggled with your starts at your last regatta, simply dedicate more time to practising starts, and spend less time on straight-line boat speed if you are confident with your boat speed. This also allows you to assess clearly whether or not you have improved at each specific skill, and to take charge of your progress: only move on to the next area for improvement when you are satisfied with your performance of the last skill set. Think critically about the skills that

you choose to focus on for each phase of your training schedule and the time that you should spend practising each one, and you will see greater improvement where you need it the most.

Equally important to the scheduling and content of your practices is the environment in which you train. In the beginning of your training season, do your best to become comfortable in a variety of conditions, but as the 'big regatta' approaches, focus your training in the sailing environment that you expect for that event. For example, if you are preparing for a championship that will take place during the summer on San Francisco Bay, logically you can prioritize training in strong wind, short breaking waves, and current, as your boat handling and boat speed skills in these conditions will predictably be of most use to you in this location and time of year.

Conversely, if you are preparing for a championship in San Diego, you should try to train in light wind and ocean swell. Because not all sailing locations will consistently have the racing conditions that you expect to encounter during the event that you are preparing for, you must be aware of the seasonal wind conditions of your training location so that you know what you have to work with and can focus your training on the days with your target sailing conditions. Go sailing on the days with the wind conditions you are targeting to train in; go to the gym, rest, do boat work, or reflect on your progress on the other days. If you sail multiple types of boats, train in the type of boat that you will race. Ultimately, however, there is no substitute for training at the location of the event you are preparing for, and maximizing the days on the water at the venue before the regatta will help you get to know any weather trends or knowledge specific to that venue.

A sailor's preparation for the Olympic Games may be the greatest example of a purposeful and effective training plan. Each country has its own system, but approximately a year before the Olympic Games, sailors are selected for the Olympics through a series of qualification events. From that point forward, all efforts are focused towards the Olympics. Sailors learn as much as possible about the sailing venue's weather trends, current, and even the available restaurants and hotels. Wherever they train, the athletes adjust their equipment and train in the wind conditions that are expected at the venue. In my experience during the few months of training before the 2004 and 2008 Olympics, these sailing venues became like my new home. I spent all my time training on the water and refining my team's technique and boat speed on the waters where racing would take place. In short, we did everything we could during our preparation to gain every possible advantage before the event.

While careful planning of the schedule, skills, and environment as they relate to the training process is critical to a sailor's success, especially at the highest levels of the sport, this is not to say that a rigid plan should hold you back from putting in time on the water. If the best you can do is find a few hours here and there to practice each week, that is far better than staying at home. This is especially true for less experienced sailors, who will benefit the most from becoming more comfortable with sailing their boat in a range of conditions and with sailing around a racecourse, rather than from an intensive, structured schedule that focuses on preparation for specific regattas. Time on the water, ultimately, will be the greatest factor in your improvement as a sailor or as a team – but I guarantee that all the top sailors will have a specific training plan for their season, and any sailor looking to raise their skills to the next level will benefit greatly from doing the same.

SHOWING UP TO PRACTICE

As a sailing coach, when thinking about the greatest factors for predicting whether or not a sailor will become successful, I will choose hard work over talent. Every. Single. Time. The talented sailor may at first have an edge over other sailors at the beginner or intermediate levels of competition, but in the long run it will be the hard-working, motivated, and reflective sailor who will be successful at the high level. As a professional sailor and as a youth and Olympic sailing coach, I have seen this rule repeat itself again and again. Simply put, the harder you work and the more time you commit to sailing, the better you will become. No matter their current level in competition, the sailor or team that is motivated to learn and succeed and is willing to put in extra days on the water will always triumph over the sailor that only shows up on race days, doesn't properly sit out over the rail, or doesn't reflect critically on their performance.

I always tell my sailors 'practice as you race'. Many youth sailing programs run practice races during their training days with a windward/leeward type course – sailors start the race at a start line, round a top mark, and sail back through the start line to finish. Practice races are a great way for sailors to put together the skills that they have developed over the training season, but the course that I set has one key difference: instead of finishing the race by crossing back downwind through the start line, each boat finishes the race by dousing their spinnaker, doing a proper leeward rounding around one of the starting marks, and completing a tack.

Why do I force my sailors to round a leeward mark and tack in order to finish the race? Because the only way you as a sailor will see yourself improving between training sessions is to challenge yourself to practice the situations that you will encounter on the race course, even if they take a bit more effort. I am sure that every sailor would find it easier to just float through the finish line and slowly douse the spinnaker after they have finished, but on the race course you will undoubtedly encounter crowded mark roundings and fast-paced, intense situations, one of which is the transition from the downwind leg to the upwind leg. By rounding a leeward gate, the sailors are forced to look ahead to see which mark is favoured, position themselves according to the other boats and fight for mark room. Then they must douse the kite and do a proper leeward rounding, just like in a real race. This is what it means to put in the extra effort, or go the extra mile, in practice. This is the X factor of success that makes a great sailor. If you don't practice these situations during your training sessions, how can you expect to have mastered them by the day of the championship, when every point on the scoreboard matters? Have the mindset during training to 'practice as you race', or you will not be at your peak performance when it counts.

However, all the hard work and motivation in the world won't get you anywhere if you don't have a structured and efficient practice plan for each day that you go on the water. The most important thing for every day's practice is that you get something out of it, that you can look back at the end of the day and describe a specific way that you have improved, however insignificant it may be.

I recommend that every practice day, before going on the water, you decide on 2 or 3 goals for the day, and you hold yourself to completing them – by the time you return to shore, at a minimum, even if you achieved nothing else during practice that day you will have completed those goals. The more specific your goals are, the more useful this exercise is. Don't just tell yourself 'I want to get better at starts'. Say 'I want to practice my accelerations' or 'I want to work on keeping control of the boat at slow speeds'. Be specific with your goals for each day so that you know that your time on the water has been well spent.

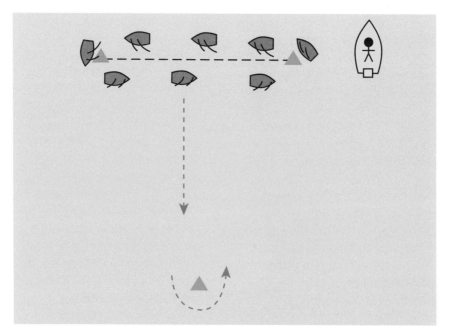

This is one of my favourite drills. The boats circle around two marks at the top of the course. When the coach blows a whistle, the boats all turn downwind and set their spinnakers, similar to a downwind start. Each boat must fight to be first around the leeward mark, after which they race back upwind to finish through the line. This drill is designed so that all the boats are forced to fight for their position at the leeward mark. It is one of the best ways to practice crowded leeward mark roundings because with most other drills, such as conventional races, the boats will become spread out by the time they round the leeward mark.

The exercises or drills that you practice during your sessions should be adaptable to variable conditions and be directly applicable to racing. For example, if you train in a shallow area and low tide reduces the area you can sail, you and your coach should have a backup plan, such as a short course exercise with lots of manoeuvres rather than straight-line speed testing, so that the practice day does not go to waste. Every drill that you do should be designed to improve your performance at some point around the racecourse.

Finally, a useful tip to keep in mind during your training sessions is to break down and name each specific skill or manoeuvre that you might use on the racecourse. When I sailed the 470 we had six different types of gybes. Each gybe had a different purpose, and we would use each one in different wind conditions and in specific situations in a race. In lighter wind, for example, the skipper would control both spinnaker sheets throughout the gybe, while in stronger conditions or when needing to make a sudden manoeuvre to surprise another boat, the crew would control the sheets and the skipper would swing over the boom. We used one of our gybes, which we called the 'rodeo gybe', only when rounding a leeward mark from a downwind on starboard onto a reach on port, because with it we could turn around the mark

without switching the spinnaker pole to the other side of the boat and be instantly ready for the reach. Every boat will have its own manoeuvres, and every team needs to have specific cues for each one that every sailor on the boat knows.

For example, many keelboats have multiple types of douses including leeward, windward, and Mexican douses. Breaking down, naming, and individually practising the manoeuvres that you will use at various times and in various conditions on the racecourse is critical to your success as a team. This is because once you have a name for each manoeuvre, you can hold yourself accountable to practice and master each one. Once you have them mastered, each manoeuvre is another tool in your toolbox of skills that you can easily pull out when the situation requires it; once you call out its name, everyone on the boat is on the same page and knows exactly what to do to perform the manoeuvre successfully.

Achieving this level of perfection is not always easy, but keep at it. The message to bear in mind here is that you don't practice until you can get it right, you practice until you can't get it wrong. With motivation, careful analysis of what you can do better, and consistent practice, you will see improvement. Just remember, there's nothing better than seeing all your hard work translate into the results you want at a regatta.

Chapter 22

POST-PERFORMANCE ROUTINE

A proper mindset is critical to the success of any athlete, and this is especially true for sailors. I don't believe there is any other sport as complex as sailing. In what other sport must you keep track of as many simultaneous factors as on the racecourse, become an expert on as many rules, theories, and weather patterns, and make as many tweaks to the setup of your boat to gain the slightest edge in speed? Sailing truly requires a unique mindset, because talent alone will not get you to a high level. As with any sport, you must

be intensely motivated to put forward your best effort during training and competition, but you must be just as motivated to analyse your performance afterwards and see where improvements can be made.

I learned for myself the importance of reflection during my time in the Israeli Defence Force. There is a rule among Israeli pilots that for every minute spent flying, a minute is spent debriefing. Likewise, there are so many facets of sailing and so much knowledge that will improve your performance around the racecourse that you have to reflect on every aspect of your performance, and you have to be truly committed to learning in order to be successful. You must absorb information like a sponge, constantly seeking out knowledge from books, speakers, webinars, other sailors, and from your coaches, to learn as much as you can about weather strategy, race course strategy, tactics, the rules, how to sail your boat fast, and everything in between. Whether it's after a day's training session or at the end of a regatta, a proper debrief and reflection on your performance is critical to learning from your mistakes, replicating what you did well, and becoming a better sailor the next time you go on the water.

The after-sailing debrief is the time that a coach can most directly affect your improvement as a sailor. It is a time to reflect on the day, with the goal of improving your level of sailing for next time. Your coach will have his or her own style of debriefing the sailors or teams they are working with, such as pointing out the general trends or giving individual feedback – as a sailor, it is your job to get the most out of it. At the end of the day during the debrief you should ask yourself the following questions: What did I learn today? What did I do well? Where can I improve?

Chances are you will already have some ideas in your head, but a good coach will help guide your answers to these questions. As an outside, big picture perspective, a coach sees your speed, manoeuvres, tactical decisions, sail setup, etc in comparison to the other boats in the practice session, and so is well equipped to give you tips for the next time around. For example, if you were slow upwind, a coach could tell you that you were moving the rudder much more than the other boats.

As a sailor, you must make use of the information you receive. What are your goals during the debrief? If you are debriefing a day's training, you will likely benefit the most from advice that focuses on long term ways to improve – for example, changing to a new method of gybing that you have never practised before. If you have just come off the water after a long regatta day and are looking to get better results the next day, you will benefit more from clear, specific advice during the debrief that focuses on improving your performance – for example, positioning yourself closer to the favoured end of the start line. Each day your coach may debrief you and your team, but it is up to you to adapt their advice to your current goals and change their words into results.

THE NOTEBOOK

I can promise you that every high level sailor has one, and if you would like to stop repeating the same old mistakes, remember what you learn, and see your results actually improve from event to event, it is an absolute necessity. Your notebook is the medium through which you use your reflection to improve your future sailing performance. As a firm rule, every sailor should have one. A notebook helps you to reflect on and remember what you have learned. You should add to it after every major practice session, clinic, and regatta.

I know many sailors, however, who consistently add to their notebooks but do not make real use of them. The whole value of a notebook comes from when you read and reread it. It is not meant just to be written in and forgotten, but to be used. You should review your notebook before each regatta so that you remember any skills or strategies that you learned about recently or that worked well for you in the past, so that you can make use of them during competition. Periodically reread it to refresh your memory of what you have done well in the past that you would like to replicate, and of the areas you might focus on for improvement.

So, what information should you include in each entry in your notebook? Here are some guidelines that I recommend.

✳ First of all: The date, location, sailing conditions (wind strength, current, sea state), weather, and any other important contextual information.

✳ The Big Picture: summarize your big-picture thoughts about how you performed, especially if this entry is an analysis of a regatta. Identify in what ways you sailed well and where you need to improve. I find that it's helpful to break this summary down into parts of the racecourse such as the start, the upwind, and the downwind. (For example: 'I did a good job defending my position on the start line, but I need to accelerate earlier.')

✳ Boat Setup: if you were fast, write down what you were doing that day so you can replicate it in similar conditions in the future – this should include the rig setup (tension, rake, etc), setup of the sail controls (mainsheet, cunningham, etc), and how you sailed the boat (kept the boat flatter, sailed higher or lower angles, etc).

✳ If you were slow, talk to a coach or training partner about why, and write down their tips.

✳ Other boats: reflect on the behaviour of the fleet or your opponents. Think back to great moments of other sailors that you noticed during the races. If you have the vision of what it takes to be at the top of the fleet, you have a better chance to be up there.

✳ Local knowledge and strategy: any wind, current, or other environmental trends that you noticed that are specific to the venue. Which side of the race course was winning, which way the wind shifted, etc. The next time you sail in this venue you can look back on this information to improve your racecourse strategy.

✳ Add any other helpful advice you receive – boat setup tips, weather trends, boat handling skills, or anything else you think is valuable to remember!

As a final note, I'd like to acknowledge that not all sailors or sailing teams have a coach, or even other boats to train with on a regular basis. It is completely possible to improve your level of sailing even if you are practising on your own, especially at the beginner or intermediate levels, but understand there are some limitations to the ways that you can practice. Even while sailing without other training partners, you can still effectively practice your boat handling skills and manoeuvres, such as tacks, gybes, or sets, because it is relatively easy to judge whether or not you executed it well and analyse how you can improve. You can also work on your boat speed, but because you aren't able to line up with other training partners and compare yourself, you will have to judge your speed yourself and make adjustments based on the feel of the boat. When practising alone, stick to boat handling skills and boat

speed, and practice your starts and other boat-on-boat drills when you are practising with other boats.

Finally, safety comes first. If you are practising without a nearby safety boat there is a factor of safety to keep in mind, depending on the type of boat you are sailing. In a dinghy there is always a risk of a capsize, which potentially can become a dangerous situation without a safety boat. If you will be sailing alone, don't challenge yourself to go out in conditions in which you are not confident that you can keep the mast up. Similarly, if the wind is very light, do not sail farther from shore than you can return to if the wind dies. You must be aware of the current and the wind forecast for the time that you are practising so you can be sure that under the forecasted conditions you will be able to return to shore safely. Use your common sense, concentrate on coaching yourself if you are sailing alone, and you will have productive practice sessions.

ABOUT THE AUTHORS

Mason Stang, Udi Gal, and Timmy Gee at the 2021 C420 National Championship.

MASON STANG

Mason Stang grew up sailing on the San Francisco Bay. He learned to sail in Club 420s and International 420s (youth versions of the 470) from Udi Gal and at the High Performance Center, the St. Francis Yacht Club, and other youth racing programs in the Bay Area. He soon began competing in youth events, and won the Paul Cayard trophy in 2018. He also competed in Flying Juniors with his high school sailing team, captaining the team to regional and state-level wins. Under Udi's instruction he achieved regular top finishes at national-level 420 events with his teammate Timmy Gee, including winning the 2020 Midwinter Championship and the John V. Hansen trophy, finishing 2nd at the Midwinter Championship the following year, finishing 2nd at the 2021 National Championship, and finishing 4th at back to back North American Championships. As a high school senior he represented Team USA at the 2021 420 World Championship in Italy.

Mason is currently a student at Brown University, where he competes for the Brown sailing team. See the Introduction to learn more about how Mason and Udi joined forces to write this book.

UDI GAL

Udi Gal is a four time Olympian athlete and coach, and a former World and European champion in sailing, having achieved 11 medals and more than 20 world cup medals over the course of his career. Udi competed in the 2004 and 2008 Olympics, representing Israel in the 470 dinghy sailing class. He also served as the Chairman of the Israeli Olympic Athlete Committee. After retiring as a professional athlete, Udi coached the Women's USA Olympic Sailing Team in the 2012 Olympics in London and the Men's Israeli Sailing Team in the 2016 Olympics in Rio.

Today, with more than twenty years of sailing coaching experience and a Master's degree in Sports Psychology, Udi is primarily focused on the mental aspects of performance and helping others achieve their potential. He works with a variety of sports organizations, teams, and individuals on performance optimization strategies and other areas of sports psychology. Udi presently lives in San Francisco, where he coaches high-school age sailors on the San Francisco Bay. He travels nationally and internationally to coach his sailors at competitions, and gives presentations and webinars about racing tactics and strategy with US Sailing.

PHOTO CREDITS

Chris Ray (www.crayivp.com)
2–3, 24–5, 47, 59, 78–9, 98–9, 106–7, 116–17, 128–9, 139, 178–9, 182–3, 185, 186–7, 196–7, 207, 217, 224–5, 228–9, 235, 248–9, 250, 256, 280–1

Matias Capizzano (www.capizzano.com)
272, 286–7

Tom Walker Photography
100–1

Amy Gee
301

ACKNOWLEDGEMENTS

MASON STANG

I want to say thank you to my parents, who first inspired me to learn sailing and since then have been totally supportive of my continued pursuit of the sport. I have been incredibly fortunate for the time and effort they have dedicated to making my training and racing over the years possible. I'd like to also thank my long-time teammate Timmy Gee, with whom I trained and competed throughout high school. I could not have been paired with a more talented and dedicated teammate. And finally, I'd like to thank Udi Gal for going above and beyond as a mentor and sailing coach. On and off the water, Udi has continuously pushed me to become a better sailor, and I credit my sailing knowledge to his teaching.

In addition to these individuals, I want to recognize each of the sailing teams I've been a part of. The HPC (High Performance Center) team was truly a family to me. Another team I am proud to have been a part of is my high school's sailing team, from Crystal Springs Uplands School. Most recently, I have been welcomed to the Brown University Sailing Team by the sailors and our head coach John Mollicone, where I was instantly struck by the incredible camaraderie and team spirit.

UDI GAL

I would like to express my gratitude to my family who, from my early days of sailing, provided me with the unconditional love and encouragement necessary to pursue this sport. My family, the wind in my sails, supported me through many career challenges and highlights. I would like to acknowledge my father, my compass, for introducing me to sailing, for always believing in me, and for teaching me the foundational life skills I needed to succeed. I'd like to thank my wife, my anchor, for supporting my passion for sailing and inspiring me.

The trajectory of my life and my career would not have been the same without my former teammate, Gidi Kliger. I am grateful to all my teammates, athletes, coaches, and opponents who challenged me, inspired me, and took me to the next level over the course of my career. I have learned a lot from each and every one of you, and I promise to continue doing so.

I would like to recognize the families of the youth sailors I have worked with over the years. You all contribute endless energy and dedication to the next generation of sailors and inspire me to provide the best guidance, mentoring and support for our youth sailors. Being a small part of the athletes' paths means the world to me.

Lastly, this project would not have been possible without my co-author, Mason Stang. I want to thank Mason for his brilliant ability to document a complex sailing philosophy in this book. An epitome of 'student of the game', Mason is a living proof that hard work and dedication lead to great results.

INDEX

INDEX